MODERN DRAMA: DEFINING THE FIELD

Edited by Ric Knowles, Joanne Tompkins, and W.B. Worthen

Theatre, like other subjects in the humanities, has recently undergone quintessential changes in theory, approach, and research. *Modern Drama* – a collection of twelve essays from leading theatre and drama scholars – investigates the contemporary meanings and the cultural and political resonances of the terms inherent in the concepts of 'modern' and 'drama,' delving into a range of theoretical questions on the history of modernism, modernity, postmodernism, and postmodernity as they have intersected with the shifting histories of drama, theatre, and performance. Using incisive analyses of both modern and postmodern plays, the contributors examine varied topics such as the analysis of periodicity; the articulation of social, political, and cultural production in theatre; the re-evaluation of texts, performances, and canons; and demonstrations of how interdisciplinarity inflects theatre and its practice.

Including work by Sue-Ellen Case, Elin Diamond, Harry J. Elam Jr., Alan Filewod, Erika Fischer-Lichte, Stanton B. Garner Jr., Shannon Jackson, Loren Kruger, Josephine Lee, David Savran, Michael Sidnell, and Ann Wilson, the collection highlights the importance of continuing to investigate not only critical texts but also the terms of the debate themselves. Incorporating both drama history and modern studies, this compilation will be an invaluable work to all scholars of theatre and drama, and as well as students of the humanities and modernism.

RIC KNOWLES is a professor of Drama at the University of Guelph and a member of faculty at the Graduate Centre for the Study of Drama, University of Toronto.

JOANNE TOMPKINS is an associate professor and reader in Drama at the University of Queensland.

W.B. WORTHEN is a professor of Drama at the University of California, Berkeley.

D1202578

MODERN DRAMA
Defining the Field

Edited by

Ric Knowles, Joanne Tompkins, and W.B. Worthen

UNIVERSITY OF TORONTO PRESS
Toronto Buffalo London

© University of Toronto Press Incorporated 2003
Toronto Buffalo London
Printed in Canada

ISBN 0-8020-8621-7

Printed on acid-free paper

National Library of Canada Cataloguing in Publication

Modern drama : defining the field / edited by Ric Knowles, Joanne Tompkins and
W.B. Worthen.

First published as the Winter 2000 and Spring 2001 volumes of the journal
Modern drama.
Includes bibliographical references.
ISBN 0-8020-8621-7

I. Drama – 20th century – History and criticism.   I. Knowles, Richard, 1950–
II. Tompkins, Joanne, 1956–   III. Worthen, William B., 1955–

PN1861.M634 2003   808.82′04   C2003-902926-3

University of Toronto Press acknowledges the financial assistance to its publishing
program of the Canada Council for the Arts and the Ontario Arts Council.

University of Toronto Press acknowledges the financial support for its publishing
activities of the Government of Canada through the Book Publishing Industry
Development Program (BPIDP).

Contents

Contents

Introduction

RIC KNOWLES

I was offered the privilege of editing the journal *Modern Drama* at a significant moment in the history of the field. Until relatively recently, periodization – the division of literary, theatrical, and cultural history into temporal units that were usually associated with particular styles and formal features felt to be characteristic of particular moments in time – was more or less taken for granted as a way of organizing areas of study in most disciplines. Similarly, until relatively recently, disciplinarity itself – the division of knowledge and ways of acquiring it into identifiable scholarly "disciplines," methods, or approaches – was more or less taken for granted as a way of organizing scholarship, research, epistemology, and knowledge itself, on the assumption that some methods were more appropriate than others for the examination of certain subjects. But those modes of constructing and dividing the archive no longer seem as natural or as neutral as they once did, nor do the types of material that might belong in an archive or constitute an "object of study" seem so clear, as more theoretically inflected and often interdisciplinary scholarship has asked questions about the interests served by the ways in which historical periods are marked and segregated from one another, and the ways in which particular disciplinary methods acquired ownership over particular archives.

When *Modern Drama* was founded, just over halfway through the twentieth century, its defining, titular terms appeared to be transparent. Modernity was in full swing, and was assumed to be so everywhere – at least everywhere that appeared to matter, in a field that concerned itself at that time primarily with European and American dramaturgies – and it was uncontroversial to dedicate a journal with that name to drama since 1850, as though the so-called Modern Age (or modernist "style") arrived everywhere at the same time and extended, always, to the present. Since then, globalization (on the one hand) and interculturalism (on the other) have, together with postcolonialism, troubled historical master narratives and the stability of modernity's starting point across cultures. Meanwhile, the "contemporary," and most especially the "postmodern" – not to mention the turn of yet another century since the beginning of the "modern" – have troubled understandings of its *terminus a quo*. In companion areas of study, moreover, the terminology that designates the field continues to be interrogated on historical, political, and generic grounds. What used to be called the Renaissance, for instance, has increasingly, if controversially, come to be called the Early Modern period, in recognition that for an over-whelming percentage of the world the period was one of literal or cultural genocide. Given all of this, and the turn of the millennium too, I felt that it was important to re-examine the assumptions on which the "modern" in *Modern Drama* rested.

But "drama" itself presented no fewer complexities as I contemplated the mandate of the journal that I had been invited to edit. When *Modern Drama* was founded, the meaning of "drama" seemed fairly clear: the term was used, in contradistinction to "theatre," to refer to a body of so-called dramatic litera-ture that was distinguished from narrative (with its story, and, crucially, its storyteller) and lyric (with its expressive and descriptive mode – storyteller with no story) as a body of writing whose narrative drive was presented directly in the words of its various actants – story with no storyteller. "Drama" was not narrative or lyric, prose or poetry, then, because it presented unmedi-ated direct discourse that nevertheless enacted a central (Aristotelian) action driven by narrative. But, crucially at the time, neither was drama "theatre"; rather, it was the more serious, literary mode, the universal blueprint upon which the ephemeral theatrical performance depended. "Theatre" was most often theorized as either the interpretative enactment of a stable, universal, dra-matic text, or the translation of that text into different (and usually unstable) codes or semioses of enunciation, gesture, embodiment, design, and so on.

For many years now, however, the primacy of "drama," of "the play" (in contradistinction to "the performance" or "the script") has come under scru-tiny. Scholars first increasingly aligned themselves with a position familiar to theatre professionals for decades, one that saw "drama" not simply as the blueprint for theatre but as its somewhat quaint residue, the mere written record of the "real" event that took place on stage before a "live" audience. For these scholars and others, theatre was lived experience, while drama took the form of archival recording, annotating for readers understood as audiences *manqués* (often through descriptive, adjectival, or adverbial stage directions) the experience that they might have had, had they been so lucky to be there in the (genuine, originary) moment.

More recently, the concept of "theatre" itself has come under attack as scholars have increasingly questioned the genuinely originary nature of the theatrical moment. Theatre has frequently come to be seen as the repository of cultural reproduction – the reinforcement of currently dominant and oppres-sive social structures and naturalized "realities." How, the argument goes (at least by implication), can a discipline based on (Aristotelian) mimesis and grounded in the always-already of a dramatic script as political unconscious avoid simply reproducing dominant, hierarchical constructions of human subjectivity according to gender, race, sexuality, ethnicity, and class? A new, more inclusive, and seemingly omnivorous discipline has therefore emerged called "performance studies," within which theatre itself is both subsumed and rendered the object of critique. In this new field, the apparently unmediated immediacy of "performance" – genuine enactment in the here and now – is set against mimetic repetitions that are seen to be at the root of theatre as the more conservative discipline. The apparent global inclusiveness of "performance," however, is set against the Eurocentrism of "theatre." (Ironically, in some of its manifestations, performance studies has elevated the private reading of a script as a "performative" act to a level of immediacy that the same discipline frequently disputes in its staged performance.)

Among the first things that I undertook to do, then, on assuming the editorship of *Modern Drama* was to think through ways of addressing these issues that seemed so central and yet so unstable as the millennium clicked over and a whole new "period" (perhaps no longer "modern"?) began in global history – while editorialists incessantly looked back in global terms on the twentieth century and theorists began to write books about the "post-postmodern." I began, in consultation with the *Modern Drama* Executive Committee and Editorial Advisory Board, to consider ways of opening up the journal to renewed consideration of the terms of its title. These included an attempt to begin to internationalize and extend the reach of the editorial team, the Board itself, and the pages of the journal. Crucially, they also included, in consultation with my new co-editors, Joanne Tompkins of the University of Queensland and W.B. Worthen of the University of California at Berkeley, inviting some of the most active, provocative, and challenging scholars working in the field(s) to a conference in May 2000 with the express purpose of interrogating the terms "modern" and "drama," and of initiating the process of (re) "defining the field."

The three-day "Modern: Drama" conference, held at and co-sponsored by the Graduate Centre for the Study of Drama at the University of Toronto, the institutional home of *Modern Drama*, was conceived primarily as a consultation on the state of the field, and was organized to allow for a maximum of discussion and debate. Outstanding scholars, both emerging and established, grappled with serious issues in always challenging ways, and each produced a coherent and articulate delineation of different aspects of a radically changing area of study. The proceedings of the conference, revised for publication, appeared in volumes 43(4) and 44(1) of *Modern Drama*, launching a new editorial vision for the journal under Joanne, Bill, and myself. Both issues were extremely well received, and went out of print almost immediately. This book, which reorganizes the essays into coherent groupings and brings them together under one cover, is published as an attempt to make them more widely available than they were in the pages of the journal itself.

The volume opens with Elin Diamond's essay, "Modern Drama/Modernity's Drama," which won the prestigious essay prize from the Association for Theatre in Higher Education when it first appeared in *Modern Drama*. The essay serves as a fitting prologue to the volume, examining as it does the problems involved in reinventing and staging historical time. In fact, Diamond historicizes modernity itself and its reinvention of time in the context of the double optic of modernity and drama, drawing primarily on the work of Aphra Behn, August Strindberg, Bertolt Brecht, and Zora Neale Hurston. Diamond's essay is followed by three others that sort through, in different ways, the cultural and institutional affiliations and boundaries that define "drama" in the modern period. Michael Sidnell's "The Aesthetic Prejudice in Modern Drama," citing Walter Benjamin, W.B. Yeats, T.S. Eliot, and Lillian Hellman, focuses on the tension between the representational (or discursive) and the performative, on the modernist crisis of theatrical representation, and on "that subordination or suppression of the performing subject that is particularly associated with realism in modern drama" (16). Shannon Jackson's "Why Modern Plays Are Not Culture" sets Robert Brustein's essay, "Why American Plays Are Not Literature," against Raymond Williams's examination of drama's participation in societal and cultural "structure[s] of feeling" (41) in order to focus on the same crisis. It does so, unlike Sidnell, by examining and problematizing the history of the institutionalization of modern drama and its disciplinary affiliations in literary and cultural studies in America. Finally, in a complementary essay to Jackson's, Erika Fischer-Lichte's analysis "Theatre Studies at the Crossroads" uses experimental performances by Christoph Schlingensief, Frank Castorf, and Elinar Schleef to illustrate the effective interdisciplinary recreation in Europe of theatre and performance studies through "culture studies," "media studies," and "art studies."

A second grouping of four complementary essays moves from the emergence of modern drama as a discursive category through to a tracing of its continuities with postmodern performance. Stanton B. Garner's "Physiologies of the Modern" examines what he calls the "'manifesto' phase" (68) of modern drama (1880 to 1940), focusing on the corporality of the modern body as a site of observation. Tracing continuities between Émile Zola's naturalism and the writings of Claude Bernard on experimental medicine (upon which Zola built his theories), Garner locates the origins of naturalism at a moment of tension "between biological and technological modes of generating persons and things" (78). Loren Kruger also traces modernist dramaturgy to an originary moment, this time in Hegel, and her essay, "Making Sense of Sensation," echoes Elin Diamond in her understanding of "the drama of modernity" (89, 98). Interrogating the theoretical writings of Hegel and Brecht as apparently opposing idealist and materialist poles of modernist thinking, and drawing examples from contemporary performances of pain (the work of Ron Athey and the theatre of the South African Truth and Reconcilation Commission), Kruger finds more continuity than rupture between "modern" and "drama," on the one hand, and "postmodern" and ("postdramatic") "performance," on the other. In "Luminous Writing, Embodiment, and Modern Drama," Sue-Ellen Case yokes together the unlikely figures of Mme Blatavsky and, again, Brecht, and finds similar continuities. She traces the move from modern to postmodern by way of the occult, the feminine, and the Internet as set against the material- ist, masculinist, and Brechtian, and she finds the "tension around the techno- logical claim of the 'new' and the indigenous association with the 'ancient'" to be central to both modernist and postmodern performance, "animating the competing practices of scripting, embodiment, and performance as they part- ner competing constructions of gender, nationhood, and the global" (103). David Savran, in "The Haunted Houses of Modernity," like Kruger and Case, sees the contemporary (American) stage as haunted by and continuous with the "spectral drama" (125) of modernity. Looking at what he considers to be three phases of ghost plays (1885–1925, the 1950s and early 1960s, and the 1990s), and focusing for his contemporary examples on Paula Vogel's *How I Learned to Drive*, Terrence McNally's *Ragtime*, and Tony Kushner's *Angels in Amer- ica,* Savran finds that each phase corresponds to a distinct phase of Western imperialism. "The very category 'modern drama,'" he concludes, "is in fact a product of imperialism, [...] its very existence [...] predicated upon a certain disavowal, a certain refusal to credit the corporal existence and the labor power of those nearly invisible others who haunt its margins" (127).

The final grouping of four essays looks more closely at the theatrical and per- formative construction of those "others" and the ways in which that construc- tion has proved to be central to the very constitution of "modern drama." Ann Wilson, in "Hauntings," replicates Savran's central ghostly trope as she turns her attention to "Anxiety, Technology, and Gender in [J.M. Barrie's] *Peter Pan.*" Eschewing traditional readings of the play as escapist fantasy, Wilson reads its Never Land as a response to middle-class anxieties over class, race, sexuality, and especially masculine identity in modern life. "*Peter Pan,*" she concludes, "is a fable of modernity, anxiously negotiating industrial technolo- gies that produced a middle class predicated on instability and which encoded impossible roles for men and women" (141). Josephine Lee's focus in "Bodies, Revolutions, and Magic" is more specifically on cultural nationalisms and the performance of race as she concerns herself with the staging of "the racial fetish" (148) in plays by Lorraine Hansberry, Alice Childress, Frank Chin, Ysidro Macias, George C. Wolfe, and Richard Wesley. Like Kruger, Case, and Savran, Lee finds problematic continuities between modernism and postmod- ernism. She finds that "racial fetishes in their new incarnation – as demonstra- tions of the power of coloured bodies – work less to inspire audiences to social action and more to compensate for the loss of [...] radical energies. What is at

stake," she argues, "is not so much whether these racialized bodies possess
magic [...] but whether this spectacular power has any use other than the generation of profit" (154–5). Alan Filewod also looks at nationalisms and racial
essentialisms, and at continuities between the representation of race in high
modernism and its deployment in plays that present themselves as oppositional
– in this case, the radical agitprop of three theatre companies from Scotland,
Canada, and Australia. Noting the grounding of such work in the rediscovery of
lost authenticities, the suppressed cultural forms of marginalized communities,
and the "meta-historical fantasy" (163) of organic community, Filewod proposes that agitprop "is not only an expression of theatrical modernism, and of
its corollary, modern drama, but is similarly situated in a historical crisis of
race" (165). The final essay in the present volume, Harry J. Elam's "August
Wilson, Doubling, Madness, and Modern African-American Drama," focuses
on the work of a single playwright, and on that playwright's use of "mad" characters as representing a connection to what Filewod might call the suppressed
cultural forms of a marginalized community, but what Elam refers to as "a powerful, transgressive spirituality," a "lost African consciousness," and "a legacy
of black social activism" (173). For Elam, "racial madness" (174) is fundamental to Wilson's "minority modernism" (192) (a concept not entirely distinct
from Josephine Lee's "cultural nationalism" [144]). Wilson's "black modernist
project," then, "is fundamentally concerned with the remaking and conservation of historical memory, the renegotiation of primal and initiating ruptures, in
African American experience" (192). Wilson, Elam argues, "asks that we recognize the significance of race, slavery, and African-American thought and cultural production as not just conditioned by but constitutive of modernity" (192).

Ultimately, and not surprisingly, this volume reports no single answer to the
questions it raises, no final definition of the field, and no easily articulated
new mandate for the journal *Modern Drama* or the project of modern drama
studies. But the essays included here do display remarkable coherence in their
accounts of the anxieties, exclusions, hierarchies, and otherings that together
have constituted the field of study that brings the terms "modern" and
"drama" together. They also display considerable agreement about the interests that the construction of this field of study have traditionally served. Perhaps equally significantly, these essays model a type of analysis – historically
grounded, archivally based, thickly described, theoretically sophisticated, and
politically engaged – to which *Modern Drama* and the field of study that it
represents aspire in the first decade of the third millennium. They point, too,
to an archive, or "object of study," that extends beyond the "modern," narrowly conceived, and beyond "drama" (or even "theatre"), narrowly understood, to include questionings and challenges of the very period and generic
categories that the terms of the journal's title have traditionally invoked, particularly insofar as both represent a "disciplining" of scholarship, an exclusion
of "difference," an exertion of control, or an exercise of power.

This volume announces, then, for the field of modern drama studies, what the editors hope is a new openness to questionings of period and generic boundaries; to questionings of scholarly and generic privilege based on class, race, nation, ethnicity, gender, and sexuality; and to questionings of all kinds, especially those that haven't yet been thought of or understood. The editors are very proud of this collection, and we hope that it signals and opens the way for a range and variety of work in the field that we ourselves are not yet able to imagine.

MODERN DRAMA: DEFINING THE FIELD

Modern Drama/Modernity's Drama

ELIN DIAMOND

I

We want continuity and we deny continuity. [...] Too much of ourselves, we say, is attached to the past, as if it could be unattached. We develop methods for denying memory. [...] [but] [h]istory is stubborn. [...] Like it or not, we *are* remembered [and the] history that is not played again as farce is, of course, played straight by the actors. It's only history that thinks it's funny. True, all this is merely theoretical; it needs fleshing out in the theater. The past always needs blood donors. The theater is a means of transfusion.

– Blau 8–9

Modern drama, the question raised by the conveners of the Modern:Drama (defining the field) conference[1] and the current editors of *Modern Drama*, has a past that is selectively remembered and denied in the institutions that support our scholarship. It is nearly absent from current scholarship investigating the times, spaces, and practices of Western modernity and modernism. It is also absent from the academic memories of those who, like me, found themselves happily ensconced in high school literature classes that, even through the 1960s, were dominated by the methods and ideology of the New Critics.[2] Focusing on the autotelic object, most often the short poem, to the exclusion of authorial biography, tradition, and historical context, New Criticism sought to create a preserve of literary language in imitation of T.S. Eliot's modernist imperative to purify the language of the tribe. In its heyday in the 1940s and 1950s, New Criticism exhorted us to never "go outside the poem" lest we merely *use* literature to defend a depleted liberal humanism or, far worse, to illustrate a Marxist analysis of social forces (Bové 95–97).

Yet history has "remembered" the New Critics, in Blau's ironic sense. With their version of a literary preserve and links to Southern Agrarian elites, they

shared a region and a time (the 1950s) with the first Civil Rights activists –
and only history laughs at that juxtaposition. There is also a more interesting
problem: in a paradox worthy of New Critical attention, Cleanth Brooks,
Allen Tate, and Robert Penn Warren became agents of change, for, in the
midst of essentializing literary discourse, they sought to identify what Gerald
Graff calls its "human relevance" (16). In *The Well-Wrought Urn*, Brooks
condemns readers and critics for going "outside the poem" yet endorses
Eliot's claim that good poetry is "mature" and "founded on the facts of experience" (254–55). In the heart of the New Criticism, then, was an untenable
contradiction. Having insisted on the essential separateness of the literary
word, they also wanted it to circulate. Having banned, for the purpose of rigorous close reading, the author's life and social-historical conditions, the New
Critics found themselves in a social-historical conjuncture to which their own
critical parameters made them blind. Such blindness, I will argue, removes the
New Critics from the ethos of modernism, where they usually lodge, and
places them in a feedback loop of longer *durée*: modernity. Their polemical
antihistoricism exposes one of the many threads of metaphysical historicism
that modernity itself has fostered. In Frank Lentriccia's summary, "History as
[...] teleological unfolding [...] history as continuity, or mere repetition [...]
history as discontinuity – a series of 'ruptures'" producing distinct periods
(xiii–xiv). Such a history, Lentriccia continues, "depends on an idealist, and, I
would add, Hegelian notion of a "unity and totality [that resists] forces of het-
erogeneity, contradiction, fragmentation and difference: a 'history' [that]
would deny 'histories'" (xii–iv).

Some of us may remember that Brooks and Warren referred constantly to
"drama" in their poetics: "Poetry [...] may best be read not as argument inviting us to debate nor as explanation inviting us to understand, but as drama
inviting our involvement" (James E. Miller, Jr., and Bernice Slote, qtd. in
Graff xii). Yet they followed the Romantics in dismissing drama (excepting
Shakespeare) from their canon of organically structured aesthetic objects.
There may be cultural and institutional reasons for this, but one is tempted to
say that the experience of imaginative "involvement" was riskier with the
drama, especially since the major dramatists of their day, Tennessee Williams
and Arthur Miller, in their works and in their lives, raised sexual and political
questions that would have made "involvement" distasteful. Risky too was
what could happen to the project of close reading in relation to drama. Though
it is certainly possible, and for many of us desirable, to do close readings of
plays (analyzing a play's formal structure as key to its meaning), it is impossible, in the case of drama scholarship, not to "go outside the text." Performance
is that messy, *historicizing* moment that interrupts the integrity of the written
document.

Still, that modern drama has been excluded from the received canons of
modernism and that the New Criticism has contributed to that exclusion is a

fact – and, I would argue, an opportunity. The antihistory position of the New Critics, so compatible with the anxiety about history that underpins much of modern drama and other modernist writing, exposes the temporal biases of modernity itself. If performance contains an irreducible material historicity, then texts written for performance may be particularly vulnerable to the new modes of historical thinking that modernity fostered. What, I wonder, would be the effect of positing the category *modernity's drama* in relation to, or instead of, *modern drama*? What critical possibilities would become open to us? Of course, in some ways this has already been done: studies of the "early modern" differentiate a form of contemporary scholarship, usually Foucaultian, that seeks to place Renaissance literature and culture in a different intellectual conjuncture. That work is fascinating, yet my interest is not to find, say, symptoms of (late modern) interiority in Shakespeare's early modern plays, or to reveal networks of power/knowledge in the social and textual environments of the early seventeenth century. My question is, How does one of modernity's key features – its way of inventing/thinking about historical time – get dramatized, and what would "modernity's drama" as a configuration *do* to the ways we think about *modern* drama? Even as I suggest a few responses below, I note that certain playwrights are way ahead of me. Bertolt Brecht and Caryl Churchill have each written at least two plays set in the seventeenth century: Brecht's *Mother Courage and Her Children* (1938–1939) and *Life of Galileo* (1938–1939), Churchill's *Light Shining in Buckinghamshire* (1976) and *Vinegar Tom* (1976). In the following discussion I will touch on *Mother Courage* only, but all four plays signal an acute awareness of what Denise Albanese calls the "interested element" (28) in modernity's temporal arrangements. Further, by showing that the future of seventeenth-century science and economics is dialectically related to our past and present, Brecht and Churchill suggest that temporality itself is an historical construction. This is the message, too, of my epigraph. The past, Blau asserts, riffing on Marx's *Eighteenth Brumaire*, may or may not replay itself as farce, but it will always need fresh actors – blood donors – because *it is always under construction*. The theatre – and the theatre's literature – is not only a means of transfusion, it is *the means* of transfusion, for what is resuscitated is what had to be invented in the first place.

II

Scholars who work on modernity take some pains to distinguish it from "modernism" (the term for Western artworks of various media, produced between the 1850s and the 1950s, that sought self-consciously to overthrow reigning formal and perceptual traditions) and from "modernization" (the penetration of everyday life by the new technologies of electricity, the internal combustion engine, the telephone, automobiles, airplanes, and so on). For Matei Calinescu, among many others, the story of Western modernity is conceivable only as a particular kind of "time awareness, namely, that of *historical time*, linear and irreversible, flowing irresistibly onwards" (13). The earliest use of *modernus* ("man of the day," a newcomer) versus *antiquus* ("one whose name has come down from the past") can be traced to the fifth century, and it was a commonplace in the Middle Ages. From Renaissance secular humanists, notably Petrarch, came the concept of three large temporal divisions: antiquity, the Dark Ages, and modernity. Calinescu writes, "Classical antiquity came to be associated with resplendent light, the Middle Ages became the nocturnal and oblivious 'Dark Ages,' while modernity was conceived of as a time of emergence [...] 'renascence,' heralding a luminous future" (20). For Petrarch and "the next generation of humanists, history no longer appeared as a continuum but rather as a succession of sharply distinct ages [...] alternating periods of enlightened grandeur with dark periods of decay and chaos." Thus the Renaissance "accomplished an ideologically revolutionary alliance with time" (21–22). That is, history was no longer understood to be based solely on a providential plan; instead, human acts were responsible for the creation of the future. With Montaigne's *Essays* (1580), Bacon's *Advancement of Learning* (1605) and *Novum Organum* (1620), Descarte's *Discours de la méthode* (1634), Galileo's *Dialogue Concerning the Two Chief World Systems: Ptolemaic and Copernican* (1632), and, later, Newton's *Principia Mathematica* (1686), modernity based on the philosophical commitment to reason and the scientific method takes clear shape, ending the Renaissance idolatry of antiquity. Descartes asserts, *"C'est nous qui sommes les anciens"* ("It is we who are the Ancients") (qtd. in Calinescu 25).

Reinhart Koselleck's theories of modernity and history give finer tuning to Calinescu's descriptions. In *Futures Past: On the Semantics of Historical Time*,[3] Koselleck argues that historical time changes between 1500 and 1800. In these centuries "there occurs a temporalization of history, at the end of which is the peculiar form of acceleration which characterizes modernity" (5). Koselleck calls these temporal changes "planes of historicity" (3–4) and isolates two planes for analysis: eschatological prophecy, the anticipation of the imminent end of the world, and prognosis, the calculus of prediction based on past events. Rooted in Christianity, eschatology was readily adapted to different political situations. During the Reformation, Luther was convinced that the Pope was the Antichrist, while to Catholics the Antichrist was Luther. Yet all parties thought the end was imminent: eschatology defined the future of early modernity. The trouble was, of course, that the world did not end. After the Wars of Religion, culminating in the Thirty Years' War (1615–1645), it became apparent that the new nation-states, and not God, were keeping the peace. Politicians hated the early prophets of doom and persecuted them. As Koselleck puts it, the "state [...] enforced a monopoly on the control of the future by suppressing apocalyptic and astrological readings" (10). In effect, the seventeenth century destroyed prophecy. Yet in England, in response to anxiety over the return of monarchical rule in 1660, millennial prophecy rose again. And in Germany, during the prolonged suffering of the Thirty Years' War, prophecy had perhaps its last gasp. What Koselleck does not tell us is that the advent of the nation-state, the spread of scientific method into all domains of social and cultural life, was coextensive with the growth of capitalism, the launch of the colonial enterprise (the Europeanization of the globe), and the beginnings of the slave trade. In an unholy alliance of religion and capitalism so familiar to us today, millenarianism morphed very quickly into colonialism – the moral imperative to fear the promised end became, by its own ineluctable logic, the equally fervent imperative to expropriate the promised land.

One can see why the future of early modernity could no longer be explained by eschatology, Koselleck's first "plane of historicity." For the nation-state, a new political calculus was required; successful governance, it was thought, depended on foresight. Hence, Koselleck argues, prophecy gave way to prognosis. Instead of eschatological expectation, prognosis implied that, based on what was known of past events, the future could be rationally predicted, and thus the old mistakes avoided (*pace* Marx and Blau), or, history played first as tragedy, then as farce. Yet this new plane of historicity also implied the "novelty of time running away with itself and prognostic attempts to contain it" (14). The future may be based on the past, but not with absolute certainty. And prognostic thinking had another effect: by introducing the past into the future, prognosis generated a sense of repetition – history as cyclical – that ultimately proved as static as the time projected by prophecy. The Enlightenment doctrine of progress changed all of this: it opened up a future that transcended the hitherto predictable notion of time and experience. According to Koselleck, the "future" of progress is characterized by two main features: the increasing speed with which it approaches and its unknowability. Gotthold Ephraim Lessing (1729–1781) described the quintessential believer in progress: "he cannot wait for the future. He wants this future to come more quickly and he himself wants to accelerate it [...] for what has he to gain if that which he recognizes as the better is not actually to be realized as the better within his lifetime?" (qtd. in Koselleck 18).

But, again, not all the world was moving at the same pace. The eighteenth century accelerated imperial aggression and codified the slave trade. Progress – what would be called modernization by the nineteenth century – also racialized time. Or, rather, the progress narrative revealed another powerful strand in the temporality of modernity: the time of the other.

In *New Science, New World*, Denise Albanese argues that the turn of the seventeenth century installs the time sense that was nascent in such documents as Thomas Harriot's *A Briefe and True Report of the New Found Land of Virginia* (1590) (qtd. in Albanese 13). Harriot's text contains images of natives that juxtapose a stylized, heavily tattooed body of an Algonquin chief with a similarly rendered body of a Pict, a member of the long-defunct tribe that inhabited ancient Scotland. The implication is that the Virginia native, contemporary to seventeenth-century viewers, was in fact coeval to the ancient Pict – that is, North American present time was the equivalent of the British past. The difference between Indian and Pict becomes, by sleight of images, a "matter of time," with "time" signifying in "a newly interested fashion [...] [both] as a measure of linear regularity, and [as] a guarantor of relation even where no prior train of geography, nationality, or other form of consequence exists" (Albanese 28). Past and present, Old World and New World, each relation "positions temporality as a neutral and universal substrate. Yet the plotting of bodies and cultures along a one-dimensional time line marks the temporal as a loaded and interested element in the emergent forms of power-knowledge" (28).

While Albanese is clearly indebted to the work of Johannes Fabian and Michel Foucault, her chief inspiration is Michel de Certeau's *The Writing of History*, a study that complements but differs crucially from Koselleck's. In Albanese's succinct summary, the modern world, for Certeau, "produces itself through othering, through discursive and material mechanisms that effectively bifurcate regions of culture, the better to legitimate some and delegitimate others" (2; see Certeau 19–113, 209–43). In this view, cause–effect historical narrative has the function of justifying such operations, rather than of explaining or clarifying how and why social and political change takes place. Indeed, "change," Albanese asserts, is merely an "invention" of "humanist historiography" (2). Albanese describes her project as a form of "redress": to show the emergence and convergence of texts of early scientific modernity is to understand how oppositional discourses (past/present, Old World/New World) helped to secure the sorts of othering on which modernity rests. Her aim is to disturb modernity's othering narratives. If we turn to what might be called "modernity's drama," however, this kind of critical narrative becomes problematic – not because it excludes modernity's divisions and modes of legitimation, but because it absorbs and resorts them in distinctive ways. Sir Isaac Newton's contemporary, the writer Aphra Behn, seems to have imagined the new temporalities in terms not unlike "planes of historicity" (Koselleck) or "othering" (Certeau and Albanese) – yet not like them either.

III

Absolute, true, and mathematical time, of itself, and from its own nature, flows equally without relation to anything external.

                                        – Sir Isaac Newton, 1687 (qtd. in Kern 11)

By 1664, Aphra Behn had traveled to Surinam and had encountered firsthand the dizzying vortex of European imperialism, colonization, and the slave trade

– the inspiration for *Oroonoko*. Entering the male preserve of London's theatrical marketplace in 1670, she was well positioned to understand that the past needed blood donors, especially female blood donors, and made her comic drama – from *The Forc'd Marriage* to *The Widow Ranter* – a form of satiric transfusion. Fleshing out the rigors of patriarchy and the economics of marriage with two, three, sometimes four sets of lovers, her busy intrigue plots are labyrinths of silly confusion and mercenary calculation: if he leaves here, and she transports her jewels there; if she travels to this place in disguise and ends up at the other place; if he thinks she is where he isn't and finds them instead; if her house is really their house, then … then … There is no real "then," but, rather, in play after play, a mockery of prognostication. Like the grand eschatological designs of her immediate forebears, the end of the comic plot – marriage – is known from the beginning, but it comes to pass only after its value has been ridiculed and debased. As if resisting and defiantly satirizing Newton's "absolute" time, and the linear historiography that was its complement, Behn's intrigue comedies rush toward their end without moving forward. It is, I think, her tampering with the "planes of historicity" – prophecy and prognosis – as much as her admirable pre-Enlightenment demand for sexual and intellectual parity in Grub Street that invites us to view her theatre work as modernity's drama.

In 1687, two years before her death, Behn wrote a farce called *The Emperor of the Moon*, based on a French opera. It has the Behn family of characters: a foolish controlling father, hemmed-in and amorous women, standard-issue male lovers, and more than usually active servants directly in the mold of commedia dell'arte, called Scaramouch and Harlequin, who choreograph the mad intrigues badly and then put everything right. Rounding out the cast are "Negroes, and Persons that dance" (395). Significantly, the heavy father is a scientist, a Neapolitan "Doctor" who, after patient observation of the lunar surface, imagines that the moon is populated and governed like the earth. Baliardo enters in Act One, scene two, "with all manner of Mathematical Instruments hanging at his Girdle; Scaramouch bearing a Telescope twenty (or more) Foot long" (402). The "(or more)" in Behn's stage directions suggests lewd stage business. When Doctor Baliardo looks through the telescope, Scaramouch attaches a picture of a nymph with backlighting to the lens at the other end, and the titillated astronomer thinks that he's looking into the bedroom of the Emperor of the Moon. Behn's unrestrained send-up of scientific observation and scientific instruments (Galileo built the first astronomical telescope in 1609, but Newton built the first reflecting telescope in 1668, just two decades before Behn's play), her pointed linking of the new science to empire building and patriarchal misbehavior, her mocking equation of the newly minted man of science with the old commedia *dottore*, all testify to a certain mocking detachment toward the glories of modernity. In the lavish and most certainly crowd-pleasing finale, Behn provides a spectacular cacophony of historicities: "eight or ten Negroes upon Pedestals" are joined by "Keplair" and "Galileus" (453) while a Chorus nudges Baliardo towards his comeuppance (upon learning that the Emperor of the Moon was his daughter's suitor in disguise, Baliardo renounces science). Are "the Negroes," speechless except when singing and dancing, trophies of the New Science, or are the Negroes and singing scientists both features of the cultural marketplace, providing a shrewd dramatist new contents for old containers? The history of modernity would, of course, exclude Behn's comedies as distorted and trivial fictions, reductive of its higher aims. But the exclusion seems to be mutual – which is to say, dialectically absorbed into the semantic texture of Behn's drama. Thus Behn's refusal to, as Albanese puts it, "bifurcate regions of culture, the better to legitimate some and delegitimate others" (2), may be a refusal of modernity's historical mandate. Interestingly, this refusal had a future. *The Emperor of the Moon* was staged with some regularity until 1777.

IV

My souls (characters) are conglomerations of past and present stages of civilization, bits from books and newspapers, scraps of humanity [...] feverishly hysterical [...] vacillating, disintegrated.

— Strindberg 65

The anti-humanist, antimimetic bias, the mocking but anxious attitude toward history, the references to fragmentation, to hysteria, to subject–object distortion, to modernization: these features of Strindberg's Author's Foreword to *Miss Julie* are everywhere in Western modernism, yet no director that I know of has taken them seriously. In Strindberg's conception, Jean and Julie are bits of the new print technologies and "conglomerations" of modernity's typical periodizing: the past and present stages of civilization. If modernity's historiography invented the past/present divide, modernism's response is to smudge the line radically with a conglomeration of temporal effects. Late-nineteenth-century newspapers were the emblem of capitalism's avant-garde, a montage object that brought together, with no obvious logic, news of the metropole, of the far-flung empire and its exotic and/or turbulent natives, of the latest consumer styles in hats, gloves, and shoes, as well as, of course, news of the market, both national and international. Strindberg makes explicit in his Foreword something that Behn also cultivated in her polemical prefaces and epistles: the cultural and political grounds of theatre production, the reasons why we must go "outside the text" to experience it. No less than Behn's but in a different formal register, Strindberg's dramaturgy in *Miss Julie* is responsive to what Koselleck has called the "planes of historicity." As Behn's theatrical intrigue plots, all future-oriented, mocked both the future imagined in modernity's gendered plots, and its modes of futurizing, Strindberg, drawing from the psychosocial contents of his own culture, has Jean and Julie reveal themselves through the prophetic and predictive logic of dreams. Dreams are another means of mocking futurity or, in Koselleck's terms, the progress narratives of modernity. According to the new Freudian psychology, of which Strindberg was certainly aware, to dream is to condense the materials and desires of the past into distorted images. According to dramatic convention, dreams speak the truth or come true. But Jean, a self-conscious *modernus*, invents his dream out of various scraps of civilization, including Freudian psychology, while Julie, tied to her *antiquus* father (a member of the old landowning aristocracy), does not deserve a future and thus dreams of falling to her death. Prediction collapses into the temporal stasis of eschatological prophecy. Indeed, *Miss Julie*'s evocation of heroic tragedy (suicide as moral duty) is an ironic reminder of teleological design triumphing over narratives of progress, where actions are understood to be the effects of individual rational choice. In Strindberg's astringent plot, as in Behn's chaotic ones, progress-orientation is stalled. Perhaps, through these brief glances at texts by Behn and Strindberg, we can specify two tendencies in modernity's drama: "conglomeration" ("past and present stages of civilization"; "Negroes" dance with scientists) and stalled progress (the planes of early modern historicity – prophecy and prediction – collapse into one another and are unredeemed by the rational promise of progress or futurity).[4]

We should, however, consider a third tendency in modernity's drama, what we might call its tendency to foster a double optic. More explicitly and certainly more self-consciously than Behn, Strindberg seems to want his audiences to assume a double optic – to respond simultaneously to the play on the stage and to the modernity bleeding through the play.[5] The double optic would necessarily be transgressive of modernity's historical project; it would deliberately subvert Hegel's powerful legacy, exemplified in his *Lectures on Fine Arts*, where he subsumes the "diversity and fragmentation of temporal experience" to the unitary unfolding of time as spirit (qtd. in Bender and Wellbery 9). To smash this universalizing history into what Lentriccia calls "histories" is a resistant measure we recognize in discussions that compare modernism's confinements against postmodernism's freedoms. Modernism, in this critical story, is dominated by epistemological uncertainty, while postmodernism contends with ontological issues, as in the confrontation with others and other realities (see McHale 53–78). Because we are still trying to rethink the conventional parameters of modern drama, I want to stay with the subject–object questions modernism raises. The double optic does indeed involve epistemology – what the I/eye sees and therefore knows – but it places at least two irreconcilable realities in view.

Two brief examples will have to suffice. In scene six of Brecht's *Mother Courage and Her Children*, Brecht explains dramatically the politics of the

double optic by enlisting the strategies of modernity's "planes of historicity."
Mother Courage sits with the Chaplain during Tilly's funeral, a "pause" in the
Thirty Years' War. The Chaplain recalls how he once thrilled his congregation
with prophecies of doom, but Courage's discourse consists of present-time
calculations about her wagon and the war. Suddenly Kattrin arrives with a
head wound inflicted by a soldier. As Courage binds her wound, the Chaplain
hears the cannon salutes marking General Tilly's interment.

> THE CHAPLAIN   Now they're burying the general. This is a historic moment.
> MOTHER COURAGE   To me it's a historic moment when they hit my daughter over
> the eye. (184)

Tilly's funeral, as an event in the Thirty Years' War, underscores modernity's
immanent progress narratives, which point toward the formation of the nation-
state in the wake of the destruction of the Holy Roman Empire. Kattrin's
wound, in contrast, is a piece of unofficial history. For the Marxist Brecht,
Kattrin represents the peasant's view of the war – in this case a "view" that
wounds, that nearly puts out an eye. Next to Tilly, Kattrin should remind us of
Behn's "extra" dramatis personae: "Negroes and Persons that dance." Her
needs and dreams are distorted by and will be subsumed into the great man's
story. His funeral, and not her wound, is the only event that modernity recognizes. As a Marxist, Brecht has to reject Strindbergian "conglomeration" and
the notion of stalled futurity. Instead, he wants to slow the pace of modernity
in order to reconstruct our view, to give us a double view that allows us to see
Kattrin's head wound as an "other" historic moment, no less significant than
Tilly's funeral.

My second example is drawn from an article by Brecht's contemporary,
playwright, novelist, and essayist Zora Neale Hurston. In her montage-like
"Characteristics of Negro Expression" (1935), Hurston explains the dynamism of a Negro folklore thought to be merely an authentic window on the
past:

> Negro folklore is not a thing of the past. It is still in the making. Its great variety
> shows the adaptability of the black man: nothing is too old or too new, domestic or
> foreign, high or low, for his use. God and the devil are paired [...] Rockefeller and
> Ford [...] talk and act like good-natured stevedores or mill-hands. Ole Massa is
> sometimes a smart man and often a fool. The automobile is ranged alongside the
> oxcart. (180)

Like Brecht's dialogue above, Hurston's language is an object lesson in the
double optic, shrewdly guiding us from conventional oppositions to ones that
we strain to "see": Rockefeller as a stevedore, the automobile alongside the

oxcart. In modernity's progress narratives, the oxcart should not outlast the Ford. But in the racial legacies of modernity to which I've alluded earlier, "past" and "present" are not ontological realities but "interested" categories that help legitimate some by delegitimating others. However, Hurston's double optic comes with an affect distinctly different from Brecht's. Kattrin cannot "use" her wound, but Hurston's black man revels in, and makes art from, the incongruities presented to his peasant's-eye view of the action. Modernity even recharges his old folk narratives, and he does modernity the favor of turning those narratives into folklore. Those who know this essay will recall the proto–New Critical attention Hurston lavishes on the metaphors, similes, double descriptives, and verbal nouns that are "characteristic" of Negro expression (176–78). In modernity's feedback loop, this would make the New Critics, who began writing just over a decade after the publication of Hurston's text, her blood donors, the actors who fleshed out her past because it had become their future – while, like actors everywhere, they tried to make us believe that they invented it all themselves! This humble (perhaps not so silly) scenario, like Hurston's performative writing, deliberately collapses the planes of historicity, challenges the futurity of progress narratives, and provides a double optic on the idea of history itself. Such, I propose, are the characteristics of modernity's drama.

NOTES

1 In reworking this piece from conference talk to published essay I am grateful to Joanne Tompkins and Ric Knowles for their helpful suggestions.

2 My eleventh-grade teacher, a graduate student at the University of California, Berkeley, seemed to think our reading assignments were wonderfully subversive. Ignorant of the cultural politics, I learned to explicate authorless poems based on the sound, meter, and metaphoric structures they presented. I loved it, and I became a feminist, an actor, and a Marxist fellow-traveler anyway.

3 I thank my colleague Matthew Buckley for bringing this study to my attention.

4 To read Strindberg through "modernity" – and through Koselleck – is to see his close connection to Walter Benjamin's famous description, fifty years later, of Klee's "Angelus Novus," the figure of the angel, its wings caught in the winds of Progress that blast the angel into the future while the wreckage of the ages, in piles at its feet, grows skyward (259–60). Here is Koselleck in brutal shorthand: prophecy without redemption, prognosis stymied, the tilt toward the future so violent that the present is evacuated. One might well ask, given the choreographed nonsense of Behn's intrigue plot and the fatalistic choreography of Strindberg's, what modernity's drama makes of the present. To stall the future is to render the present meaningless, a thematic of modern drama from Büchner to Beckett, but one emphasized and specified if "modern" is understood to mean "modernity."

5 I say this knowing Strindberg's well-known insistence on rapt audience attention for his "intimate" theater and, even in his early Author's Foreword to *Miss Julie*, his call for greater naturalism in acting (if not set design). A double optic does not have to mean distraction.

Aesthetic Prejudice in Modern Drama[1]

MICHAEL J. SIDNELL

The aesthetic prejudice chiefly in question is that subordination or suppression of the performing subject that is particularly associated with realism in modern drama. It stands revealed as such not only in the staging but also in the performative elements of the verbal texts in which dramatic realism, rather paradoxically, defined itself. The incommensurability of an act of representation and a corresponding embodiment of a performing subject is often made quite obvious in the juxtaposition of modern dramas and their operatic versions, and it is a given in the aesthetics of physical theatre. In the earlier twentieth century, such aesthetic issues were so embroiled in fateful political struggles as to induce such crises of representation as those instanced here: the transmutation, in Walter Benjamin's theory, that brought with it an acceptance of didactic performance; the severe problems encountered in Marc Blitzstein's operatic and remedial transformation of Lillian Hellman's flawed aesthetic in *The Little Foxes* and its associated moral blindness; and the divergent theatre practices of W.B. Yeats and T.S. Eliot with respect to speech, music, and dance. In these instances, performativity *versus* discourse is a critical issue, and it remains so in contemporary practice, though hardly the dangerous one that it has been in the past.

The long-drawn-out iconoclastic crisis of early Byzantium, for instance, was a dynastic struggle in which the aesthetic preferences of the rivals were explicit motivations for violence. In the early stages of the crisis, the iconoclastic Leo III ruthlessly suppressed anthropomorphic religious images and their veneration.[2] He couldn't "bear," he said, "to see Christ represented by an image that could neither breathe nor speak, and preferred a symbol" (Lassus 86). After more than a century of conflict and persecution, figural religious imagery was restored in Byzantium, and with it the veneration of the divinity immanent in the icon.

A contemporary approximation to the Byzantine opposition might be found in the dramatic character, as a function of realism, contrasted with the performing subject, which conflates signifier and signified in the immanence of the enactment. There need be nothing magic about this hypostatization or embodiment of the performing-self as such. It might appropriately be called performative iconicity but for the fact that semiotics has boldly appropriated the term "icon" to mean a kind of sign, whereby instantiation defers to interpretation. Resistance to this co-option of the performing subject as sign has been taken to be a justification for the continuation of theatre and even for the theatricalization of social life; at the same time, the reception of theatre has remained mostly a *reading* practice, the interpretation of a so-called performance text.

In the 1930s, the crises of representation were more acute and dangerous, perhaps, than ever before. The prejudices of realism and aestheticism were organized on a massive scale and aspired to total domination – and not just in art. As Walter Benjamin famously observed, fascism was an aestheticization of political life (*Gesammelte Schriften* 1.2.506–8; *Illuminations* 241–42).[3] And Benjamin himself was one of those driven by the exigencies of the time to forge a radically new aesthetic. In relation to theatre, he had to come to terms with what is immanent in the non-linguistic presentation; he did so, though in a manner constrained by his unqualified acceptance of Brechtian epic theatre. Earlier, in his pre-Marxist writings, Benjamin's attention was sharply focused on language. Greek tragedy he conceived as nothing other than a form – the only form, moreover – of pure dialogue; and baroque tragedy, or *Trauerspiel*, in his view, consisted mostly of emotive dialogue, though it sprang from nature and found its fulfilment in music (*Selected Writings* 60).

The early Benjamin contested the critical reception of drama whereby its contents or meanings are privileged over its (verbal) embodiments. "Truth, bodied forth in the dance of represented ideas, resists being projected, by whatever means, into the realm of knowledge" (*Gesammelte Schriften* 1.1.209; *Origin* 29), is his lapidary pronouncement.[4] This doctrine is easier to assent to than to abide by, since the meanings derived from artistic representations, though incommensurate with their truth, can be rendered as discourse, as truth cannot. "Discourse," indeed, in its contemporary usage, signals precisely the assumption that the earlier Benjamin vigorously contests: that the embodiments of art can be converted into knowledge and moral insight. To which it might be added that insofar as modern drama has been read discursively – not just as text but as theatre – that is largely because its own assumptions have enabled such reading. When, for example, dramatic texts offer to prescribe theatrical presentations, they declare those presentations *readable*. This assumption has characterized – at least in its younger days – the distinguished journal that has hosted us on this occasion. It might even be called the original mission of *Modern Drama*. Certainly, in 1958, its founding editor was intent on saving modern drama, and the performance and criticism of it, from the obscurity that had, he asserted, beset modern poetry and the novel (Edwards 1).

Attempting to restrain the habit of deriving moral significance from art's representations, the early Benjamin set himself the Nietzschean objective – though limited – of dislodging the assumptions of realism and Socratic rationalism.

> Although, in general, one hardly dare treat it so unquestioningly as a faithful imitation of nature, the work of art is unhesitatingly accepted as the exemplary copy of moral phenomena without any consideration of how susceptible such phenomena are to representation. The object in question here is not the significance of moral content for the criticism of a work of art; the question is a different one, indeed a double one. Do the actions and attitudes depicted in a work of art have moral significance as images of reality? And: can the content of a work of art, in the last analysis, be adequately understood in terms of moral insights? (*Gesammelte Schriften* 1.1.283; *Origin* 104)[5]

Benjamin's rigorous answers are, first, that "[e]verything moral is bound to life in its extreme sense [...] where it fulfils itself in death, the abode of danger as such" (*Gesammelte Schriften* 1.1.284; *Origin* 105),[6] so that it would be sentimental or insincere to treat art as a primary site of moral activity and naïve to assume that "the actions and attitudes encountered in fictional characters may be used in the discussion of moral problems" (*Schriften* 1.1.283; *Origin* 104);[7] second, that "art cannot [...] allow itself, in its works, to be appointed a councillor of the conscience and it cannot permit what is represented, rather than the actual representation, to be the object of attention" (*Gesammelte Schriften* 1.1.284; *Origin* 105).[8]

By "what is represented" Benjamin means the signified, and by "the actual representation" something like the artistic form that embodies truth in all its quiddity or whatness. And at this point he dissents from Nietzsche; for artistic form absolutely cannot survive in the Nietzschean "abyss of aestheticism [Abgrund der Ästhetizismus]," where no demarcation between form and formlessness is possible (*Gesammelte Schriften* 1.1.281–82; *Origin* 103). In the theatre, the necessary demarcation is between stage and audience, which, says Benjamin, is demonstrated by the very fact of the orchestra pit (*Gesammelte Schriften* 1.1.282–83; *Origin* 104).[9] Later, as we shall see, he would identify this same architectural feature as a negative indicator of a required transformation in the relations between audience and performers.

In his critique of the prejudice that privileges "contents" or "meanings" of representations, Benjamin was endorsing a characteristically modernist and formalist discontinuity between art and morality, truth and meaning. In this respect, he was in agreement with T.S. Eliot, who, in 1933, described the unseasoned reader's need for understanding as the equivalent of "stage fright," which a dollop of meaning could pacify:

> The chief use of the "meaning" of a poem, in the ordinary sense, may be [...] to sat-
> isfy one habit of the reader, to keep his mind diverted and quiet, while the poem does
> its work upon him: much as the imaginary burglar is always provided with a bit of
> nice meat for the house-dog. (*Use of Poetry* 151)

While the reader's mind was thus occupied with the consumption of meaning, the burglarious poem could ransack the receptive house – that is to say, act directly on the "nervous system," which is, in fact, what Eliot thought a play should do (Introduction xii).[10]

Such physiological effects, whether of poetry or of theatre, were far from Benjamin's concerns. And when he asserts that the "actual representation" *is* what it *is*, whereas meaning is open to question and subject to change, he is speaking of dramatic texts, not their staged counterparts. But, since actuality of representation is a phenomenon of the stage performance as well as of the text, the textual embodiments and the staged ones have a relation to each other, as well as to their attributed meanings. Benjamin would come to recognize this; Eliot, moving in the opposite direction, would turn away from the corporeal expression on which he had set such store, opting for a more purely dialogic and static dramatic form.

Undoubtedly these choices were inseparable from political pressures, but there was, and is, no symmetrical alignment of the opposing pairs: modern realism *versus* modernist discontinuity, on the one hand; corporeality and writing, on the other. If modern realism links textuality with moral signifi-cance, the modernist aesthetic privileges performance in both the literary and the theatrical dimensions. And though some modernists were led by an anti-humanist, anti-rational, and performative aesthetic into a politics of authoritar-ianism and force, totalitarian regimes themselves favoured beautified realism with clear moral content.

Benjamin's critique of the overweening claims for moral signification in art did not, of course, take the modernist turn to the right. Instead it took on a rather rabbinical cast:

> "Thou shalt not make unto thee any graven image" – this is not only a warning
> against idolatry. With incomparable emphasis the prohibition of the representation
> of the human body obviates any suggestion that the sphere in which the moral
> essence of man is perceptible can be reproduced. (*Gesammelte Schriften* 1.1.284;
> *Origin* 105)[11]

In effect, Benjamin had already applied this ingenious adaptation of the

Mosaic prohibition in postulating Greek tragedy as the transmutation of a silent, ritualized agon of the body into pure dialogue, which had to do not with moral ethos but with legend (*Gesammelte Schriften* 1.1.280; *Origin* 102). And in his view of baroque tragedy, the characters are figures in the carpet, by no means possessing human individuality. As to the performers playing the characters, the early Benjamin does not consider them at all. It was under the pressure of intense, systematic cruelty that Benjamin was forced to see that purely linguistic "actual representations" could have quite different effects and meanings from corresponding corporeal representations, and he would come to appreciate the special difficulty that a German actor in exile would confront if called upon to play a storm trooper (*Gesammelte Schriften* 2.2.517; *Understanding Brecht* 22).[12]

In our time, physical theatre distinguishes quite clearly between the verbal and the corporeal in verbal representations of arduous acts, on the one hand, and arduousness in the representation of even easy acts on the other. *Really* arduous acts of representation are a feature of the productions of Carbone 14, as in their 1991 adaptation of the *Alcestis*. This work was partly based on a short prose poem by Heiner Müller and took Hitchcock's *The Birds*, the Noh play *Kamasaka*, and the Odyssean descent into the underworld as intertexts. In performance, the prodigiously athletic Johanne Madore and Rodrigue Proteau, among other exhibitions of power and grace, smashed a number of enormous blocks of ice; and even we in the audience suffered a little from the flying chips. I cite this production partly because the title of the work could stand – in fact, does stand – as a motto for stage corporeality in general. The title, *Peau, chair et os* ("Skin, Flesh, and Bone"), comes from the anatomical analogy that Zeami uses with respect to the Noh stage. One of his several triads of theatrical embodiment is great strength (bone), consummate skill (flesh), and unfaltering grace (skin). These qualities, says Zeami, are rarely found in one performer, though that is the perfection aspired to (69–71).[13]

Peau, chair et os is one in a long series of tributes paid to the Noh drama by Western theatre in the twentieth century. In the earlier years of the century, the Noh provided W.B. Yeats with a long-sought model. Thereafter, nearly all of Yeats's plays would include music and dance. This, for a poet who had steadfastly proclaimed the sovereignty of the word in drama, was a radical transition, and the mark of an uncompromising artistic integrity. In Yeats's later plays, the poetry is held in abeyance while room is made for the original contributions of dancers, choreographers, and musicians. And there is ample compensation for the loss of verbal sovereignty, for when words are no longer called upon to govern the whole performance, their "poeticity" – to use Roman Jakobson's term (378) – may be fully registered: they can assume a more performative function of their own. In Yeats's last play, *The Death of Cuchulain*, dance is invoked not just for its own sake but also as the alternative to inadequate verbal enactment: "I wanted a dance because where there are no words there is less to spoil," says the irascible Prologue (1052).

The phenomenon that so annoys Yeats's Prologue is a special instance of a linguistic bodying forth being reduced to its mere content, as when a speech is so mangled in delivery that the original poetic performance is nullified. More typically, poetic acts are deliberately subordinated to the realism of characterization. "There is not nothing, no, no, never nothing,/ Like clashed edges of two words that kill," writes Wallace Stevens (13). In their staged utterances, however, "the clashed edges" of words are frequently dulled by the pretence of impromptu utterance accompanying the clashing of *characters*. The words, that is to say, become *what* is represented rather than, to use Benjamin's phrase, "actual representation."

In the earlier twentieth century, this convention of characterization was so ingrained as almost to be considered a universal aesthetic of theatre, though it was challenged by formalist theorists such as Jiří Veltruský (25).[14] Yet even Sigmund Freud, who was prone to read dramatic characters as "different interlocutors" (Veltruský 25), ventured to suggest that Lady Macbeth and her husband could be considered as a single "character [split] up into two personages," with *his* incipient insomnia dramatized in *her* sleeplessness, the blood on *his* hands provoking *her* intensive hand-washing, and so on, "like two disunited parts of a single psychical individuality" (323–24). Freud's observation, as he perfectly well knew, was in the realm of poetics, not psychopathology. Likewise, Jonathan Pryce's 1980 playing of both the Hamlets, father and son, was in no need of clinical analysis. The Ghost's unearthly voice, issuing from the depths of the convulsed body of young Hamlet, clashed with the Prince's efforts to comprehend his situation. This dialogical clash resonated with those of the soliloquies in a way that would hardly be possible with the customary material ghost.

Nowadays, realism's convention of a unified character is quite often repudiated by distributing a single role between several actors, as Robert Wilson did in *Doctor Faustus Lights the Lights*, his 1992 production of Gertrude Stein's modernist text of the same name. Where Stein herself had written a Marguerite-cum-Helena as "at once singular and plural," Wilson distributed three of the roles between eight actors, including three sharing the title role.[15] This brought clearly into view not only the performing subjects on stage but also the poeticity of Stein's text, which was also emphasized by the speech of performers whose English came to them from this text and not as a mother tongue.[16]

An informative example of the opposite tendency was the thoroughgoing displacement of dialogic acts by interpersonal ones in Fiona Shaw's 1997 staging of T.S. Eliot's *The Waste Land*, which she chose to populate rather than to "do [...] in different voices."[17] In Shaw's performance of it, Eliot's modernist poem was recast as "absolute drama," as it has been called, in which nothing is represented except through interpersonal exchange (see Szondi 8–10). But the fact of Shaw herself as a single performing subject limited this tendency, which could be carried much further by a group of sufficiently misguided actors.

The given examples are by way of indicating that the "actual representations" may belong both to the theatrical and poetic realms, though it is often taken for granted that they belong only to the stage, as, for instance, in the following review of a production of Pinter's *The Room:*

What makes a play dramatic is not how its words work when read, but what happens when they are acted. A play's real existence is in performance, and lines that may seem inert on the pages brighten and fizz in the air of the theatre. (Reynolds)

But in what the reviewer regards as its unreal, offstage existence *The Room* is demonstrably performative in the Austinian sense and, I would say, in a general sense also (Sidnell, "Authorizations"). You can almost hear the dialogue speaking on the page. Pinter's stage directions, however, are conventionally inert and defer to a hypothetical staging.

A type of writing that restricted its page life in anticipation of a " real existence" on the stage was the "well-made play." The model has been extensively analysed, often with a sardonic recognition of the gap between the theatre for which it was made and the one it no longer suits. A late-arriving and enduring example of the kind is *The Little Foxes.* Lillian Hellman's play has frequently been produced, right up to the present; it was regularly used as a model in Josefina Niggli's esteemed course in playwriting, and it is also one of a select group of plays from the modern canon that have been made into operas. Some of the other members of the group are *Wozzek, Lulu, Juno and the Paycock, Purgatory, A View from the Bridge, The Crucible, A Streetcar Named Desire, Six Characters in Search of an Author*, and, joining it very recently, *The Silver Tassie.* All these plays have so far survived their operas, and one or two of the operas have dropped out of view, at least for the time being; so, overall, they don't – or don't yet – support the notion that plays wear out with their themes while operas are kept as fresh as paint by their performances. But the salient point is that the drama/opera pairs are telling examples of contrasting aesthetics of representation with different significations and effects.

For instance, *Six Characters in Search of an Author* by Hugo Weisgall, with a libretto by the Irish playwright Denis Johnston, is a sprightly opera-within-an-opera satirizing operatic conventions and their attendant machineries. Weisgall and Johnston elide Pirandello's modernist discontinuities by means of a musical contest of performing subjects: the quality and style of the singing are the real tests of the characters' authenticity, rather than their ontological claims. That is to say, the theatrical engagement is performative rather than discursive, with all that that implies for audience response. More prob-

lematically, when Marc Blitzstein made an operatic version of Lillian Hellman's *The Little Foxes,* its performativity constituted an unintended but
devastating critique of the play's aesthetic and moral prejudices, which were,
to a degree, those of its genre.

The Little Foxes employs an arsenal of devices for developing its themes
with realism and suspense; and its dialogue is so highly indexical that the two
most frequent words, by a statistical count (Potter), are, rather astonishingly,
not "the" and "and," but "you" and "I" – these pronouns constantly and anxiously signalling the fictive presence of characters. Given the play's themes of
voracious greed, racism, fraud, betrayal, wife abuse, cruelty, whoremonger-
ing, mercenary marriage, and manslaughter in turn-of-the-century Alabama, it
is worth considering where the spectators' pleasures lie. Certainly not in
music, though the play has often been called "melodramatic" and music is of
considerable *thematic* importance in it. The interrupted scraps of piano playing, along with the fragment of a violin, are signs of vanished aristocracy, and
they also signify the antipathy to music of the money-obsessed Hubbards.
Hellman's Hubbards, indeed, suppress music not only in their fictive homes
but on our actual stage. There is pleasure, no doubt, in the suspense; in the
vigorous stirring of emotion, even though it is mostly disgust; and probably in
the comforting reflections that things are worse in the South or that they *were*
worse in 1900, or in 1939, when the play was first performed; and, of course,
in the reflection that a Hubbard is somebody else.

A vital something that Hellman leaves entirely to the staging is the "Southern dialect," which is called for but specifically not written. What *is* repeatedly written is a grossly pejorative label for African-Americans, which would
now reverberate beyond the fictional characterization and action: it could by
no means be received as merely historical and harmlessly mimetic. Moreover,
the fact that Hellman let it stand in her revised and "definitive" text of 1972
(*Collected Plays*) is an indication of an enduring aesthetic prejudice, which
resides not in the linguistic racism that exposes it but in false assumptions
about written and played performatives.

The plotting and characterization of the play are said by Judith Barlow to
constitute "Hellman's own racism." Here is Barlow:

Working class, Black and female, Addie is the only major character in the play who
cannot be implicated in the evil doings because she clearly has no power. Hellman was
in many ways ahead of her White colleagues in the 1930s in giving so crucial a role to
an African American woman: Addie is a voice of reason throughout, and she is present
at the final curtain to provide wisdom and support for Zan. Still, Hellman's own racism
is revealed in the fact that Addie, unlike the White women in Foxes, has no "story" of
her own. It may comfort Whites to believe that the Black women who work for them
are dedicated exclusively to their White "families," have no ties to their own kin or

African American communities, but it is a fiction grounded in a biased world view. (162)

I would agree with Barlow about the "biased world view" embodied in Hellman's fiction but would add that the bias would be even more forceful in the staged representation if the colour-coded distribution of roles in Hellman's text were followed. But, of course, this need not be done, and cross-colour casting might nicely counter the aesthetic prejudice of the text.

In *Regina*, first produced in 1949, Marc Blitzstein had implicitly anticipated Barlow's criticism of the racism of *The Little Foxes* by giving some black characters a story of their own, notably Jazz, the leader of the Angel Band, and his young brother Chinkypin. Blitzstein also deftly foregrounds and erases the play's objectionable term for African-Americans in a single utterance, to which Addie's response is, "don't you use that word around here." And the opera doesn't, ever again. Blitzstein, of course, was modifying not only the fiction but, with great deliberation, what was immanent in the representation. Hellman disapproved of his alienation device, whereby the characters momentarily become a chorus (as in Eliot's *The Family Reunion*) to comment on themselves. And she intensely objected to Blitzstein's transformations of the representation of race, which she found gratuitous, especially his introduction of a jazz band (Gordon 307).[18] But if it was inescapable that music should dominate the opera, so was it, given the Alabama setting, that a lot of the music should be black. Even the 1941 film had ventured in this direction, though its Swanee River score and imagery betrayed its own bias. What is profoundly transvaluative in *Regina* is that, though some of the music is sinister enough, Blitzstein also makes a point of letting his lyrics do much of the dirty work by going against the grain of the music. And in the black music especially there is a soaring hopefulness for which there is no counterpart in Hellman's grim play. Blitzstein was forced to make different major cuts for the various productions of *Regina*, to the effect that the opera has never been staged in full. But it has been recorded in a version that convincingly claims to fulfil Blitzstein's original scope and vision.

Blitzstein's approach to opera owed much to Brecht's example, and, indeed, to Brecht's personal advice, which had been the instigation for *The Cradle Will Rock* (Gordon 113). And what Blitzstein had learned was something like what Benjamin learned from the same teacher: that text and theatre are "actual representations" of their own aesthetic assumptions, and that these assumptions may be consistent with their discursive meanings, or otherwise. But in *Regina* there is also an unrestrained empathy and joy that seem remote from epic theatre.

My last example is a prime instance of a deep-considering dramatist who adopted a modernist and theatrically performative aesthetic in the 1930s and backed away from it as its implications became clearer to him. The work in question is T.S. Eliot's partly familiar, partly unknown, scenario for a play called *The Superior Landlord*. The familiar part of this scenario is the one fragment that it incorporates from the published work *Sweeney Agonistes: Fragments of an Aristophanic Melodrama*. The rest of the scenario remains unpublished, unplayed, and almost unknown (Sidnell, *Dances* 263–65). The published fragments have often been restaged since Hallie Flanagan's first production of them at Vassar in 1933 and the entirely independent production by the London Group Theatre in the following year (Sidnell, *Dances* 91–107). Brecht (who attended on the same night as Yeats, as it happened) declared *Sweeney* the best thing in London, or so it was said. It has been regretted that Eliot did not take the *Sweeney Agonistes* experiment further: but, in fact, he did, in the complete scenario for *The Superior Landlord*.

In the scenario, Dusty and Doris are throwing a bottle party. Two drummers – one Jewish, one black – have brought banjos with them. The party is interrupted by various "Intruders," one of whom, Pereira, pays the girls' rent. He is defeated in argument by Sweeney, who reveals that he in turn is *Pereira*'s landlord – the "superior landlord" of the title.

Mrs Porter, long awaited, eventually arrives singing a modified version of the ballad of *Casey Jones:*

And the neighbours knew by the shrieks and the groans
That the man at the throttle was Casey Jones.

She is killed by Sweeney; probably not for the first time, since he shows no surprise at her later resurrection, which occurs in time to conclude with a wedding procession led by the two of them.

The scenario is divided into two parts separated by an interlude consisting of a short ballet by a pair of dancers in period costumes against a sky-blue drop and a passage of poetry, spoken by a hidden *diseuse* and "in complete contrast" to the verse of the play. Eliot thought better of this extravagant interlude and deleted it, perhaps because it was inconsistent with the structure that he had taken over from Francis Cornford's *The Origin of Attic Comedy* (1914), in which Cornford proposed just such a ritual origin of Greek comedy as Nietzsche had proposed for tragedy. The *Superior Landlord* scenario attempts to fill out that original structure in a contemporary ritual and in a manner consistent with the younger Eliot's idea of a poet of the theatre with "a part to play in society as worthy as that of the music-hall comedian" (*Use of Poetry* 154). Though utterly different in style, Eliot's scenario has something in common with Yeats's dance plays in its performative emphasis on corporeal, musical, and poetic events as such.

In Eliot's later plays, urbane, mostly upper-middle-class characters would talk to each other, seated or standing still, in unrhymed verse, and the vestigial chorus became a psychological phenomenon. In his earlier plays and experiments, including *The Rock* and *Murder in the Cathedral*, music, dance, fixed metres, rhyme, and chorus work had been vital elements of the presentation. The revolution in Eliot's work for the theatre, associated as it was with acute political and religious pressures, was a highly symptomatic episode in a crisis of theatrical representation, though it has hardly been seen in this perspective. Rather like the earlier Benjamin and, for that matter, the aforementioned Byzantine Emperor, the later Eliot subordinated stage corporeality in all its profane sensuousness in favour of the word as the proper abode of spirit or Logos.

As I have mentioned, the earlier Benjamin designated the orchestra pit as a necessary division between the onstage chorus and the audience, protecting form from formlessness. In his later writings he precisely reverses this position:

> The point at issue in the theater today can be more accurately defined in relation to the stage than to the play. It concerns the filling-in of the orchestra pit. The abyss which separates the actors from the audience like the dead from the living, the abyss whose silence heightens the sublime in drama, whose resonance heightens the intoxication of opera, this abyss which, of all the elements of the stage, most indelibly bears the traces of its sacral origins, has lost its function. The stage is still elevated, but it no longer rises from an immeasurable depth; it has become a public platform. Upon this platform the theater now has to install itself. (*Gesammelte Schriften* 2.2.519; *Understanding Brecht* 1)[19]

The demarcation between the forms on the stage and the formless realm of the spectators is no longer functional or wanted. Formerly, Benjamin had posited an artistic embodiment poised between Nietzschean aestheticism and discursive moralizing; now he was so extremely anti-Nietzschean as to endorse a Socratic relation of hero and audience. In this new relation, the performing subject is recognized as such but immediately conscripted by writer and director into a dialectical process that denies to subjecthood − even in the auratic personage of Charles Laughton − the status of unified, immanent truth. In this aesthetic, forged under great pressure, the fracturing of the performing subject powerfully represented the cruelty of its time.

NOTES

1 To the following people I owe special thanks: to Stephen Davis of the Blitzstein Estate for permission to play a recorded extract from *Regina,* and the Toronto Public Library and Lee Ramsay for making it available; to Natalie Rewa for advice

about the preparation and use of audio and visual materials, and to Paul Stoesser for his technical skill in presenting them; and to Ric Knowles for inviting me to give this talk at the "Modern:Drama" conference convened at the Graduate Centre for Study of Drama, Toronto, in May 2000.

2 See Barnard; Barasch; and Lassus.

3 *"Der Faschismus läuft folgerecht auf eine Ästhetisierung des politischen Lebens hinaus. [...]* Ihre Selbstentfremdung hat jenen Grad erreicht, der sie ihre eigene Vernichtung als ästhetischen Genuß ersten Ranges erleben läßt. *So steht es um die Ästhetisierung der Politik, welche der Faschimus betreibt. Der Kommunismus antwortet ihm mit der Politisierung der Kunst."* / "The logical result of Fascism is the introduction of aesthetics into political life. [...] Mankind['s] [...] self-alienation has reached such a degree that it can experience its own destruction as an aesthetic pleasure of the first order. This is the situation of politics which Fascism is rendering aesthetic. Communism responds by politicizing art." References to Benjamin's *Gesammelte Schriften* are to volume, part, and page. They are followed by references to corresponding English translations.

4 "Die Wahrheit, vergegenwärtigt im Reigen der dargestellten Ideen, entgeht jeder wie immer gearteten Projektion in den Erkenntnisbereich."

5 "Dem Kunstwerk, das man so leichthin sonst als naturgetreue Wiedergabe kaum zu fassen wagt, traut man bedenkenlos die exemplarische Kopie moralischer Phänomene zu, ohne die Frage nach deren Abbildbarkeit auch nur aufzuwerfen. Es steht dabei durchaus nicht die Bedeutung moralischer Sachverhalte für die Kritik eines Kunstwerks, sondern ein anderes, ein doppeltes vielmehr, in Frage. Eignet den Handlungen, Verhaltungsweisen, wie sie ein Kunstwerk darstellt, moralische Bedeutung als den Abbildern der Wirklichkeit? Und: Sind es moralische Einsichten, als in denen zuletzt der Gehalt eines Werks adäquat zu erfassen ist?"

6 "Alles Moralische ist gebunden ans Leben in seinem drastischen Sinn, dort nämlich, wo es im Tode als Stätte der Gefahr schlechtweg sich innehat."

7 "Handlungen und Verhaltungsweisen, die bei erdichteten Personen begegnen, seien für die Erörterung moralischer Probleme so zu nutzen wie das Phantom für anatomische Belehrung."

8 "Denn ihrerseits kann Kunst in keinem Sinn es zugestehn, sich zum Gewissensrat in ihren Werken promoviert und das Dargestellte statt der Darstellung selbst beachtet zu sehen."

9 "Vor allem sind die Chöre und das Publikum durchaus nicht Einheit. Das wird, soweit der Abgrund zwischen beiden, die Orchestra, durch ihr Vorhandensein es nicht belegt, zu sagen bleiben." / "Above all, there is no kind of unity between the choruses and the public. This needs to be said, insofar as the gulf between them, the orchestra, does not demonstrate it by its very presence."

10 "The play, like the religious service, should be a stimulant to make life more tolerable and augment our ability to live; it should stimulate partly by the action of vocal rhythms on what, in our ignorance, we call the nervous system."

11 "'Du sollst dir kein Bildnis machen' – das gilt nicht der Abwehr des Götzendienstes allein. Mit unvergleichlichem Nachdruck beugt das Verbot der Darstellung des Leibs dem Anschein vor, es sei die Sphäre abzubilden, in der das moralische Wesen des Menschen wahrnehmbar ist."

12 "It is easy to see that to play a stormtrooper or a member of the 'people's courts' is a very different task for a refugee actor than it is, say, for a good-hearted actor to play Iago. For the former, empathy is no more suitable than it would be for a political fighter to identify himself with his comrades' murderer. A different mode of acting – the epic mode to be plain – may find a new justification here and achieve a new kind of success." / "In der Tat ist es leicht zu erkennen, daß die Darstellung eines SA-Mannes oder eines Mitglieds des Volksgerichts für einen emigrierten Schauspieler eine ganz andere Ausgabe bedeutet als z.B. die es Jago für einen herzensguten." See the end of "What Is Epic Theater" (2nd version) (*Understanding Brecht* 22).

13 *Peau, chair et os.* See Massoutre. In his program note, Maheu refers to another triad: sight (skin); hearing and dance (flesh); spirit (bone).

14 "Dramatic dialogue is not, in actual fact, a sequence of speeches said by different interlocutors but a single, uninterrupted and intrinsically unified utterance by the dramatist. The interlocutors are just meanings – as immaterial as any other meaning – deriving from that utterance."

15 Three actors played Marguerite and Helena, two played Mephisto, and three played Faustus. See Savran 25–27.

16 The distinctively modernist plays of Gertrude Stein appear to have been designed to resist the transmutation of verbally embodied representations into the mere contents of staged ones, or to be used as prescriptions for such. Hence the absence, variously, of character names, of definitive distribution of speeches, of stage directions and scenic assumptions and other conventional attributes of playscripts. Stein's plays are often indistinguishable from her non-dramatic writings, her libretti from her drama. She appears to render unto the theatre those things that are theatre's.

17 "He Do the Police in Different Voices" was Eliot's original title. See Eliot, *The Waste Land* 5. A *Times Literary Supplement* review of the BBC film version offers a detailed account of Shaw's approach to the performance of the poem. See D.S.

18 Gordon quotes Hellman's letter to Blitzstein of 27 June 1949: "I still feel that the whole approach to the Negro in the play, whether it is the jazz band, or Jabez's singing to Birdie, or the Negroes at the party, is sentimental. I think the original play already had too much of such sentimentality and it was an artistic mistake. But I don't think we should increase the mistake" (307).

19 "Worum es heute im Theater geht, läßt sich genauer mit Beziehung auf die Bühne als auf das Drama bestimmen. Es geht um die Verschüttung der Orchestra. Der Abgrund, der die Spieler vom Publikum wie die Toten von den Lebendigen scheidet, der Abgrund, dessen Schweigen im Schauspiel die Erhabenheit, dessen Klin-

gen in der Oper den Rausch steigert, dieser Abgrund, der unter allen Elementen der Bühne die Spuren ihres sakralen Ursprungs am unverwischbarsten trägt, ist funktionslos geworden." The later version of this passage, in "What Is Epic Theater?" (2nd version), is more specific to the epic and didactic theatres. This limitation may contain a hint of reservation about the applicability of the remark to theatre in general. See Benjamin, *Understanding Brecht* 22.

Why Modern Plays Are Not Culture: Disciplinary Blind Spots[1]

SHANNON JACKSON

"[The] lack of communication with the other disciplines gives the drama a peculiar insularity."

> – Robert Brustein, "Why American Plays Are Not Literature" 245

"I learned something from analysing drama which seemed to me effective not only as a way of seeing certain aspects of society but as a way of getting through to some of the fundamental conventions [with] which we group as [a] society itself. These, in their turn, make some of the problems of drama quite newly active."

> – Raymond Williams, "Drama in a Dramatized Society" 20

My title is taken, with significant modification, from the same essay in which Robert Brustein chastised "the drama" for not being interdisciplinary. In that piece, "Why American Plays Are Not Literature," Brustein made clear that something called "literature" was the discipline with which drama most needed contact. Not only was it, in Brustein's view, the only discipline with which the drama needed contact, but its models of value were those to which all drama should aspire. Condemning the fact that American dramatists almost never sought representation in "the literary periodicals," his 1959 use of the term "interdisciplinary" was thus a way of rationalizing a formula for the cultural legitimation of the drama, American and otherwise. My second epigraph is from a drama scholar who was Brustein's contemporary, if also, at some level, his antithesis. Before and between renowned texts such as *Culture and Society* and *Keywords*, Raymond Williams published a series of books in the field of drama – *Drama from Ibsen to Eliot*, *Drama in Use*, *Modern Tragedy*, and a revised *Drama from Ibsen to Brecht* – a "set" that he considered a formative "critical study" of the dramatic form (Foreword n.pag.).

Robert Brustein and Raymond Williams published some of their most

widely read studies of drama in the fifties and sixties, in two different countries and in intellectual environments that bore a vexed if interdependent connection to each other. Both began their intellectual lives as drama scholars,
and both would go on to become "cultural critics" of sorts. However, while
both would take up the question of whether or not "plays" were "culture,"
their answers differed significantly – a difference that depended on varying
notions of the term "culture." For Brustein, the cultural denoted a realm of
artistic preserve and artistic excellence, free from what he would later call the
sociologizing of aesthetics. Williams's name and thought, on the other hand,
would become synonymous with another cultural project – the project of "cultural studies." As someone who figures prominently and repeatedly in the origin narratives of this movement, Williams thus helped to advance the theories,
politics, and methodologies whose "sociology" Brustein would later condemn. How "the drama" could serve as point of entry to two very different
relations to "the cultural" is one of the concerns of this essay.

It seems useful to ask such a question in light of a number of other debates
currently at issue in the field(s) of drama, theatre, and performance studies.
Certainly, the journal *Modern Drama* has redefined itself and re-signified the
terms of its title in part as a response to such debates – many of which turn on
the question of drama's relation to traditional concepts of culture, as well as to
newer methods of cultural critique. Of course, questions, debates, and ad hoc
conversation about the future of – and interrelations between – various components of our field are often subject to severe reduction. In some circles, scholars of performance studies and self-labeled "progressive" theatre studies claim
a particular kinship with cultural studies. This means promoting an approach to
performance that unsettles divisions between high and low; that advocates a
radically contextual and socially grounded analysis; that takes seriously feminist, antiracist, and intercultural critiques of identity and globalization; that
deploys cutting-edge interdisciplinary methodologies; and that links scholarship to modes of praxis outside the academy. To claim a kinship with cultural
studies and thus to assert one's "newness," in turn, tends to recast other orientations as "old" and as antithetical to a cultural studies project. Such identifica-
tions can have the effect, for instance, of retroactively construing the scholarly
project of modern drama as traditional and as metonymically aligned with all
that cultural studies is not. To study "drama" in this caricatured light is thus to
perpetuate a narrow, elite, and Eurocentric line of inquiry, one that reproduces
cultural divisions between high and low, one that disavows both theatrical and
materialist relations of production and whose "literary" mode of analysis presumes and reifies the artistic autonomy of the isolated dramatic text. Such
characterizations are typically peppered with supporting quotations from contemporary cultural theorists such as Stuart Hall, Paul Gilroy, Lawrence Grossberg, and Angela McRobbie, as well as the luminaries from whom so many of
them claim to have descended – including Raymond Williams himself. This

essay is thus also an exploration of a complicated and undertheorized history between drama and cultural studies, one whose disavowal paradoxically deploys the intellectual genealogy of a drama-cum-cultural theorist such as Williams to serve as ammunition for a critique of drama scholarship. Rather than conceiving cultural theory solely as a contemporary means of revising traditional drama scholarship, I suggest that we also recognize the ways in which the epistemologically fraught "life of the drama" has propelled the development of cultural theory itself (Bentley, *Life of the Drama*).

As a way to focus questions about the vexed genealogies of drama, theatre, performance, and cultural studies, the argument of this essay will return to the concept of literature – the unproblematically valued term in Brustein's world, the ambivalently devalued term in some cultural studies arenas. Recent debates in cultural theory, theatre, and humanities scholarship often revolve around the role of so-called "literary" approaches in cultural critique – as well as around adjacent notions of "textual," "discursive," or "linguistic" analyses. Indeed, arguments of legitimation and delegitimation often pivot and twist around conflicted uses of such terms. Some performance studies scholars might associate a "literary" method with an elite, textualist, anti-materialist study of modern drama. However, when some of the same performance studies scholars engage in de-contextualized analyses of the tropes of avant-garde performance art, it is not entirely clear who is being less materialist, which analyses are more text-based, nor what performance forms are actually less "high." Conversely, scholars of modern drama might reject a piece of scholarship on a non-theatrical performance event as "unliterary" without acknowledging the indebtedness of the analysis to formalist and/or textualist methods of critique. Consequently, it seems important to remind ourselves of the extraordinarily large number of associations attached to the literary and its attendant list of catch-all adjectives. As I continue, I hope that such reminders will help to expose some blind spots in current oppositional debates amongst and within our fields and subfields. To investigate such a genealogy is, after Foucault, to challenge assumptions of disciplinary singularity, even when such assumptions may be expedient for both self-labeled "traditionalist" defenses and self-labeled "counter-traditionalist" appeals. The genealogical consciousness makes it less easy to uphold divisions between "old" and "new" approaches, sometimes reversing convenient notions of who is borrowing from whom and sometimes also reversing the categories of intellectual precedence and descent. As a result, it can unsettle our conceptions of what fields are foundational and derivative, of what scholarship is interdisciplinary and intra-disciplinary, and of what approaches are narrow and expansive. The conflicted referentiality of the literary is just one arena where such binary delineations are made in drama, theatre, performance, and cultural studies; hence, the investigation of literature's conflicts is also one way of destabilizing those delineations.

The concept of literature is also important from an institutional perspective. The profession of literature has served as the primary vehicle for establishing the cultural capital of modern English-speaking universities and, hence, has also served as the barometer for gauging the legitimacy of other humanistic fields. Additionally, as the professionalizing field that reluctantly housed the study of drama in the early twentieth century, as the professionalized field from which theatre's academic promoters broke free throughout the rest of the twentieth century, literary studies has long served as foil, shadow, and sometimes foundation to the emerging disciplinary identities of drama, theatre, and performance studies. Along the way, Literature and English departments have produced some of the most significant and widely circulated critical paradigms in the humanities, models and frameworks that many in drama, theatre, and performance studies have adopted despite their own anti-literary rhetoric and institutional location. At the same time, the status of drama and theatre within literary studies has remained suspect, despite critical paradigms that, to varying degrees, might have been illuminatingly concretized by the example of dramatic performance. Consequently, current conversations about the institutional legitimacy of our fields are linked implicitly to this complicated institutional history. Furthermore, literary studies is thoroughly enmeshed in the development of cultural studies. Perhaps the most formative cultural studies critiques of literature have emerged from within the field of literature itself. The movement "from literary into cultural studies," to use Anthony Easthope's phrase, was initiated most often by professors of English who sought to enlarge literature's objects of study to include a variety of print and nonprint forms, as well as to expand the range of questions asked of traditional literary documents. Such a movement has been neither harmonious in its execution nor complete in its transformation. This essay is thus also an attempt to install the concept of modern drama next to such disharmonies and partialities. Modern drama is a cultural form that has always inhabited a reluctant position inside and outside the field of literary studies. An exploration of the blind spots around modern drama clarifies and defamiliarizes the conflicts that inhere in the transformation from literary to cultural studies. Drama's ill fit in both "older" literary studies and "newer" cultural studies suggests that there may be more continuity between past and present approaches than contemporary paradigms admit. Finally, I hope to make connections among terms and subfields that are often too conveniently opposed, as well as to defamiliarize the defensive postures and persistent ambivalences that seem to keep those oppositions in place.

DRAMA AND CULTURAL CAPITAL

I would like now to investigate different associations attached to the word "culture," and with them an awareness of the institutional context in which humanistic knowledges emerge, circulate, and accumulate value. From there, I hope to offer a longer reflection on the historical status of "drama" in the academy, or, more specifically, on the status in the academy of the associations that have been ambivalently attached to the term "drama." These associations vary widely and are often not reconcilable. Drama can be both low and high, contextualized or de-contextualized, commercial or avant-garde, feminized or masculinized, literary or unliterary, cultured or cultural, a text or an event, practical or impractical, more fake or more real, depending upon the legitimating or delegitimating context. Within literary studies, drama's associations have been plotted along such contradictory axes, and it is along these axes that Robert Brustein's essay also turns. The essay is perhaps most useful as an index of the kind of available metaphors and unprocessed tropes characteristic of such exegeses. Brustein accuses dramatists of being too "anxious to please," of going for "climactic emotional effects," of developing an "unsavory reputation through [drama's] alliance with the market place," and of having a "tainted imagination" (247, 248). In a characteristically contradictory relationship to European legacies, he manages to accuse American dramatists both of being less distinguished than European playwrights and, at the same time, of catering to cosmopolitan influences. Brustein perhaps made a correct assessment in recognizing that detachment from the realm of literary production and its world of "literary periodicals" would threaten the status of drama as a legitimated cultural form. As John Guillory writes in his study of cultural capital in the university humanities curriculum, "An individual's judgment that a work is great does nothing in itself to preserve that work, unless that judgment is made in a certain institutional context, a setting in which it is possible to insure the *reproduction* of the work, its continual reintroduction to generations of readers" (28). When Brustein worried about whether drama was or was not literature, he was effectively worrying about whether drama was or was not "Culture" in a particular, credible form. In so doing, he reiterated concerns about drama's illegitimate status in a process of acculturation, arguments that had shadowed the curricular position of drama in the academy for more than half a century. The terms of Brustein's argument further employed a national division to support a hierarchy of cultural capital, shoring up the literary legitimacy of drama in general by renouncing its "bastard" American offspring (Smith). The structure of such an argument would be repeated in our field as various drama scholars engaged in a nationalist process of internal self-splintering – subordinating African-American drama to American drama, Irish to English, English to French – in order to save some aspect of drama from complete literary anomie.

Around the turn of the twentieth century, the concept of "literature" consolidated as a curricular and professional category. Literary credibility was determined by the degree to which a pedagogic text fulfilled the sometimes nebulous but persistent standards of a humanist liberal culture, one that sought to secure a position within a U.S. university system increasingly preoccupied with utility, with technical knowledge, and with the paradigms of scientific inquiry. As Laurence Veysey has argued in *The Emergence of the American University,* the latter borrowed a revised version of a Germanic model in which lines of inquiry were made more rigorous by installing them within the conventions of scientific research. Some early literary scholars worked to adapt philological methods to make literature into a science and to promote an ethic of literary research whose constructed sense of "rigor" we live with, in different form, today. More pernicious for the status of literature, however, were the effects of industrialization, a rising business class, and a distrust of intellectualism; this milieu produced a concern for practicality and "real-world" sensibilities in higher education, one that dangerously positioned literature within the realm of non-utility. Reacting within and against both "the German method" and a hyper-practical emphasis that threatened to divest higher education of a "spiritual" dimension, scholars of literature joined promoters of "liberal culture" to argue for the preservation of a higher

human character, shaped "by the deliberate choice of whatever is noble and helpful." The man of culture was "positive, but reverent ... chastened in manners and voice." [...] He possessed breadth: "breadth of understanding and learning, breadth of sensibility and artistic feeling; breadth, both of aspiration and endeavor – of deference and charity." (Veysey 186)

As Veysey concludes, "[a]n aesthetic, a moral and a tacit social code were all to be found intermingled in the conception of culture as it existed in American academic circles of the late nineteenth century" (191).[2]

Brustein's 1950s articulation was thus embedded in this concept of culture, chastising the vulgar sensibility of American drama for not aspiring to Arnoldian goals. Furthermore, when he criticized dramatists for pandering to crowds or for sullying the theatre with the forces of economic rather than cultural capital, he resuscitated the anti-utility arguments of early cultural dissidents, condemning the effects of the "real-world" ethos of American business on the products of culture.

Brustein's essay condemns only American drama; however, drama's real-worldness and manifest enmeshment in economic relations had made its academic status as "literature" (that is, as "Culture") shaky for quite some time. Indeed, the significant aspect of modern drama, initially called "drama other than Shakespeare" in a hesitant literary curriculum, was its equivocal status as literature that was not quite literature, a humanist form that, by virtue of its saturation with "the practical," made it not quite humanist after all. Academic promoters of theatre responded to this liminality in varied and often contradictory ways. While some, such as Eric Bentley, created compensatory arguments for drama within accepted literary categories, others reversed the terms of value to characterize drama as a rugged, masculine pursuit that countered the fastidious preoccupations of the literary reading room. Indeed, Brustein's corpus can be seen as a constant ride over a disavowed ambivalence. While his 1959 essay on American plays aspires to make the cultural position of a "man of the theatre" equivalent to that of the "man of letters," other essays and speeches would find it more expedient to emphasize the numerous ways in which theatre differed from the conventions of lettered transmission and literary pedagogy. This vacillation is symptomatic of pervasive classed and gendered patterns in quests for cultural legitimacy. While certain circumstances prompt legitimators to invoke classed cultural hierarchies unproblematically, other contexts prompt some of the same proponents to condemn such standards as feminized, as judgments and preoccupations derived from the prescriptive and peripheral tastes of a feminine imagination.

DRAMA AND CRITICISM

In the 1950s, gentlemanly notions of liberal culture only vaguely represented the field of literary studies as it was being practiced and legitimated in the university at the time. By mid-century, the English methods of "practical criticism" and the American practices of "new criticism" had penetrated most English departments on both sides of the Atlantic, working to replace nebulous, belletristic notions of cultured literature with a method of rigorous "close reading" and decontextualized explication. New Criticism argued for literature less as the moral vehicle of liberal culture than as an object whose understanding required a formalized method of expert reading, one whose feats of interpretation matched the rigor, difficulty, and degree of specialization found in scientific research. Terry Eagleton isolates "the brisk, bloodless" prose of I.A. Richards as the most extreme of new critical originators: "Far from questioning the alienated view of science as a purely instrumental, neutrally 'referential' affair, [Richards] subscribes to this positivist fantasy" (39). New criticism thus served as a mid-century response to the consolidation of a so-called Germanic research university, fending off accusations of literary fuzziness by formalizing its study. While new critical practitioners such as John Crowe Ransom, Cleanth Brooks, R.P. Blackmur, and William Empson varied in tone and perspective, they generally conceived literature – most ideally embodied in poetry – as a "self-enclosed object" to be deciphered by "the toughest, most hard-headed techniques of critical dissection" (Eagleton 40, 42). Meanwhile, as movements for coeducation and democratic legislation such as the British Education Act and the American G.I. Bill opened the doors of English and North American universities to a varied student population, humanities professors had to devise wider methods of cultural dissemination. In such a context, as both John Guillory and Gerald Graff have noted, the text-focused, genius-tracking methods of new criticism made for easy syllabification and efficient lecturing, allowing the professing of literature to fit more easily within a managed university concerned that its curriculum "scale" to meet the demands of an increasingly large, and presumably unlettered, clientele. The trajectory of this "critical technocracy" advanced another level with the structuralist developments of "genre criticism," most famously and formatively embodied in the work of Northrop Frye. His *Anatomy of Criticism* (1967) incorporated a circumscribed notion of literary history into new critical formalism, developing an elaborate system of categories in which to place each instance of literary production. Significantly, this system expelled "any history other than literary history: literary works are made out of other literary works, not out of any material external to the literary system itself" (Eagleton 80). Frye's genre criticism – and the genre criticism that would follow – thus had the satisfying character of scientific and historical paradigms while, at the same time, severely limiting the content and character of the history it brought to bear.

Some mid-century critics – such as Cleanth Brooks and, to some extent, Eric Bentley – worked to situate the drama within the legitimating structures of new critical frameworks. Of the formative new critics, Brooks's scholarship and textbooks perhaps best exemplify new critical analyses of "the drama" and "the dramatic." A comparison of textbooks such as *Understanding Poetry*, *An Approach to Literature*, and *Understanding Drama* demonstrates this circumscribed critical sphere, one that located drama in a relational field that measured its distance from poetry. Brooks and Robert B. Heilman's *Understanding Drama* (1948) divides its table of contents into "Problems of the Drama," "Simpler Types," "More Mature Types," and "Special Studies in the Tragic Mode," whereas Brooks and Robert Penn Warren's *Understanding Poetry* (1960) divides chapters under far more secure categories such as "Narrative Poems," "Descriptive Poems," "Metrics," "Tone," and "Imagery." "Problems of the Drama" also includes extended essays that compare drama to "other literary forms" in order to recount the "vast amount of materials accessible to fiction and poetry [that] are not accessible to drama" (Brooks and Heilman 24). *Understanding Poetry*, on the other hand, includes no such comparative essays and seems not to need references to other genres to serve as illuminating counterpoint. Under such frames, the fundamentals of drama, such as "place," "exposition," "tempo," and "overt action," were conceived as "problems" – as "compensatory adjustments" (Brooks and Heilman 26) – rather than as "accessible" materials on a par with the poetic materials of metrics, tone, and imagery. In its pedagogical presentation of several genres, *An Approach to Literature* (Brooks, Purser, and Penn Warren, 1952) also reproduced similar hierarchical comparisons. Meanwhile, Eric Bentley's widely circulated essays and books offer a related illustration of a mid-century dramatic discourse, one that in many ways mixed the language of cultural capital with the language of new criticism for self-legitimation. In *The Playwright as*

Thinker (1946), for example, Bentley deploys the disparaging tones of Arnoldian cultural analysis, lamenting that "drama as a high art has appeared only sporadically" (75) and quoting Bernard Shaw's statement that "[t]he theater is *always* at a low ebb" (xix). Echoing and anticipating Robert Brustein and others, Bentley condemns the debased contextuality of the theatre – its commercialism, its audience relations – as well as the particular debasement of American theatre's "low ebb." At the same time, Bentley could be found justifying his approach to drama by invoking new critical language. He opposes himself to those

who [hold] that a good play is not a thing that can profitably be examined in detail and that criticism of great drama is therefore fruitless or impossible. My own conviction is that any good thing is a *very* good thing and that any good work of art can bear the closest scrutiny. The better, the closer. (xxii)

Bentley's references to "close reading" and to the kinds of "scrutiny" associated with practical and new criticism suggest how fully a type of formalist appeal could legitimate a mid-century critical endeavor.

Other academic promoters of drama addressed the fundamental ways in which new critical methods altered both the object of literature and the concept of cultural capital. Written in 1952, John Gassner's peremptorily titled essay "There Is No American Drama" exemplifies a much more suspicious response, as well as the anxieties that circulated around theatre's institutionalization at mid-century. I will focus on it at length because such anxieties will also help to foreground an alternate genealogy between drama and cultural studies. Like Brustein, Gassner chose American drama's equivocal status as the basis for a lengthier meditation on cultural hierarchy. However, by exploring the disconnect between new critical models and the examples of American drama, the thrust of his argument takes a much different direction. He cites, for instance, the political commitment of drama in the twenties and thirties, an avowed contextuality that resists the decontextualized strategies of new critical interpretations. He continues, moreover, by reciting all of the associations that have clung to the drama ever since the project of literary legitimation began in the academy. His ardor suggests his own internalization of the dilemma, an ambivalence that continues throughout the essay:

We were deficient in taste and intellect. We were debased by Broadway vulgarity. We were banal, blatant, and shamelessly sentimental. When we evinced sympathy with the common man, we descended to bathos. When we left plain realism, we gave ourselves up to vapid abstractions and to puerile, undergraduate metaphysics. (24)

Within this provisional acceptance of a debased condition, Gassner nevertheless works to develop a reverse snobbery as a kind of defense. He replicates contemporaneous attacks on the new criticism by invoking the threat of its "European orientation," reproducing a 1950s critique of Europeanization in much the same way that earlier scholars invoked the threat of Germanification in the study of literature. For Gassner, T.S. Eliot figured prominently in this orientation: "It is European *cum* Eliot-sponsored aristocratic traditionalism *cum* erstwhile aristocratic southern agrarianism transposed into the key of so-called New Criticism" (25).

Gassner, however, was more than knee-jerkedly dismissive of new criticism, rightly anticipating a paradigmatic shift in literary studies that would not bode well for American drama:

The charges they make directly and by implication are serious and should be received seriously. They are important, too, because the attitude they reveal may well pervade the educated members of an entire generation upon which the fate of any significant theatre we may have in the 1950's will largely depend. (84)

Gassner, in fact, agreed with new critical objections even as he tried to argue from a different position. "The new criticism," he continues, "is often so acute that it must be respected, but so sweeping in its condemnation of American drama that it must be refuted" ("Answer" 59). Gassner made the choice to refute not by arguing for American drama within new critical paradigms but by arguing that such paradigms could not track the significant interrelations of the American theatrical event. Indeed, he went so far as to suggest that adherence to new critical principles would compromise the "Americanism" of that event. To subscribe to this dominant paradigm, an adherence embodied in the figure of Eric Bentley, whom Gassner calls "the most Europeanized of the critics" ("No American Drama" 24), would be to "reject everything that has been distinctly American in our playwriting" ("Answer" 60). Imagining over-cultivated playwrights writing "with the fastidiousness, the mental discipline, the refined or sharpened taste" of a new critical sensibility, he issues dire warnings for American playwrights:

Let them make full use of the various devices of "irony," the various types of "ambiguity" discussed by William Empson, the multiple levels of meaning so adeptly ferreted out in recent literary studies. [...] My suspicion, as already stated, is that the results will be rather ineffective [...] One important reason is that an ultra-intellectual or ultra-refined kind of drama will lack any substantial basis in American manners and attitudes. [...] There is no widely held tradition in America that is not democratic, and this tradition possesses no particular subtleties, cautiousness and restraint. ("Answer" 60)

Theatre and America were both, in his view, for better and for worse, spaces of "spontaneity," of "sympathy," and of "convictions" – all of which have "a way of getting out of hand" (60).

Obviously there are many difficulties with this argument. At the starkest level, Gassner invokes a nationalist and masculinist allegiance in the service of an anti-theoretical, anti-interpretive position. The threat of Europeanization also reifies a threat of feminization, couched in language that castigated subtlety, fastidiousness, and refinement in order to bolster a drama that was "masculine, buoyant, hard-driving and uninhibited" (61). These problems notwithstanding, I would like also to emphasize that what Gassner limitedly refers to as "Americanism" was also a site within which to speculate on dramatic performance's relationship to the social – perhaps even to "sociology" – and to material histories other than those emphasized in Frye-based genre criticism. In this way, Gassner promoted the analysis of theatre as cultural, albeit a different type of "culture" than the Arnoldian or new critical associations, one that approached the kind of relation that Raymond Williams might have had in mind when he suggested that drama offered a key into the "fundamental conventions [with] which we group as [a] society itself." Gassner writes of the dramatist's ability to reproduce "the idiom or tone of contemporary life in America," but adds that catching this idiom means not "fastidiously avoiding contact with an often coarse-grained reality," something that happens when "we treat playwriting as divorced from social reality and practiced in a vacuum" (61). He was aware of a theoretical turn toward a different conception of culture in the English context via T.S. Eliot's notion of the "medieval synthesis" between persons and the cultural context they mutually produce. He uses the reference to speculate on its limits, suggesting that appeals to the communal would remain circumscribed by new critical hesitancies.

I do not by any means ignore the fact that there has been, indeed, much writing about the need for a communal or cultural context by T.S. Eliot and his associates in the field of criticism. But, specifically, the "context" to which they generally refer is non-existent in the modern world; and strictly speaking, it has been non-existent since the Middle Ages. [...] I do not believe the "medieval synthesis" is actually desired for themselves even by the gentlemen who point toward it. There have been too few Thomas Mertons among them to act upon their beliefs. (61)

For Gassner, American theatre called the bluff of the literary establishment's tentative and perpetually formalist quest for communalism. To act on an alternative conception of culture, one that could not be confined to the literary object, was to risk letting things "get out of hand", and, hence, a hypocritical limit point in Eliot's writings. "Meanwhile," Gassner wrote, "there *is* a cultural context – a rough, bouncing and democratic one – in which to function, precariously perhaps, but vigorously" ("Answer" 61). Without accepting the gendered and polarizing terms in which Gassner articulated such enthusiasms and defenses, it is worth acknowledging the social phenomena and affective structures he was trying to emphasize. The messier elements of a theatrical "contextual" aligned with the messier elements of a theatrical "communal"; both resisted the epistemological boundaries of the literary object in ways that anticipated another critical redefinition of the "cultural."

Drama both challenged prevailing conceptions of culture and provided an all-too literal illustration of them. Hence, drama's promoters could be found defending and critiquing the same targets, expediently taking up positions in one context and just as expediently dropping the same positions in another. John Gassner's alternative cultural argument was still hampered by its defensive posture toward new criticism, one that homogenized the movement, equated all its thinkers, and refused to read carefully between the lines of a text like William Empson's *Seven Types of Ambiguity* for the open readings and savvy awareness of social context that others would find. Gassner's argument was also hampered by its defensive posture toward Europeanization. Such reductions – in which available terms of delegitimation are invoked ahistorically and without restraint – appear frequently in polemical encounters where something is at stake. The blind spots created by such rhetorical, conceptual, and nationalist moves are unfortunate for a number of reasons. Most significantly for the purposes of this essay, they would keep such academic promoters of drama from recognizing a related intellectual development happening over in England, one that, had its importation happened sooner or differently, might have positioned drama as a linchpin in the transformation from the study of literature to the innovations of cultural studies. Indeed, to reread the insights, defenses, illuminations, and confusions of mid-century drama criticism is to discern the stops and starts of a theatre-to-culture genealogy.

Francis Fergusson, for instance – perhaps one of the more insightful and widely read drama critics of the period – engaged contemporaneous models of literature and culture. Fergusson adopts a more cautious and considered argument on the relation between drama and New Criticism in his widely printed *The Idea of a Theater* (1949). He praises Ransom, Blackmur, and Empson, who have "done much to make the arts of letters understandable," seeing connections between "the dramatic situation" and Blackmur's "language as gesture" and Empson's studies of ambiguity and the pastoral (21). At the same time, he forthrightly states that, since drama is "not primarily a composition in the verbal medium," other approaches were equally necessary. Hence, he decided to integrate Cambridge anthropology into his study of the drama in order to analyze the "ritual" function of a form whose "own essence is at once more primitive, more subtle, and more direct than either word or concept," an aspect best conceived by "writers who are students of culture rather than literary critics" (22). In contrast to other drama critics, Fergusson foregrounded an anthropological notion of culture throughout his text. Positioning anthropological analysis as fundamental to his approach to the drama, he thus installed an early connection between drama and anthropology. While his approach reproduced the primitivist and structuralist reductions of such earlier anthropological models, it is still noteworthy that the contingencies of the dramatic event served as a bridge between New Criticism and classical anthropology. Thus his drama scholarship can be located on a discontinuous genealogy in literary and cultural studies, indirectly anticipating the mutual enthusiasms between literature and anthropology that would underpin the "blurred genres" and "new historicisms" of a later generation.[3] Fergusson is also obviously a figure in a discontinuous genealogy between drama and performance studies. It is thus worth remembering that "drama" could and did provide an earlier occasion for thinking about the sociocultural dimensions of the textual artifact and for thinking about the nature of "restored behavior," something that does not always appear in the counter-traditionalist appeals of progressive literary studies and of performance studies. The historical link suggests that there is never one singular disciplinary tradition that any contemporary project can claim to be countering.

With this discontinuous genealogy in mind, I would like now to return to that other 1950s drama theorist, Raymond Williams. To position Williams as a drama theorist is to emphasize aspects of his legacy that are often ignored or unknown, particularly in the U.S. context. Connections between the principles behind cultural and theatre studies are brought into bracing light when one remembers that Raymond Williams preceded and interspersed his foundational scholarship in cultural studies with his less famous series in dramatic criticism between 1952 and 1968. As suggested in my introduction, I have found it more than intriguing to think about these early writings in light of Williams's developing models of culture. From this angle, the transition from literary to cultural studies can be seen to take place through the vehicle of "modern drama." For instance, Williams's *Drama in Performance* attempts to place dramatic literature in a production context by borrowing the language of utility, language that destabilized the literary status of his project and thus deployed drama as springboard toward a materialist cultural analysis. Moreover, it is perhaps no coincidence that a theatre-oriented scholar coined the term "structure of feeling." Meanwhile, later works, notably *Culture* (1982), or what in the United States would be titled *The Sociology of Culture*, made considerable use of theatre as a case study for theorizing the institutional, organizational, political, and social dimensions of aesthetic forms. To emphasize this disciplinary genealogy is thus to position drama not only as something that might make an alliance with cultural studies (as Jill Dolan and others have argued) but, more profoundly, as a site that helped to propel the cultural studies project (see Dolan).

Developed through the rewriting of Williams's drama books and into the publication of *The Long Revolution*, the concept of "structure of feeling" was meant to give some formal ballast to his concept of culture. As Fred Inglis writes,

"Structure of feeling" was a concept designed to catch the point of intersection between art and historical experience as individually, and therefore as socially lived. Williams's project [...] had been to grasp a cultural history as experience; that is to say, to interpret the movement of change caught and held in the peculiar lenses of art. (233)

It was thus less a model of how art reflected society than a method by which to catch emergent moments in "the active processes of learning, imagination, creation, performance" (Williams, *Problems* 29). In *Drama from Ibsen to Brecht*, Williams's definition of structure of feeling uses drama to articulate realms of affective experience that match but exceed the conventions of literary critique:

It is as firm and definite as "structure" suggests, yet it is based in the deepest and often least tangible elements of our experience. [...] Its means, its elements, are not propositions or techniques; they are embodied, related feelings. [...] we can look at dramatic methods with a clear technical definition, and yet know, in detail, that what is being defined is more than technique: is indeed the practical way of describing those changes in experience – the responses and their communication; the "subjects" and the "forms" – which make the drama in itself and as a history important. (18, 20)

While Williams often found such active, recursive processes in novelists such as Dickens, Hardy, and Lawrence, who, he felt, had listened to the voices of English culture and developed artistic conventions both to match and to advance them, he often conceived drama as the form that allowed him to "look both ways" between the aesthetic and the social. In his inaugural lecture as Professor of Drama at Cambridge University, he used dramatic form to speculate on his wider hopes for a theory and practice of a social culture. He elaborates, for instance, on the significance of Anton's Chekhov's dramaturgy:

It is a way of speaking and of listening, a specific rhythm of a particular consciousness; in the end a form of unfinished, transient, anxious relationship, which is there on the stage or in the text but which is also, pervasively, a structure of feeling in a precise contemporary world [...] I don't think I could have understood these dramatic procedures as *methods* – that is to say, as significant general modes – if I had not been looking both ways. I could have seen them, perhaps, as techniques [...] [but] it is where technique and method have either an identity or, as now commonly, a significant fracture, that all the hard questions of this difficult discipline begin. ("Dramatized Society" 21)

Williams's discussion of structures of feeling in Chekhovian dramatic dialogue echoes the language he used to analyze Dickens's dialogic power. Not coincidentally, Williams isolated the kind of realm that John Gassner invoked in his account of an American dramatic idiom, suggesting that Gassner's Americanist label was serving as a stand-in for an account of cultural processes in general.

Hard questions about the fracture between technique and method, between consciousness and language, between feeling and world, appear throughout Williams's drama scholarship. In *Modern Tragedy*, Williams uses such impulses to engage and critique a legacy of dramatic criticism. Though specifically replying to George Steiner's philosophy of tragedy, he argues against a general critical strain that too easily married the systemics of structural anthropology with the systemics of literary genre criticism (43). Such a union resulted too simply in a model of tragic form that transcended social and historical particularity. For Williams, this universalizing tendency bypassed what was most intriguing about the drama – its dynamism, its mutability, its embedded social structures.

[T]ragic experience, because of its central importance, commonly attracts the fundamental beliefs and tensions of a period, and tragic theory is interesting mainly in this sense, that through it the shape and set of a particular culture is often deeply realised. If, however, we think of it as a theory about a single and permanent kind of fact, we can end only with the metaphysical conclusions that are built into any such assumption [...] the assumption of a permanent, universal and essentially unchanging human nature. (*Modern Tragedy* 45)

Condemning theorists who presumed an ahistorical equation between Greek, Renaissance, and modern tragic forms, Williams goes on to redefine the significance of tragedy in terms that resonate with his paradigms in cultural theory:

Tragedy is then not a single and permanent kind of fact, but a series of experiences and conventions and institutions. It is not a case of interpreting this series by reference to a permanent and unchanging human nature. Rather, the varieties of tragic experience are to be interpreted by reference to the changing conventions and institutions. The universalist character of most tragic theory is then at the opposite pole from our necessary interest. [...] It is in any case necessary to break the theory if we are to value the art [...] [instead] to see its controlling structure of feeling, the variations within this and their connections with actual dramatic structures, and to be able to respond to them critically, in the full sense. (45–6)

Foregrounding the interrelations among experience, convention, and institu-

tion, Williams focused on technical and social shifts in the theatrical event –
upon the choral structures of Greek tragedy, upon the later secularist
impulses that replotted tragic action, and upon the modernizing forces that
generated and isolated the psychic conventions of the tragic hero in the
twentieth century. Seeking the variations within and between dramatic structure and "structures of feeling," Williams's investigation in *Modern Tragedy* thus provides the lens and the language for theorizing cultural process,
anticipating and echoing the analytic paradigms of "dominant," "residual,"
and "emergent" for which his cultural theory would become known (*Sociology of Culture* 204).

The "hard questions of this difficult discipline," whether that discipline be
modern drama or culture in general, may have had a beginning for Williams in
such structures of feeling, but the endings of such questions are still uncertain.
I have endeavored, in this investigation, to link Williams's intellectual genealogy with those of drama and thereby to position the latter as oft-unrecognized
precursor. At the same time, dramatic performance is also interesting in a Williams genealogy as a metaphor for expressing a certain kind of ambivalence in
progressive literary studies, ambivalences that persist in literature's transmutation into cultural studies. Checkered throughout Fred Inglis's biography are
constant references to the parallel ambivalences with which Williams greeted
both participation in "actual" theatrical events and participation in "actual"
social relations. In fact, Inglis tells his readers that Williams accepted his
endowed chair as Professor of Drama despite "hardly [having] been to a theatre for years" (241). Without recounting all of these references or overly psy-
chologizing Williams, I think that this reluctance is an intriguing symptom,
not simply of hypocrisy, but of the basic conundrums built into our "difficult
discipline." Drama seems to function both as a springboard for extra-literary
cultural engagement and as a limit point past which literary-derived cultural
analysis seems unwilling to go. This kind of ambivalence and Eliot-like slippage persists even in Fred Inglis's own way of treating drama as a cultural
event, that is, as a form that is made analyzable and useful in the moment
when it is turned back into a trope.

Drama matters so much for Williams because, more than any other form except opera
[...] it is a communal form of art. Among dramatists, Ibsen was the first key subject,
because Ibsen dramatised heroism as hopefulness, even when – most of all when – the
hero or heroine was pulled down to death by desire. Ibsen prefigured the essential tension between Williams's pervasive feelings of inheritance and his equally strong drive
to break away and keep away, keeping other people away at the same time. (Inglis 105)

It is noteworthy that Inglis follows the first sentence about theatre's ensemble
form with a thematic discussion of the content of Ibsen's plays, as if one were
an extension of the other. The "communal" alliances and frictions of theatre-

making, of course, embody the simultaneous urges of collective inheritance and of breaking free; however, Inglis reorients that shaky communalism from the interactive realm of actors, writers, and designers to the internal dynamics of the play text. That kind of move is reproduced again and again in literary-derived studies of both culture and modern drama, demonstrating the persistence of new critical methods even in attempts to break free from new critical objects. Such tendencies seem to perpetuate the formalist quest for communalism.

That persistence reflects back on modern drama's continued shaky relationship to culture, an instability that appeared in culture's early formations as a gentlemanly moral form, continued in its later formations as a rigorously studied new critical mode of cultural capital, and now reappears in culture's most recent anthropological transformations in cultural studies. That this shakiness should continue within the socially oriented, praxis-friendly, materially contextualized project of cultural studies seems curious. It seems curious that such cultural revisions of a literary studies project have not repositioned drama, a form whose literary status was circumspect because of its occasional vulgarity, its embedded practicality, its extra-literary aesthetics, and its hyper-contextual and relentlessly non-autonomous status as an epistemological object. Rather than lamenting this oversight, however, it might be useful to use its persistence to reflect back on debates about the status of "text," "language," and "the literary" in cultural studies. If the relationship between literature and society has turned into a cultural studies fascination between text and social process, then the liminal life of drama in the academy re-situates and is re-situated by such methodological questions. When Meaghan Morris asks would-be cultural theorists to move beyond "[a] literary reading of a shopping mall that does not seriously engage with questions that arise in history, sociology and economics" (qtd. in Grossberg 14), her argument alights on similar inertias that have produced blind spots around modern drama. Indeed, methodological questions about the role of "text-based" criticism in cultural studies rest upon concerns that have plagued the study of drama within and without literary studies since the turn of the century, even before Francis Fergusson's literary wariness prompted him to contact those "students of culture" in Cambridge anthropology.

The ambivalent status of drama might well be continuous with, to cite Dorothy Hale, a lingering social formalism in progressive literary and cultural studies. Hale investigates the "slippery materialism that creates a bridge [...] between Marxist literary criticism and Anglo-American literary formalism" (13). Reading this slipperiness next to contemporary scholarship in cultural studies, she cites examples of literary scholars such as Eve Kosofsky Sedgwick, Barbara Johnson, and Henry Louis Gates, Jr., who use novels as the basis for wider cultural theory. Hale maintains that such work is ultimately formalist, derived from traditional new critical literary paradigms and an undertheorized belief in a tropic connection between literature and the social. Thus, the lure of new criticism's textual self-sufficiency lingers despite a rhetoric that seeks to destabilize the status of literature and to reach toward a progressive politics in gender, race, and queer studies.

If the novel in Sedgwick's criticism is no longer a formalist world apart, it nonetheless retains much of the representational autonomy it enjoyed under the old new critical regime that Sedgwick has helped to supplant: the cultural critic who has dedicated herself to depriviledging the novel on aesthetic grounds finds herself reinstating the novel's formal privilege on the grounds of its social representativeness. (5)

Intriguingly, both Hale and Catherine Gallagher trace that slippage back to scholars like Raymond Williams, figures whose quest for materialist analysis ultimately remained mystified about how material production "dissolved" into the literary artifact (12).

When such solid, material objects as shoes and potatoes are themselves "read" as signifiers within complex signifying systems, the distinction between material and symbolic products breaks down. The physical object becomes a signifier, and the physical properties of conventionally recognized signifiers (e.g., the aural and visual qualities of spoken and written words) are emphasized. Everything can then appear equally autonomous and dependent, determined and determining, referential and self-referential, symbolic and real. (Gallagher 635)

Writing from within the institutionalization of cultural studies, Lawrence Grossberg agrees about the inertias built into certain strains of literary-derived cultural studies scholarship. Despite Williams's assertions about the need to break down conceptual divisions between "culture" and "society," despite arguing that "Cultural studies had to reinsert culture into the practical everyday life of people," "Williams was never able to actually escape this separation – both in his privileging of certain forms of culture (literature) and in his desire to equate culture with some sort of totality and/or ethical standard" (Grossberg 16). While Hale and Gallagher remain unconvinced by Williams and his descendants' attempts to foreground the materiality and embodiments of the literary text, drama's materialism and its bodies beckon for critical recognition. Nevertheless, drama's decidedly embodied bodies (not to mention its shoes and potatoes) continue to occupy a blind spot in critical theory, cumbersomely literalizing cultural studies principles, cumbersomely exceeding social formalist analysis.

Finally, I think that this discontinuous genealogy is chastening to those of us who have an announced affiliation with performance studies. As a varied intellectual and artistic movement galvanized by a cultural studies milieu, as an increasingly large body of scholarship regularly supported by formative thinkers such as "Johnson," "Gates," "Sedgwick," and their colleagues, performance studies bears no singular or unfettered relationship to disciplinary traditions in literature, culture, and drama. I do not mean to suggest that we unthinkingly embrace Raymond Williams as an intellectual predecessor, nor that we entirely accept all critiques of formalist or "literary" cultural studies. Nevertheless, it seems important for performance studies scholars and affiliates to situate our subfields, our methods, our textualist impulses, our mystified materialisms, and our most cherished insights within a complicated institutional genealogy. When I think about my recent work in performance studies, I consider one of its major efforts to be something akin to the analysis of structures of feeling in aesthetic, recreational, and everyday spaces – moments when convention and emotion, technique and force, a gestural movement and a social movement, collide, rework, undo, and advance each other. And for a while, I think, I imagined this project as something unlinked to the project of modern drama. It has been useful and humbling for me to recognize a different genealogy, albeit a discontinuous one, among categories such as drama, literature, culture, and performance. Before comprehensively endorsing the connection between the disciplines of performance studies and cultural studies, I have found it important to step back from this equation – historically, institutionally, curricularly, methodologically. An awareness of a longer, complicated disciplinary genealogy makes oppositions between old literary studies and new cultural studies, and between old theatre studies and new performance studies, less easy to maintain or to elide. Thinking genealogically about literature's relationship to theatre before cultural studies, about Williams's theatrical relationship to literature, about cultural studies' reproduction of supposedly supplanted literary methods, and about the different types of methodological traditions perpetuated and refracted in performance and cultural studies reveals more unexpected discontinuities and disavowed connections. These various disciplinary beginnings have not always produced analytically helpful endings, but perhaps their future has yet to be imagined.

NOTES

1 I would like to thank the participants of the Modern:Drama conference, especially William B. Worthen, for their helpful responses and suggestions.
2 Internal quotations are from C.F. Thwing, *The College of the Future* (Cleveland, 1897) 12–3; and J.J. Lewis, "Culture and Limitation," *Report* (U.N.Y., 1878) 429.
3 See Geertz; Greenblatt.

Quo Vadis?
Theatre Studies at the Crossroads

ERIKA FISCHER-LICHTE

I. PROLOGUE

Theatre studies as an academic discipline was founded in a programmatic way, as a discipline devoted not to text but, rather, to performance.[1] Since its very origins, it has been understood as an "interdisciplinary" subject within which many other fields of study intersect and merge: art history, musicology, literature studies, cultural history, communication and media sciences, philosophy, religious studies, anthropology, sociology, economics, and law. Whether it is defined and practised as culture studies, as media studies, or as art studies, the study of theatre constitutes, by definition, an interdisciplinary field.[2] Nearly a century after the founding of theatre studies, on the threshold of a new millennium, it makes good sense to take stock of the challenges and prospects, problems and risks facing theatre studies today because of, and in terms of, its interdisciplinary nature.

For the sake of clarity, it seems appropriate to embark upon this enterprise by dealing with different aspects of theatre studies separately – as culture studies, as media studies, and as art studies. By using the terms "culture studies," "media studies," and "art studies," I do not intend that these highly contested terms should serve to define concepts or clearly demarcated fields of research or even particular disciplines. Rather, I am considering them in terms of their relation to theatre specifically. Considering theatre studies as culture studies entails viewing theatre as a particular genre of cultural performance, to be investigated in the context of and in relation to the different genres of cultural performance, which in their sum total constitute this particular culture. When dealing with theatre studies as media studies, theatre is regarded and examined as a particular medium compared to other media, such as the print or the electronic. When theatre studies is practised as art studies, the focus is on theatre as a particular art form that, in many ways, is related to other art forms such as music, poetry, the visual arts, film, dance. The three terms as they are used here, accordingly, describe three different perspectives on one and the same object.[3]

The following three sections are devoted to these three perspectives. I shall begin each section by referring to a theatre performance produced within the last three years by one of the highly subsidized state theatres in Germany, that is, from the so-called mainstream. The rationale for this procedure is twofold. On the one hand, the development of theatre studies, even in the field of theatre historiography, is, in more than one respect, closely related to the development of contemporary theatre. On the other hand, I believe that theatre studies finds itself, in many ways, in a similar position to contemporary theatre. Both have to navigate between the twin dangers of Scylla and Charybdis. Today's theatre moves between the two extreme poles: the process of exchange with other genres of cultural performance, other media, other art forms, which sometimes allows it to merge or even transform itself into other cultural performances, media, art forms; and the proclamation of a poor theatre, a theatre of empty space, a theatre reverting to its "essentials." In terms of theatre studies, Scylla may appear as such a broad expansion that it runs the risk of merging into general culture studies, media studies, and art studies, while Charybdis represents the tendency to narrow the approach down to only a very limited number of theatrical genres that, however, some theatre scholars claim to be our proper subject. Thus, the question I shall deal with is how theatre studies can avoid being shipwrecked either at Scylla or at Charybdis and can instead regain the strength and flexibility to sail daringly and safely into the open sea. And since contemporary theatre is haunted by similar ghosts and spirits, it might be useful to start the discussion by taking a closer look at a theatre performance and its particular way of challenging these dangers.

2. THEATRE STUDIES AS CULTURE STUDIES

In 1998, an election year in Germany, Christoph Schlingensief presented *Election Campaign Circus Chance 2000* in a circus tent in a production by the Berlin Volksbühne. Beside Schlingensief himself, who directed the course of each performance, praising, blaming, commanding, abusing, and intervening in all kinds of ways, the performers included some well-known actors from the Volksbühne and the Berlin Ensemble, such as Bernhard Schütz and Martin Wuttke; a family of circus artists who performed stunts and tricks; some disabled people; a group of unemployed; the so-called Schlingensief "family"; and, again and again, the spectators. It is almost impossible to define the event clearly and properly. Was it theatre or a circus performance? Was it a freak show or part of an election campaign? A talk show or a coming-out? The foundation of a political party or a sales promotion? The spectators were never in a position to make out distinctly in which kind of cultural performance they were participating at any given moment. As for the multitude of different genres being performed simultaneously, the spectators not only faced the problem of deciding whether to focus on one performance only and miss the others, or to let their gaze and attention switch between different performances; moreover, they also had to clarify for themselves under which genre of cultural performance to subsume what was going on. This proved fatal for many a spectator.

Usually the spectators can rely on their knowledge of the specific rules that constitute a particular genre of cultural performance and a certain framework that clarifies which rules to apply. Such knowledge helps participants at a cultural performance to behave "appropriately." In Schlingensief's production, however, such frameworks were permanently displaced, forced to collide with and collapse into each other. This experience was not only a result of the simultaneity of the different genres of cultural performance being realized. It was also triggered by a device that meant that the transformation of one genre into another took place without any warning or any clear markers, let alone any preparation. Thus, it happened that the different genres not only commented and reflected on each other but, moreover, questioned and annulled each other. To give an example: during one part of the performance, Schlingensief ordered tables to be brought into the arena. He explained to the audience that lists were laid out on the tables where they could sign up as founding members of the new political party, "Chance 2000." While many of the spectators followed Schlingensief's invitation and poured into the arena, Martin Wuttke grabbed the megaphone, climbed up to the small gallery over the artists' entrance, and abused the spectators for fifteen minutes for complying with Schlingensief's demand, for following the leader like sheep. As he did so, he repeated over and over again the same nonsensical, yet highly allusive, phrase: "I am the people's exciter / germ and you are an autogenous stress-sculpture / plastic."

Such permanent transgressions of the borderlines between the different genres of cultural performance resulted, for the spectators, in a deep uncertainty as to which framework to apply and by which rules to abide. The general rule of the game seemed to dictate that if one genre of cultural performance transgresses the borderline over into another, merges into it, or transforms it, the rules constitutive of one will annul those of the other. That is to say, either there were no particular rules to follow at all any more or the rules openly contradicted each other.

As a consequence, spectators attempting to relate the events to one particular frame – that of a circus performance, election campaign, or theatre performance – became totally confused. Not only were their expectations crudely crushed; they also felt completely irritated and often did not know how to respond at all. They felt insecure, even disoriented. Disappointment, anger, frustration, even aggression, were often the consequences observed. On the other hand, there were many spectators who obviously enjoyed the situation, who more than willingly seized the opportunity to play with frames, rules, expectations, to experiment with the feeling of insecurity and destabilization, to transgress or even to dissolve and annul borderlines. In Schlingensief's performance, all parties involved, performers and spectators alike, found themselves in a situation *between* all the rules, between all fixed and stable positions. Such a radical "betwixt-and-between" (Turner 40), as a permanent transgression and transformation of borderlines, genres, frames, and expectations, may open up new and unforeseen potential for innovation; because of the lack of clearly marked differences, however, it may equally well result in chaos and violence (Girard 50). Here, theatre acted and worked as a kind of catalyst, inducing a crisis through artistic means that, in terms of its very structure, was similar to the crisis afflicting the surrounding culture. In a kind of laboratory situation, it allowed, even forced, the participants to find and try out their own ways of coping without establishing a set of rules that everyone must follow (see Garfinkel 76–103). This seems to be an almost Solomonic solution. Perhaps we shall be able to find a similar solution in terms of theatre studies as culture studies.

When theatre studies in Germany was first defined as culture studies, the same problems arose that theatre studies redefined as performance studies faces today. From the late 1920s, the German theatre scholar Carl Niessen (1890–1969) claimed that besides theatre performances, theatre studies should include all theatrical genres – festivals, processions, ceremonies, games, dances, rituals, ballad-singing, storytelling, and other performances from all cultures and all times – as objects of research. He conceived theatre studies as a discipline devoted not only to what Europeans, at different times in their cultural history, understood and defined as theatre but to all kinds of cultural performance – that is, more or less, as performance studies understands and defines the field. He argued that all human performative activities derive from a particular anthropological condition, namely the innate human urge to act out all kinds of spiritual, emotional, and mental states physically, by carrying out particular performative acts. In order to describe this urge, he used the Latin term *mimus* (see Niessen). That is to say, in order to master the problems arising from a definition that embodies all kinds of cultural performances in all cultures and all times in one discipline, Niessen left aside the enormous differences between the manifold objects of his research by reducing them to one common aspect: the so-called anthropological given – *mimus*. In this way, the vast bulk of performances were to be investigated in terms of this one aspect alone. Fieldwork, analysis, and theorizing were carried out with the sole purpose of passing them all off as manifestations, examples, and illustrations of a theory of *mimus*, regardless of their cultural, historical, social, or other differences.

Such a solution, naturally, is unacceptable to today's performance studies. On the other hand, the idea that we are in a position to deal with all kinds of cultural performances in all cultures and all times competently is an illusion. Culture manifests, constitutes, creates, explains, disputes, and recreates itself in and through performances, objects, and texts. Let us suppose that a systematics of culture studies could be devised from this idea: culture studies as text studies, as object studies, as performance studies. It does not matter whether this is the "correct" systematics. Systematics are never correct or incorrect but, rather, either manageable or not manageable; either they lead to results that are relevant or no important insights are gained at all. What can we expect from a discipline such as "text studies"? The first prerequisite for scholars working in this discipline would naturally be knowledge of all languages and of the particular kind of writing in which texts are written. But even in the most unlikely event that this prerequisite is met, what kind of findings and insights can research generate if the context in and for which the texts are/ were written is not known? One can assume that the cultural, historical, political, and social situation in which the researchers live will be the yardstick by which to measure the texts being investigated. The outcome of such research will most likely serve to confirm the researcher's own prejudices, opinions, ideologies, aspirations – to prove the researcher right. But is this kind of research relevant? Do we really need it? On the other hand, what can textual scholars do to avoid the trappings of dilettantism?

They will have to specialize in, let us say, texts from Japanese or Assyrian culture, in legal or religious texts, in narrative texts or in poetry or in whatever kind of categorization of the whole field might seem promising to them. Then they will have to form centres for these specialists and develop a network between these. In the end they will discover that they cannot manage without extending the network to corresponding centres in the fields of object studies and performance studies. Naturally, the fields of specialization, the centres, and the networks will have to be created in as flexible a way as possible so that they can change, shift, be regrouped, or otherwise be transformed whenever necessary. I could tell the same tale in terms of object studies or performance studies, no doubt, but the point is clear.

What conclusions can be drawn from this scenario for theatre studies? First, that a definition of the discipline such as that provided by Niessen and performance studies will inevitably result in dilettantism. In this respect, theatre studies, as defined here, resembles a Schlingensief performance. For it is an all-embracing definition that blurs the borderlines and furthers a merging of all kinds of cultural performances of different cultures and different times. But in contrast to a Schlingensief performance, theatre studies does not act and work as a kind of catalyst by inducing a crisis through scientific means – as Schlingensief does through artistic means. Rather, it can be regarded as the expression and consequence of a crisis existing not only in our discipline but in the humanities in general. For, to a large extent, the humanities have proved incapable of productive interdisciplinary work. They tend either to insulate themselves in the narrow compartments of neatly defined disciplines or to transgress the borderlines between the disciplines – which is absolutely necessary – but, alas, without being sufficiently methodologically prepared and able to move and act professionally and efficiently on new and unknown ground. Well – *avanti dilettanti*!

This dilettantism also recalls Schlingensief's performances, with their quite charming and amiable dilettantism, which, none the less, is rather ambivalent and quite often becomes dangerous and threatening. Such an ambivalence is also characteristic of our discipline's dilettantism. But while Schlingensief's performances might provoke some fruitful responses and insights in the spectators and so, in the end, prove quite successful, ours is to be regarded and judged much less favourably. The attitude of cheerful dilettantism, it is true, may help us to overlook and ignore some problems entailed by the performances under investigation that, were they to be realized, would discourage us in our efforts to explore such performances. However, by overlooking and ignoring the problems, we rob ourselves of any reliable basis for dealing with such performances effectively. There is no way leading out of this dilemma other than a close cooperation with other disciplines that focus on exactly those problems that we tend to miss.

In developing performance theories, theories of performativity and theatricality, theatre studies has provided a theoretical basis from which different disciplines exploring cultural performances – such as religious studies, sociology, political sciences, and law – can investigate rituals, ceremonies, festivals, games, trials, executions, and even theatrical processes in social life. Such theories can be used most productively by all these disciplines as heuristic tools.[4] This by no means implies that because theatre studies has worked out the heuristic tools, it is only theatre scholars who may apply them and the whole field belongs to them. Of course, I can extend my research at any time to sports competitions, political party conventions, trials, or whatever, provided that I have made myself competent in the field. But this makes sense only if the perspective of theatre studies contributes something special by dealing with a particular problem and, thus, discovering and highlighting an important aspect that the other disciplines dealing with these kinds of performances, such as sociology, political sciences, or law, were not able to reveal. Just another plain sociological, political, or legal study from the pen of a theatre scholar is not worth all the effort made to gain sufficient competence, let alone a pseudo-sociological or a poor political or legal study.

If this is the state of affairs in theatre studies as culture studies, what can be done in order to limit the field of research in a reasonable and justifiable way? In the end, no rules can be established that determine the selection of a particular kind of performance for the object of our research. However, a general guideline is quite conceivable: each theatre scholar and each theatre department would only carry out research and teaching in terms of the genres of performances for which they are qualified, competent, and authorized, whether these are performances from their own or from other cultures. The limitations can change any time when an individual scholar acquires new qualifications and skills or when a new colleague with other qualifications and skills joins the department. Additional rules, in my view, do not make any sense. I am afraid this is a solution somewhat in the manner of a Schlingensief performance. But since I called that almost Solomonic, it cannot be too disastrous for theatre studies.

A second consequence might be the foundation of interdisciplinary centres of performance studies, assembling scholars from all disciplines dealing with performance. Of course, no single centre would be in a position to cover the whole field; each would have to develop its own research profile regarding the particular problems it will deal with. Theatre studies, no doubt, would be among those disciplines that could contribute most to such centres. Accordingly, it would take an important, if not the leading, position, without, however, losing its independence and merging into cultural studies. For theatre studies is not only culture studies but media studies and art studies as well.

3. THEATRE STUDIES AS MEDIA STUDIES

In 1997, the Berlin Volksbühne premiered Frank Castorf's production of *Trainspotting*. It was his theatrical adaptation of Irvine Welsh's first and highly successful novel, *Trainspotting*, and its 1996 adaptation for film by Danny Boyle. The performance made excessive use of film, video clips, and recorded music. The film clips showed, for instance, pictures of a landscape in spring, filmed from the window of a moving train, or a documentary on the singer of Velvet Underground, Nico Icon; the music included recordings by Velvet Underground, Iggy Pop, and Lou Reed, as well as Karel Gott (a German pop-singer, born in 1939, performing mostly lightweight music with folksy tunes and themes) and Arnold Schoenberg. The performance was realized as an intermedia event and an intermedial reflection on theatre in the age of the new media. Part of such reflection was the particular use made of film, video clips, and recorded music, as well as the play on different theatrical conventions. The effectiveness of the theatrical and the media conventions are made possible by theatre's mediality, the communication in theatre enabled by the bodily presence of actors and spectators.

The actors addressed the spectators directly – as when one actor violently stamped on the ground in front of a spectator, looking directly at him and threatening him till the spectator moved back terrified, or when the same actor abused a woman in one of the upper rows as a "fucking bitch" and bellowed at her to stop her "idiotic gawping." In any case, the spectators had a hard time trying to claim the position of distanced observers. The production did its utmost to make them part of the performance.

The spectators were seated on scaffolding at the back of the stage. To take their seats, they had to cross the stage, where some lighting equipment was laid out. Those spectators who had already taken their seats watched later arrivals stumble over the stage, sometimes destroying parts of the "set," although the ushers at the Volksbühne had kindly asked the spectators to watch their step when walking over the lighting equipment. Here, obviously, the roles of spectator and actor were being played with. The arriving spectators took on the roles of actors before the gaze of the spectators already seated, whether they wanted to or not. At the same time, the performance toyed with the conventions that mark the beginning of a play. Did it start as soon as the first spectator had reached the scaffolding and started to watch others arriving, or when the first actor from the Volksbühne entered the stage?

Even the end of the performance was arguable and negotiable. The actors tried hard to draw as much applause from the audience as possible in order to extend the performance. They not only jumped and smiled and stretched out their arms, they also addressed spectators who tried to steal away in order to stop them and ask why they were leaving so soon, whether they did not like the performance, or scolded them for being so stingy with applause; they mingled with the spectators, shaking – or, in the case of female spectators, kissing – their hands, saying "thank you"; in other words, they tried all means by which to prevent the spectators from leaving, and thus to prolong the performance. In the end, it was the spectators who decided on the conclusion of the performance: when the last one left, it was over.

Castorf's *Trainspotting* seems to be a promising starting point for the discussion of theatre studies as media studies – in particular with regard to the current debate on the relationship between live performances and mediatized performances and on the notion of "liveness." This performance incorporated the latest in the technology of image reproduction – just like Piscator's productions in the 1920s and just as theatre has always incorporated the newest technology for its purposes, whether it was the different kinds of stage machinery in the Baroque theatre, electric light and the revolving stage at the turn of the twentieth century, or, most recently, lighting systems run by computers, video, and sound recordings. Does the use of such technology impair or even reduce the sense of liveness? Is liveness ultimately only possible in Grotowski's poor theatre? Of course, the answer depends on the definition given for "liveness." It has been used as a normative and even as an ideological concept. I use it as a descriptive term, by which I mean the bodily co-presence of two kinds of people in one space, those who perform and those who look on; the roles of performer and spectator are not necessarily fixed to particular groups of people.

Such a definition does not suggest, let alone entail, notions such as "authenticity" or "subversion" – both highly loaded, ideological concepts. Authenticity, a concept first coined in the eighteenth century, is the result of particularly careful and clever staging strategies – whether in live performance, film, television performance, or everyday behaviour. On the other hand, a live performance can be just as affirmative or subversive as any text or any mediatized performance, depending on the kind of performance or text and the context in which it is used and in which it functions. The Nazi *Reichsparteitage*, without doubt, were live, highly affirmative performances, as were Leni Riefenstahl's films portraying these events, *Sieg des Glaubens* ("Victory of Faith," 1933) and *Triumpf des Willens* ("Triumph of the Will," 1935). Thus, the concept of liveness, as I use it here, has no implications whatsoever regarding authenticity and subversion.

On the other hand, this definition would suggest that the use of image reproduction technology in a theatre performance cannot serve as a criterion by which to measure its liveness. The use of such technology does, however, affect the modes and habits of the spectators' perception, as the critics already noted after Piscator's production *Trotz alledem* ("Despite Everything," 1927)[5] and as could be seen in Castorf's *Trainspotting*. However, such a change in the modes and habits of perception can be compared to the change brought about through the introduction of the Italian stage in the seventeenth century or to the changes initiated by Max Reinhardt when he deserted the box-set stage and played in a circus arena, in a forest, on a marketplace, or in a church or built a *hanamichi* through the auditorium, as well as by many directors of the 1960s who turned away from theatre buildings or rebuilt them in order to introduce new models and perspectives of perception. In terms of the history of European theatre, the incorporation of reproduction technology appears to be just one more device with which to challenge spectators' modes and habits of perception and to adapt to the new modes and perspectives made possible by the new media – as was Serlio's application of the central perspective in painting to the stage 450 years ago. But such a change in perception does not reduce the quality of liveness, let alone annul it. Rather, it emphasizes the fact that live performance and mediatized performance are not so different from each other in each and every respect and that they can have much in common with each other, even share important features, depending on the perspective from which we compare them. Nonetheless, the one requires and displays the physical co-presence of two kinds of people in the same space, while the other does not. And in terms of what a performance makes out of this basic distinction, it either makes all the difference in the world or amounts to nothing more than a *quantité négligeable*.[6]

Castorf's *Trainspotting*, for instance, suggested that actors and spectators alike could make use of the possibilities offered by the bodily co-presence of actors and spectators in the same space. And among such possibilities are the reversal of gaze and the exchange of roles between performers and spectators, which as such are not given in mediatized performances. This possibility always exists, often haunting the actors like a nightmare; a spectator may not only irritate the actors by coughing or laughing at the most improper moments but actually intervene by making loud remarks or by starting an argument or even a fight with another spectator and thus opening another "stage," another focus of attention, to the other spectators.[7] Such audience responses may be caused by provocations from the stage, as often happens in performances by Castorf or Einar Schleef – who are masters at provoking all kinds of innovative audience response. Such responses may also be caused by the efforts of some spectators to exploit the public event of a performance for their own purposes in order to put themselves – metaphorically and sometimes even literally – onstage. In any case, they have an effect on the course of the performance itself.

It is up to the actors whether they become confused and irritated by such responses or whether they enjoy them as welcome opportunities for an *extempore*. Whatever way the actors react to this kind of audience response, the performance will be immediately affected by it.

It is this that makes the basic difference between live performance and mediatized performance. Whatever the spectators' reaction may be, in mediatized performance the film or the television show to which they respond does not change. Even in shows such as the German version of the TV series *Big Brother*, where the spectators were asked to intervene by voting to eliminate one participant from the Portakabin in which the show took place, the result was, at best, the consequence of a majority vote (assuming that it was not preplanned by the producers and only passed off as the spectators' vote). The spectator has no immediate, face-to-face access to or even impact on the performers and their performances that would force them to act differently.

This constitutes a big difference between live performance and mediatized performance. Of course, there are live performances where some actors pretend to be spectators, where the audience's responses and the actors' reactions to them are staged and rehearsed. On the other hand, there are also live performances where no observable audience response interrupts the performance taking place. Nonetheless, the potential always exists. And all performers, as well as all spectators, are aware that it could happen and are either horrified or enthusiastic about the mere idea.

This holds true also for the opposite possibility that the performers leave the stage, address a spectator, and transform him into a co-player on whom the other spectators direct their gaze and attention. Here, the roles of actors and spectators are redefined. Any actor can act as a spectator, any spectator as an actor. The gaze of the spectator on the performer, which seems to be irreversible, is met and returned by the performers – as was the case in *Trainspotting*. The spectators are being exposed to the gaze of the performers and of the other spectators. It is the liveness of performances that allows for such a possibility. It opens up the opportunity not only to represent the gaze of the other on stage but to perform and to negotiate it in the process of interaction between both parties involved. The object of perception (the performer) becomes its subject, the subject (the spectator) its object. The gaze of/on the other may unfold its dynamics. The performative acts of one group and the gaze by which the others perceive them, in their interplay, open up the possibility of a permanent redefinition of roles.

Liveness, in this respect, is one criterion by which theatre performances can be distinguished from film presentations and TV shows, for instance. This statement does not imply any value judgement. Liveness per se is not better or worse than mediatization. A value judgement comes into play, however, when one considers how the inherent possibilities of liveness and mediatization are employed. The simple fact that one performance is live, the other mediatized, does not tell us anything about its quality or how it functions within a particular social or political context. It merely informs us about a certain potential that may or may not be actualized.

Each medium possesses its own means, each opens up possibilities that another medium does not offer. Yet, as Lessing stated in the preface to his *Laokoon* (1766), it not only is conceivable but actually often happens that one medium makes use of means developed by another, that it tries to copy or at least to simulate the possibilities emanating from another's particular mediality: *ut pictura poesis* ("poetry shall be like a picture"). And sometimes it is so successful that a recipient will not perceive the difference any more or, at least, will perceive the difference to be marginal and irrelevant to his reception.

This is a phenomenon to which Philip Auslander refers in his stimulating book on liveness. Here he sketches a "particular historical pattern" where,

[i]n many instances, the incursion of the mediatized into the live has followed [...]. Initially, the mediatized form is modeled on the live form, but it eventually usurps the live form's position in the cultural economy. The live form then starts to replicate the mediatized form. This pattern is apparent in the historical relationship of theatre and television. Those involved in early television production first took the replication of the theatre spectator's visual experience as their objective. [...] since the late 1940s, live theatre has become more and more like television and other mediatized cultural forms. To the extent that live performances now emulate mediatized representations, they have become second-hand recreations of themselves as refracted through mediatization. (158)

The history of the relationship between theatre and television, as Auslander recounts it here, is the story of a transfer of modes and perspectives of perception from one medium to another. Television began from the visual patterns known to the spectator sitting in front of a box-set stage; later on it developed its own modes of perception, which the stage then re-imported. This may be a correct description of the process regarding some theatre forms; in my view, it rather provides a good example of the processes of exchange carried out between different media. While some forms of theatre may have taken some perception modes from television, television, in its turn, makes use of a dramaturgy in family series and soap operas that was developed by the domestic play and melodrama of the eighteenth century. Thus, it is a constant give and take, certainly not to be thought of as a one-way street.

On the other hand, American avant-garde theatre and European theatre since the 1960s have by no means modelled themselves on television. Quite the contrary: in a productive encounter with the new media of film, television, video, and, later, computer, they experimented with the most diverse modes and perspectives of perception; they developed and tried out a number of possible new ways to realize and display their liveness, whether in different kinds of audience participation, such as "offending the audience" (Handke), or in other ways of provoking and exciting the spectators to a marked response. As in *Trainspotting*, theatre often plays with and reflects on other media, as well as on its own particular mediality, its liveness. It is intermedial in its use of the possibilities the other media have to offer without merging into the other media, without losing its liveness. This is because it is liveness, understood as the physical co-presence of performers and spectators in the same space, that seems to be a constitutive and defining concept of theatre.

Thus I come to the conclusion that the concept of liveness – a demystified concept, as a matter of fact – is indispensable to theatre studies as media studies. It has proven to be a basic concept – not for ideological, political, or essentialist reasons, nor for the sake of ensuring advance value judgements, but as something that enables the media scholar to define differences, to describe the possibilities offered and developed by the different media, regardless of whether they can be copied or simulated by other media. For in order to make such a statement – that methods or devices developed in one medium are transferred into another, where they often have to serve other functions and purposes – it is necessary to make distinctions. The concept of liveness is a useful tool that allows such distinctions to be made. However, it is not the only one. In order to discover, describe, and analyse processes of transferring, copying, or simulating possibilities of one medium to or by another, it is absolutely mandatory to know all the media and their particular potential. Theatre studies as media studies will always have to consider the other media – in each and every respect in which they are related, in whatever way, to theatre.

4. THEATRE STUDIES AS ART STUDIES

In 1997, Einar Schleef staged Oscar Wilde's *Salome* at the Düsseldorf Schauspielhaus. At the end of the season, in May 1998, the production was shown at the Berlin Theatertreffen. When the iron curtain rose, the spectators were confronted with a *tableau vivant*. Grey-blue twilight filled the stage space, offering to the gaze of the spectators the sight of eighteen figures, dressed in grey or black, standing absolutely motionless in picturesque constellations on the floor, which was partially sloped. The picture was very beautiful; it was shown for ten minutes. Then the iron curtain fell and the spectators were released to the intermission.

Like a painting in a gallery or a museum, the *tableau vivant* invited the spectators to behold the picture, to contemplate it. As the iron curtain rose, the revelation of the picture was met by some admiring, or just surprised, "ahs" and "ohs," but when the image lasted more than a minute, a number of spectators made it clear that they had no intention of behaving in the theatre as if they were at an art gallery. They responded by drawing a clear line between beholding a picture and participating in a theatre performance. They explicitly displayed conventional theatre performance behaviour: they applauded, they hissed, they shouted "bravo" and "da capo," they booed and catcalled. Thus, they made it very plain that they were determined to adhere to the framework given by a theatre performance, to apply the rules that regulate the response to this particular art form and to reject those valid for dealing with the visual arts and painting in particular.

Other spectators, relying on the quality of liveness in theatre performance, tried to provoke responses from the actors that might destroy the picture and restore the performance by making them move or laugh and shouted all kinds of more or less witty or silly remarks. Still the actors did not respond. Yet other spectators were apparently happy to follow the invitation to behold and contemplate the picture as they would a painting at an art gallery. They felt disturbed by the noisy responses of the others and claimed their own right to enjoy the performance by asking them to stop what they called their "bad behaviour."

What was happening here was a confrontation between two art forms and the kinds of behaviour they presuppose, if not demand, as well as the kinds of experience they trigger. During the long ten minutes when the picture of a *tableau vivant* was presented onstage for viewing, a performance was actually taking place in the auditorium. Whereas some spectators insisted on their new roles as beholders of a picture, others took the part of performers and yet others the parts of spectators amusing themselves by observing the attempts by "the performers" to get a response from the actors – which would return the part of spectator to them again – or to fight for their rights as beholders of a picture. In this way, picture and performance co-existed in the same space for ten minutes, provoking very different experiences and responses.

Since the 1960s, one can say that the different art forms and, in particular, theatre and visual arts have come closer to each other, sometimes to such an extent that they merge. In theatre, painters and stage designers work as directors, creating what is commonly called a "theatre of images." Moreover, theatre plays with all the other art forms. On the other hand, the performing mode is often characteristic of the fine arts, as in the fields of action painting, body art, land art, light sculptures, and video installations. Here, a redefinition of the role of beholder is taking place: it is split up into the roles of actor/performer and spectator. Either the live body of an artist is displayed before an audience or the beholder is challenged to move around the exhibit and interact with it while other visitors may observe him or her doing so. The roles of performer and spectator alternate accordingly, so that a visit to a museum or an art site, nowadays, quite often means participating in a performance, partly as performer, partly as spectator. This is particularly true with regard to the actions of artists such as Joseph Beuys, Wolf Vostell, Yvonne Rainer, Ann Halprin, the FLUXUS artists, or the Viennese actionists. In the 1960s and the early 1970s, they promoted and realized the "new" genre of action and performance art. Here the fine arts merge into theatre.

So, what is noteworthy about Schleef's production of *Salome* is not that because he was a painter – as well as a playwright, a novelist, and an essayist – he used devices and means used in the fine arts; rather, it is the confrontation of picture and performance, of the different responses they trigger and the different experiences they make possible. In this way, Schleef's production posed a problem that is, in my view, crucial to the issue of theatre studies as art studies today: what is the aesthetic experience caused by a theatre performance? This question implies or presupposes two other questions. Firstly, what do we regard as aesthetic experience: which kind of objects, text, performances can trigger it, and how do they do so? Secondly, provided that works of art are capable of provoking an aesthetic experience in a particular way, will it differ according to the specific art form that arouses it, in particular its materiality and mediality? Does theatre's liveness, for instance, enable another kind of aesthetic experience than mediatization (film, video) does?

It was not until the eighteenth century that such questions were asked for the first time, although, of course, similar notions such as *catharsis* have been discussed since Aristotle. This, no doubt, had to do with the declaration of autonomy in the arts around 1800. The issue was introduced, investigated, and discussed at great length by Baumgarten, Burke, and Kant. By the nineteenth century, it was not only the philosophers who continued the debate; artists and theorists from the different arts also joined in. In recent years the question has been taken up either by psychologists such as Mihaly Csikszentmihalyi, who defines aesthetic experience in a general way as "flow experience" (7), or by philosophers who focus on aesthetic perception in contrast to non-aesthetic perception.[8]

Oddly enough, theatre scholars have seldom participated in this debate, even those who specialize in audience research. It is only with great hesitancy that they put the problem on their agenda.[9] The question of aesthetic experience seems to be a blind spot in theatre studies.

This seems all the more surprising because theatre scholars working in the field of performance studies and investigating different kinds of rituals put a great deal of emphasis on the particular kind of experience that the participants of a ritual undergo. Following van Gennep's suggestion to structure rituals in three phases, namely the separation phase, the threshold or transition phase, and the incorporation phase (10–11), and Turner's definition of the concept of liminality,[10] they label the particular experience of participants as liminal experience and declare it a unique kind of experience, not to be made in other cultural fields. It seems that the liminal experience is, in fact, a fundamental human experience, to be found in people of all cultures, although, of course, in each case not only triggered in different situations by most diverse phenomena and processes but also sensed and felt in different ways. That which in one culture, one epoch, or even one particular genre of ritual will provoke a liminal experience does not necessarily work the same way in another genre of ritual, another epoch, another culture.

What justifies the assumption that aesthetic experience is a less fundamental human experience than the liminal experience? Only that we are used to according it to the recipients, the beholders, spectators, listeners, and readers? This is hardly reason enough. Why not proceed from the hypothesis that the aesthetic experience is a modern version of the liminal experience – that it is a particular kind of liminal experience undergone by the recipients – an idea that Turner himself brought up when suggesting the concept of the liminoid? As mentioned above, it was not before the late eighteenth century that the concepts of aesthetics and of aesthetic experience were developed. That is to say, they were elaborated at a time when many traditional rituals in Europe did not function any more – at least not for the members of the educated middle classes. Instead, beholding the beautiful and sublime in the newly autonomous arts as well as in nature – which was also accorded a new meaning – excited a new kind of experience called aesthetic experience because it was caused by a particular kind of sensuous perception (*aisthesis*). Thus the concept of aesthetic experience was understood and defined as a very particular combination of sensuous, emotional, and cognitive components.

Nowadays it is a common saying that everyday life in Western cultures is undergoing a process of aesthetization, whether in the fields of fashion, design, architecture, and commercial advertising or in the creation of particular atmospheres in different everyday environments (for instance, in shopping malls) or musical environments – in short, an aesthetization of our lifestyles. But what does this entail? Does it mean that the phenomena and processes that are able to evoke an aesthetic experience multiply? That our attitude towards everyday life becomes more and more aesthetic?

In order to understand what is going on here, it is necessary to get a clearer insight into the particular experience that we are in the habit of calling aesthetic. Since the concept of aesthetics was developed in the context of the arts becoming autonomous, it is to be assumed that it will be greatly affected by the aesthetization of everyday life, since such an aesthetization can be understood in certain respects as a loss of autonomy, in terms of aesthetics, as a new kind of merging between art and life. Thus Kant's definition of the aesthetic experience as *"Das Wohlgefallen [...] ohne alles Interesse"* (or, "detached pleasure"; 69) probably cannot be applied anymore. How can we define aesthetic experience today? In order to answer this question we must first clarify a number of problems. Is aesthetic experience a unified experience in the sense that it is always the same, regardless of the different phenomena and processes that are able to trigger it? Or does it change in accordance with them? And if it changes, what kind of transformation does it undergo in each case, and how can we argue that it is still, basically, the same kind of experience? What does aesthetization bring about in terms of our potential of experience?

Since, on the other hand, this aesthetization is, to a great extent, carried out as a theatricalization of everyday life, it would be not only justifiable but also most desirable if theatre studies were to take up the challenge. This is all the more true when we consider that, as the above-mentioned examples show, theatre today has a certain tendency in and through its performances to transgress the borderline separating it from other arts, media, and cultural performances – as the process of aesthetization transgresses the borderline of art and life. Thus, a theatre performance would seem to be a highly suitable object of research into the question of aesthetic experience. Theatre performances must be examined closely in terms of the particular kind of experience they provoke in spectators. It is to be assumed not only that different kinds of performances will cause different experiences but also that one and the same performance will generate different experiences within different spectators, as well as in one and the same spectator at different moments. So how will it be possible – leaving aside the methodological problems of how to access the experiences of the spectators – to abstract from all these different kinds of experiences one particular experience that we can identify as aesthetic?

Particularly important in this context is the question of how and to what extent the materiality and mediality of the arts affect the aesthetic experience. In Einar Schleef's production of Elfriede Jelinek's *Sportstück* ("Sports Play") at the Burgtheater Vienna in 1998, a chorus of male and female actors in sports dress performed the same strenuous exercises for forty-five minutes in permanent repetition, shouting the same sentences over and over again with sustained energy. Some spectators apparently felt tortured by this procedure and left after the first few minutes. Those who remained and exposed themselves to it until the very end participated in a most unusual experience. The spectators fell into a kind of trance-state in which they sensed both physically and with great intensity the energetic field that came into being between the performers and the spectators, which intensified the longer the exercises went on. The spectators were not only affected but were offered the opportunity of new experiences and were perhaps even transformed. Was this an aesthetic experience that only the liveness of a theatre performance can create? How can we compare it to an experience triggered by a painting or a film? On the other hand, what is the difference between the experience of many spectators during the performance of *Sportstück* and a liminal experience of a certain ritual? There seem to be, at the very least, strong affinities between both kinds of experiences, supporting my argument that aesthetic experience is a modern version of liminal experience.

Regarding the question of aesthetic experience, moreover, we must not forget that the idea of autonomous art and the concept of aesthetics is a truly European, Western concept, not to be found in non-Western cultures. As far as theatre is concerned, there are concepts that are, in more than one respect, comparable to it, for instance, the concept of *rasa* in Indian theatre or the notion of *yugen* in the Noh theatre. How can we deal with such different concepts? How do we relate them to each other? And, most importantly, what can we conclude from the basic differences between such concepts: that the experience is different, or that the experience is the same but subsumed under another concept or left with no concept, for whatever reasons?

In order to be able to deal properly and successfully with all the questions posed here, theatre studies faces a challenge not only as art studies but as media studies and cultural studies as well. Moreover, in dealing with the problem of aesthetic experience, it will have to cooperate with all other arts studies, as well as anthropology, psychology, and many other disciplines. The exploration of the particular experience that we label aesthetic, in any case, will be carried out as an interdisciplinary project. Theatre studies will contribute to it by investigating the particular experience that spectators may have while watching a theatre performance.

5. EPILOGUE

"The curtain down and all the questions open" (*"Der Vorhang zu und alle Fragen offen,"* Brecht 1607; my translation) – Brecht's words seem most appropriate here. The discussion I have laid out on the prospects, challenges, problems, and risks that theatre studies confronts because of and in terms of its interdisciplinary nature has yielded more questions than answers, although they are questions that raise and may provoke relevant solutions. The general question, *"Quo vadis?"* cannot be answered – at least not definitively. There are no clear and generally accepted rules to guide theatre studies over the crossroads. However, there are some guidelines on which many theatre scholars could agree. Thus, the situation in which theatre studies finds itself is rather like that of a game being played. For play is not "either/or"; it is "as well" in ever-changing constellations; it combines the rules of a game and the freedom to change those rules; it is chance and necessity. Play is not the opposite of seriousness; it is, as Schiller, Huizinga, Caillois, and Turner have emphasized, seriousness itself. It is able to make order out of the chaos of the world, but only through a precarious interplay of order and chance.

Of course, it is not by chance that the concept of play takes a rather prominent role in the examples that introduce each section of this article. The theatre performances to which I have referred play with other genres of cultural performance, other media, other art forms; they play with different frameworks, expectations, borderlines, and spectator responses, and they both allow and partly invite and seduce the spectators to do the same: to play. Playing in this way, theatre sails boldly, if not too safely, between Scylla and Charybdis, enjoying the straits as if they were the open sea.

It is the interdisciplinary nature of theatre studies that challenges it to take this risk-filled route, to play with all the borderlines, frameworks, and rules set up until today, whether they seem too strict and narrow or whether, on the contrary, they appear too misty, wide, and general. It is not a question of either one or the other. It is only by playing theatre studies, by trying out and testing, forming new parties, looking for new allies and enemies, permanently regrouping, reformulating, and recreating that which has already been grouped, formulated, and created, that we will be in a position to find – even if only tentatively – intriguing answers to the questions at stake. Our problem today is not whether to widen or to narrow down our field, to claim more territory or to cede territory to someone else. It is, rather, to recreate the discipline in such a way that it will be able to generate relevant answers to the relevant questions in a competent, understandable, and convincing manner. Since we are in such a serious situation, let us play theatre studies.

NOTES

1 At least in Germany. Cf. Fischer-Lichte, "From Text to Performance."
2 Cf. Fischer-Lichte, "Thoughts on the 'Interdisciplinary.'"
3 The German equivalent to such a use of these terms would be the terms *Kulturwissenschaft*, *Medienwissenschaft*, and *Kunstwissenschaft*.
4 In 1996, the German Research Council funded a six-year interdisciplinary research project titled "Theatricality: Theatre As a Model in Cultural Studies," initiated and coordinated by the Department of Theatre Studies at the Free University, Berlin. About thirty projects, coming from twenty different disciplines, are currently involved in this very successful program.
5 Monty Jacobs wrote: "Whether performances of this kind put the spectator under too strong a strain, the future will tell us" (qtd. in Rühle 2:794, trans. Jo Riley).
6 For discussions of liveness, see Phelan; Auslander.
7 This reminds us of some notorious theatre scandals like that caused by the behaviour of the gynaecologist Isidor Kastan at the first night of Gerhard Hauptmann's

Before Sunrise (Berlin, 20 October 1889). He pulled a pair of forceps out of his bag and swung them over his head to offer his services at the very moment when, off-stage, the character supposed to be giving birth was about to start labour.

8 See Seel's introduction to *Eine Ästhetik der Natur,* especially 11–33, and Welsch.

9 Cf. the discussions on "catharsis" by Schoenmakers, McConachie, and Rokem in *Assaph* and by Eversmann.

10 See Turner's essay "Liminal to Liminoid in Play, Flow and Ritual" in *From Ritual to Theatre,* especially 24–7. For Turner's reading of van Gennep's ritual structure, see 24.

Physiologies of the Modern: Zola, Experimental Medicine, and the Naturalist Stage

STANTON B. GARNER, JR.

In 1953, on the anniversary of the French premiere of Luigi Pirandello's *Six Characters in Search of an Author,* playwright Georges Neveux reflected on the play's impact:

> Just thirty years ago today, an elevator came down on the stage of the [Théâtre des] Champs Elysées and deposited on it six unexpected characters whom Pirandello had conjured up. [...] [I]t will be impossible to understand anything about today's theater if one forgets that little flying box out of which it stepped one April evening in 1923. (qtd. in Bishop 49–50)

Characterizing Pirandello as "the greatest prestidigitator of the Twentieth Century, the Houdini of interior life," Neveux elaborated on the playwright's theatrical achievement: "In his most important play, *Six Characters,* he took the very center of the real world and turned it inside out right in front of us, as the fisherman turns inside out the skin of an octopus to lay bare its viscera" (qtd. in Bishop 136).

I open with Neveux's tribute because it foregrounds an important intersection in the discourse of modern drama. In his reference to "today's theater," Neveux employs the language of the modern familiar to the late-nineteenth- and early/mid-twentieth-century theatre's discourse about itself. Theatre "today" – and by this Neveux means the theatre of Jean Giraudoux, Armand Salacrou, Jean Anouilh, and himself – achieves its contemporaneity through reference to an earlier moment of disclosure. The newness of this disclosure – its modernity – is represented, in part, through the language of bodies and bodily penetration. If the "real" world is a body, then Pirandello's theatre constitutes an operation on that body, crossing its thresholds, turning it inside out, revealing in the organic matter of its entrails *"the other side of ourselves"* (qtd. in Bishop 136). To the extent that the world of the "real" and of "ourselves" is

something living, then the drama of Pirandello offers itself, before the specta-
torial gaze, as a kind of theatrical vivisection.

This conjunction of the modern and the corporeal/somatic is central to the
emergence of "modern drama" as a discursive category. This article is concerned with the making of this "modern" drama, the genesis and genealogy of
its animating terms, and the strategies with which those who deploy the discourse of "modern drama" seek to resolve its inherent instabilities. For while
"modern" is (as Henri Lefebvre notes) "a prestigious word, a talisman, an
open sesame" (185), its cultural currency also occasions an anxiety of reference, an awareness that, like the present moment itself, the modern is a site of
vanishings, of self-obsolescence. In what we might call the "manifesto" phase
of modern drama (roughly 1880 to 1940), those who used the term sought to
ground and legitimize the "modern" through the language of the body – both
the theatrical body (described in the languages of radical actuality) and the
body as it was simultaneously being constructed within medical discourse.

This connection between the corporeal fields of theatre and medicine
should not surprise us. Peopled as it regularly is by doctors, nurses, and medical students, the drama of this period shows a recurrent interest in the institution and practice of medicine. The presence of such figures as Pirandello's
il dottore signals a deeper preoccupation with the body and the embodied
mind as medical subjects. Given that the body underwent discursive and theoretical transformations within medical science during the latter half of the
nineteenth century and the first third of the twentieth, it served as a useful,
even inevitable, referent for a theatre that was undergoing its own interrogation of the body as a site for observation. To the extent that the nineteenth
century witnessed a deepening of the relationship between medicine and the
physical sciences, the cultural authority of medical discourse provided the
modern theatre with a language through which its modernity could be "bodied" forth.

An awareness of the connections between theatre and medicine, in other
words, situates the earliest formulations of modern drama within a wider discursive field concerned with the body, its languages of disclosure, its pathologies. It also positions late-nineteenth- and early-twentieth-century theatre in
relation to medical and other emergent technologies involved in rendering the
body visible. This article focuses on one of the earliest convergences between
modern theatre and medicine: Émile Zola's appropriation of the physiological
body within his theory of the naturalist stage. As a way of tracing this convergence, I am interested in the discursive link between Zola's texts and Claude
Bernard's writings on experimental medicine. Exploring this connection
reveals much about naturalism's attempt to articulate the body it sought to
stage and its equally deliberate concern to advance a mode of observation, or
spectatorship, modeled on the scientific gaze. In addition, this interchange
between the languages of theatre and medicine provokes a rethinking of natu-

ralism and modernism, their complex relationship to each other, and the sometimes ambivalent place of theatre within both.

* * *

With its image of that elevator, the "little box" that disclosed new possibilities
for drama, Neveux's description is a resonant one, for it encapsulates the
appearance of the new that characterizes the modern, particularly in its avant-
garde articulations. The image of emergence, of stepping forward, is related,
of course, to notions of dislocation, rupture, declaration. As the leading edge
of the contemporary, the modern is forward-looking, yet the future to which
it points is often unclear in outline and feature; indeed, its indeterminacy
increases as the modern outstrips the structures of the cognitive world it
enters. In Neveux's words, when Pirandello's Six Characters took the stage,
"hundreds of characters loomed up before us, but we could not yet see them"
(qtd. in Bishop 49). In this sense, Pirandello's "play about the theater in the
theater" stands as a parable of the modern emerging, indeed erupting, within
the space of the non-modern; bathed in the "*tenuous light*" that surrounds
them, "*almost as if irradiated by them*," Pirandello's Characters carry with
them the aura of the new (Pirandello 214).[1]

Like the other extratheatrical texts that frame performance (programs,
posters, critical reviews), the manifesto served an essential function in fram-
ing the modern *as* modern in late-nineteenth- and early-twentieth-century
drama. Performative in intent and function, these manifestos call forth, render manifest, the modern that they take as their subject. Often located as
prefaces or afterwords to specific dramatic texts, such statements trope the
fields of enactment and reception in terms of difference and arrival. But
while the tone of the manifestos of early modern drama is often triumphalist,
the values and goals with which the modern is invested are multiple and
unstable. Like the terms *modernity, modernization,* and *modernism,* with
which it is contiguous and upon which it draws, the word *modern* is characterized by conflicting, often opposing, meanings. Its theatrical deployments
reveal its contested articulations and allegiances: technological versus classical, positivist versus irrational, progressivist versus anarchist, urban versus
rural, nationalist versus international, theatrical versus non-theatrical. Indeed,
the differences that constitute the contemporary are sometimes forged in
terms of rival notions of the modern. John Millington Synge, for instance,
rejected the metropolitan, "intellectual" modern drama of Henrik Ibsen and
Zola, dealing (as it did) with the reality of life "in joyless and pallid words"
(4), in favor of an aesthetic grounded in non-urban primitivism and literary
ethnography (transcribing an authentic Irish speech through a chink in a
Wicklow floor), which are themselves modernist projects. In view of the
fault lines of this intertextual discourse, its conflicting allegiances and repu-

diations, clearly one of the most pervasive subjects staged by modern drama is the nature of the modern itself.

Internally contradictory meanings are not the only instability that those using the term *modern* must face. The question of legitimation is central to the dynamic, and the anxiety, under which the modern must labor. *Modern*, after all, is a relational signifier, and it acquires its meanings by proposing a set of differences from that which precedes it. Joseph Roach observes, "The concept of a 'modern' drama rests on an imaginary border that separates modernity from what has come before. Modern drama thus assumes its own estrangement from the past" (113). Even when the *modern* is articulated in terms of historical development, as it is (for instance) in Bertolt Brecht's theoretical writing, the boundaries of its meanings depend on its singularity: this is the new; the future starts here. Oppositional in its self-assertion, the modern is always accompanied by the problems of origin and self-definition. The result is an anxiety of legitimation, a fear that the values and goals by which it grounds itself may not prove adequate. Jürgen Habermas describes this uneasiness:

Modernity can and will no longer borrow the criteria by which it takes its orientation from the models supplied by another epoch; *it has to create its normativity out of itself.* Modernity sees itself cast back upon itself without any possibility of escape. This explains the sensitiveness of its self-understanding, the dynamism of the attempt, carried forward incessantly down to our own time, to "pin itself down." (7)

As part of this struggle for demarcation and legitimation, the modern playwright may allude to earlier moments of the modern in order to establish a contextualizing genealogy (Antonin Artaud and Roger Vitrac's Théâtre Alfred Jarry, for example), but such gestures do not preclude the vulnerability of the modern to the very temporality from which it derives. Nothing is more out of date than yesterday's newness, and the modern is haunted both by the elements within it of the tradition from which it has severed itself and by the ghosts of impermanence and novelty (Zola, as we shall see, used the language of clothing to enact and contain the fear of modernity as fashion). To the extent that the modern defines itself as singular, it carries its obsolescence within itself, and it continually finds itself receding behind the leading edge of the *contemporary*. "[M]odernity is different tomorrow from what it is today," Milan Kundera writes in his novel *Immortality*; "for the sake of the *eternal imperative* of modernity one has to be ready to betray its *changeable content*" (138). In other words, "to be absolutely modern means to be the ally of one's gravediggers" (141).

The critical discourse on modern drama has not been immune from the anxiety that this slippage brings. In his Foreword to the second issue of *Modern Drama* in 1958, four months after the first issue of the journal appeared, the editor, A.C. Edwards, was already in the grips of the instability of the modern: "it is sobering to learn that what we had thought was vanguard is now already becoming rear guard. Ionesco and Beckett, we are told, are no longer new. And we were just beginning to get caught up on them!" (69). The further one gets from the drama of Ibsen through Brecht, the more the two conflicting meanings of the modern – in this case, the modern as modernist and the modern as contemporary – diverge. At a historical junction defined by the *postmodern*, when the former avant-garde is now well ensconced in the canon, the term *modern* has even, in some instances, acquired conservative meanings; certainly, the intellectual career of Robert Brustein displays more than a touch of what Jean-Pierre Sarrazac calls *la nostalgie du moderne* (109).

* * *

Modern theatre writing between 1880 and 1940, then, involves an attempt to consolidate the term "modern" and ground its meanings. The language of the body is central to the various discursive and rhetorical strategies employed to this end. As that which inhabits performance and orients the visual scene in terms of its sentient presence, the body is used to anchor the discourse of the modern through the rhetoric of radical actuality. In the case of naturalism – and in the writings of Zola, its chief theoretician – the discursive body stands forward with particular clarity. Indeed, Zola's theatrical writings propose the body as the somatic center of an emerging naturalist modernity.[2]

This modernity is linked, in Zola's 1881 treatise, *Naturalism in the Theatre*, with the revolutionary overthrow of a despotic monarchy and the birth of the French Republic. In the Classical period, tragedy "reigned as an absolute monarch" (*Naturalisme* 12), and the Romantic revolt represented an uprising against its artifice. The excesses of Romanticism, in their turn, paralleled the excesses of the Revolution itself, reflected (as they were) in the behavior of people whose spirits were "excited, bewildered, violently unleashed ... still racked by a dangerous fever" (19). Animating this revolution, of course, and eventually overthrowing Romanticism itself, is the true spirit of the modern age: that of positivist science and its methods of inquiry and analysis. Zola describes the movement and its transformations in the context of the modern disciplines:

The natural sciences date from the end of the last century; chemistry and physics are less than a hundred years old; history and criticism have been renewed, practically re-created since the Revolution; an entire world has arisen; it has returned us to the study of documents, to experience, made us understand that in order to start afresh we must first take things back to the beginning, come to know man and nature, verify what is.... To trace the history of [the naturalist] movement ... would be to trace the history of the century itself. (*Naturalisme* 17)

Experimental medicine occupies a privileged place in this evolution for theatre and the novel because of its concern with the physiology of the human
body within its organic and non-organic environments. As Zola states in *The
Experimental Novel*, "If the terrain of the experimental physician is the body
of man as it manifests itself through its organs, both in their normal and pathological condition, our terrain is equally the body of man in its cerebral and
sensory manifestations, both in their healthy and morbid condition" (*Roman
expérimental* 33). The corporeal volume and somatic registers of this body –
asserting itself, impeding abstraction – inhabit the figural substratum of Zola's
writings on theatre: the contemporary theatre is dying of moral "indigestion"
(*Naturalisme* 46), whereas classical tragedy in its late stages was "a tall figure,
pale and emaciated, without a drop of blood beneath its white skin" (13). Of
Romanticism, Zola writes, "For a sluggish [*lymphatique*] rhetoric, the movement of 1830 substituted a nervous and passionate [*nerveuse et sanguine*]
rhetoric" (15). Against the inanimateness of conventional representation – the
characters of which are little more than statues or marionettes – naturalism
"comes from the very entrails of humanity" (17), an origin (like that in
Neveux's description) that both constitutes and legitimizes it.

The history of naturalism, for Zola, is summed up in the gradual substitu-
tion of "physiological man" for "metaphysical man" (*Naturalisme* 92). The
dramatists of classical tragedy and romantic drama pursued idealization and
abstraction: "Never the thoroughgoing analysis of an organism," Zola writes,
"never a character whose muscles and brain function as in nature" (23–24).
Such claims set Zola's writings in dialogue with contemporary medical writers, particularly Claude Bernard, whose 1865 *Introduction to the Study of
Experimental Medicine* deeply influenced Zola. Indeed, sections of *The
Experimental Novel* are little more than a gloss on Bernard, as Zola himself
acknowledges: "I plan on all points to entrench myself behind Claude Bernard" (*Roman expérimental* 11). Bernard, who himself derided the figure of
the artist as "a man who carries out a personal idea or feeling in a work of art"
(232), advocated the application of experimental methods to physiology,
pathology, and therapeutics. Rejecting the tradition of vitalism, which saw
human phenomena as following their own laws, Bernard argued that the interior of the organic body functions as an environment and that this environment
follows the same fixed laws that govern non-organic bodies. As a "science of
living bodies" (200), experimental medicine sought to uncover the determin-
ability of phenomena – that is to say, the equations by which physiological
objects of observation react to stimuli in predictable ways.

Bernard's writing, and experimental medicine in general, provided Zola
with a model for marking the body, reading and penetrating its surfaces, and
disclosing the interactions between body and environment. Bernard states,
"There always come under consideration the *body*, in which the phenomenon
takes place, and the outward circumstances or the environment which deter-

mines or invites the body to exhibit its properties" (103). Zola theatricalizes
this physiological model and the structures of observation through which the
body discloses the laws governing its operations and interactions. He
describes the goals of the naturalist (or experimental) novel, which he considered a precursor to the naturalist theatre, as follows:

> to master the mechanisms of the phenomena inherent in man, to show the inner
> workings of his intellectual and sensory behavior (under the influences of heredity
> and environment, such as physiology shall show them to us), then to exhibit man as
> he lives in the social milieu that he himself has produced. (*Roman expérimental* 25)

By modeling itself on scientific observation, naturalism in the arts "continues
and completes physiology" (27), expanding its field of analysis from the individual to a social body that is itself characterized by the normal and the pathological.

In order to attain the ideal transparency of the scientific gaze and to reveal
the workings of the organic environment, the scientist, for Bernard, must
remain suspicious of words; he must "always cling to phenomena and see in
words only expressions empty of meaning" (217). Armed with this linguistic
wariness and with the tools of experimental inquiry, medical scientists
become, in words that echo the aesthetic aims of realism and naturalism,
"photographers of nature" (221). The linguistic argument is important here,
for it highlights the conflict in Zola's own attempt to "speak" the body, to render its legitimizing presence within the discourse of naturalism. When Bernard warns against words, it is (not surprisingly) rhetorical, chiefly figurative,
language that he targets. Rhetoric is the enemy of Zola's naturalist theatre, as
well. The failure of Romanticism, for instance, derives from the fact that it
challenged the rhetoric of Classical tragedy only to replace it with a rhetoric of
its own. The argument against rhetoric as dressing and disguise plays directly
into Zola's own rhetorical strategy (one of the reasons Zola is so engaging to
read, of course, is that he conducts his anti-rhetoric campaign with an extrava-
gantly rhetorical arsenal). Not surprisingly, Zola's most explicit discussion of
"physiological man" in *Naturalism in the Theatre* can be found in his observations on costume. Clothing, costume, and disguise constitute a site where the
representational battle over the "real" takes place. The battle between Classi-
cal·tragedy and Romanticism was "a simple skirmish" (*Naturalisme* 14) over
dress and modes of speech, nothing more: "togas were torn up in favor of dou-
blets" (14). Clothing becomes the marker of dramatic evolution as fashion,
with styles replacing each other in sequences of artifice, while the uncovered
body stands as the site of the real in its stability and perseverance. Like Bernard's scientific discourse, Zola's description of the naturalist theatre imagines a stage free of ornament, and in its call for a "true drama of modern
society" (27) it envisions a transparency of representation: "Today the natural-

ist thinkers are telling us that the truth has no need of clothing; it must walk naked. That, I repeat, is the quarrel" (23). *Il doit marcher dans sa nudité*: through a kind of anti-rhetoric, the exposed body offers itself, here and elsewhere in Zola's theatre writing, as a site where the real steps out of the conventional and artificial. Elsewhere, Zola praises Molière and Corneille for the *"nudité,"* or bare simplicity, of their dramatic action (*Nos auteurs* 9, 21).

What is at work in Zola's theatrical naturalism is the effort to discipline the theatre's signifying mechanisms that we encounter elsewhere in the history of modern realism.[3] Crucial to Zola's notion of the physiological theatre is the imagined erasure of the stage's histrionic channels – its swaggering and swordplay, its "grand spectacle and grand words, the play filled with lies parading before the crowd" (*Naturalisme* 22). In the face of such rhetoricity, naturalist theatre can ground itself in the "real" of the physiological body and install a medicalized gaze as its normative optics only by eliminating the stage's intrinsic theatricality.

* * *

A much longer version of this article might explore some of the particular ways in which late-nineteenth-century drama and its theory play out the implications of naturalism's physiological body. It might consider, for instance, the strategies through which Ibsen's plays both take up and repress the body's somatic language, exploring the physiological dimensions of the ethical and motivational spheres while challenging the notion of transparency intrinsic to pathological anatomy and other branches of nineteenth-century experimental medicine. It might look, as well, at August Strindberg, the dramatist who, at the beginning of his career, saw himself as the "genius" of the theatre that Zola called for and who extended Zola's naturalist prescriptions in what one might see as modernist directions. It might consider how the stagecraft and acting changes that formed part of the movement of theatrical naturalism put into practice the theatrical discipline that Zola's theory articulates and enacts. Finally, it might look at the ways in which naturalism, despite its internationalist appeal, intersected with late-nineteenth-century nationalist movements (especially in Germany) – the ways, in other words, in which the body serves to ground not only notions of theatre but a modernity of national community as well. In Zola's telling words, "Everything meets in the real" (*Naturalisme* 26). Zola's main treatises on naturalism, it is important to remember, were published in the aftermath of the Franco-Prussian War of 1870–1871, and one of the essays in *The Experimental Novel* ends with the following exhortation: "Let the youth of France hear me: patriotism is here. It is by applying the scientific formula that you shall one day retake Alsace and Lorraine" (*Roman expérimental* 88). As Robert A. Nye has argued, medicalized concepts of individual and social degeneration emerged after the 1870–1871 war in response to French anxieties over the country's changing geopolitical role and the military dangers posed by a declining birth rate (*Crime* 132–44; "Medical Origins" 14–16). The implications of this medicalization and the attendant concern with pathologies (crime, violence, sexual deviance) are certainly relevant to naturalism's representation of the individual and collective body.[4]

Rather than pursuing these particular directions, I will reflect on the broader implications of the medicalized discursive body and its legitimizing function within Zola's writings on theatre. For one thing, attending to this body's somatic discourse provides a way to begin thinking about the uncanny overlaps and relays between the institutions of theatre and medicine during the early period of modern drama. The biographical intersections are well known. Both Ibsen and Strindberg studied medicine before entering the theatre, and Chekhov became a practicing physician. As part of his military service during World War I, Brecht worked as a medical orderly at an Augsburg medical hospital treating epidemic and venereal disease. Claude Bernard, for his part, started out as a playwright, left the Rhone Valley for Paris in order to write for the theatre, and entered medical school only when his playwriting efforts were discouraged (Olmsted and Olmsted 14–20). The risks of anecdotal generalization notwithstanding, these career trajectories suggest the interpenetration and mutual reflections of the two fields during the late nineteenth and early twentieth centuries. Theatre and medicine, after all, each involve discourses and technologies of the body, and the presence of medicine in the discourse of theatre reflects a shared concern with what Felicia McCarren calls "the body as a site of meaning and [...] vision as a theater of knowledge" (14).

Indeed, the birth of what we call modern drama took place against a set of unprecedented cultural, professional, and technological developments in the discipline of medicine. The nineteenth century saw wide-reaching developments both in medical technologies for penetrating, measuring, and representing the body – the stethoscope was first used in 1816, the microscope and thermometer at mid-century, and the x-ray in the late 1890s – and in the cultural circulation of medicine and medical science. Linked with the experimental sciences and increasingly a discipline of the laboratory as well as the clinic, medicine enjoyed considerable cultural authority, particularly in France; this authority was heightened by its adoption of the epistemology and vocabulary of science and technology, themselves culturally ascendant during the nineteenth century (see Crawford 3–5). As Ann La Berge and Mordechai Feingold note, medical discourse permeated all areas of French society, from the learned institutions to newspapers, the arts, and daily life (3). Literacy rates rose steadily during the nineteenth century, and a large popular and scientific press developed to bring the expanding medical knowledge to the new reading public (Micale 201). All of this reflected, and contributed to, the nineteenth century's growing preoccupation with the body and its capacity for illness.

This widespread medicalization and the prestige accorded what Gustave

Flaubert called the "clinical view of life" ("*le coup d'œil médical de la vie*," qtd. in Gray 81) bear on the discourse and practice of theatre in crucial ways. In a specific sense, the cultural authority enjoyed by scientific medicine contributed powerfully to the legitimizing power of the body within literary and theatrical texts that appropriated its tropes. More broadly, the development and cultural expansion of what Michel Foucault (in *The Birth of the Clinic*) calls "the medical gaze" provided the discourse of theatre with broader models of embodiment and perception. The presence of theatre within medical discourse is obvious enough – we speak of "theatres" of operation – but the parallel, even more extensive presence of medical ways of seeing within the discourse of theatre is less frequently analyzed. For Foucault, the clinic made possible a specific relationship of body and gaze; it also helped produce the body by negotiating the relationship between inside and out, the normal and the pathological, institutions and individuals. Foucault's account of the "organic individuality" (153) that emerged from the science of pathological anatomy bears similarities to Zola's discussion of naturalism's physiological body, and the implications of the medical gaze for our understanding of theatrical spectatorship and the ways it was theoretically modeled in late-nineteenth-century theatre are equally significant. Bert O. States has written of realism as an "imprisonment of the eye" (69); naturalism in the theatre seeks to effect both a restriction of "semiotic" reference and an empowering of spectatorship in terms of certain analytic operations.

A focus on the body and its medicalized articulations, in other words, helps us position the theatre within a wider field of disciplinary developments within the nineteenth-century physical, biological, and social sciences. It allows us, as well, to re-examine disciplinary boundaries and evolution in light of the century's broader preoccupation with somatic observation and intervention. The development of psychiatry and psychology in the middle and latter parts of the nineteenth century, for example, were strongly influenced by medicine's physiological body. Psychiatry, which emerged as a medical specialty in the late eighteenth and early nineteenth centuries, drew upon neurology and neuropathology while also conducting its own research into the brain as the organic site of mental disease. Psychology, for its part, began emerging from the philosophy of mind to claim its own scientific and medical authority. The German philosopher-physician Wilhelm Wundt published a treatise on physiological (or "experimental") psychology in 1873 and opened the first psychological laboratory at the University of Leipzig in 1879. Sigmund Freud trained in Vienna in medicine and physiology, and he earned his MD in 1881 with a specialty in clinical neurology. While Freud would reject the physiological and neurological focus of his earliest professional years, the psychoanalysis that he developed in the 1890s and early 1900s remained deeply embedded in medical concepts and practices. As Dianne F. Sadoff has recently argued, "psychoanalysis innovatively revised even as it emerged from nineteenth-century psychiatric, neuropathological, and sexological theories of psycho-physical correlation, family relations, and sexual desire" (9).

Spectatorship, embodiment, pathology, contagion, degeneracy, symptom, neurosis – the medicalization of corporeality and observation in the nineteenth century provided the theatre with a network of issues concerning visuality and somatic presence. Attending to this network allows us to recast the field of modern drama, its internal history, relationships, and conflicts. Looking backward, we can appreciate anew the importance of Georg Büchner in clearing discursive and dramaturgical ground for the drama that followed. Büchner, a trained physician, offers in *Woyzeck* one of the first attempts to subject the body on stage to a kind of experimental attention and to model theatrical watching on the clinical gaze. In naturalist drama, the medicalized body functioned as the site for competing images of embodiedness, sociality, gender, and ideology. Considerable work has been done in cultural and theatre studies on the construction and representation of certain late-century pathologies – Elin Diamond's chapter on realism and hysteria in *Unmaking Mimesis* is one of a number of studies of the body and hysteria, and other culturally oriented studies have considered neurasthenia and homosexuality as medicalized categories – but there is much to say about the medical construction of embodiment within and against which notions of the pathological were articulated.

In terms of the twentieth century, this emphasis on the body reopens the question of naturalism's relationship to modernism. The exchanges between modernism's theatrical body and medical discourse and practice are intricate, as is the place of both within a broader modernist obsession with physicality and physical culture (see Segel). Not all of the nineteenth century's medical/ somatic legacy, of course, is mediated through naturalism. It was Friedrich Nietzsche, after all, who defined man, in *On The Genealogy of Morals,* as the "sick animal" (121).[5] But the continuities and divergences between naturalism and modernism in this area are particularly striking. Aspects of the modernist body are both resisted and latent in the physiological body that Zola appropriated in his theory of a naturalist theatre. Zola concentrates on the organicity of this body, and he consolidates this naturalness by opposing it to the mechanicalness of traditional theatre (imaged in terms of statues, puppets, machines). Doing so, he attempts to unify and naturalize what is, in his medical intertexts, a more complex model. The modern medicalized body is also a technologized body, and from naturalism on its organicity is complicated by the discursive and material intervention of machines. As Tim Armstrong suggests, by the early twentieth century the body could be penetrated by a range of devices; the singular body was resolved into a complex of different biomechanical systems; and other technologies and regimens were applied to it (2). For Mark Seltzer, the theoretical and procedural base for such changes occurred earlier, with the emerging problem in the late nineteenth century of "the body in machine culture" (3). Naturalism's fascination with the rivalry between biological and technological modes of generating persons and things is reflected in the range of practices and discourses that sought to coordinate body and machine. Claude Bernard regularly speaks of the organism as a living machine, operating through mechanical laws. Zola also writes of "*la machine humaine*" (*Naturalisme* 93) – and he further gestures toward this mechanization in his remarks on environment determining action – but it will be the modernists who, under the influence (in part) of later medical technology, write and stage the machine–body interface latent in late-nineteenth-century medicine and theatre.

Finally, there are other ways in which the modernist body is anticipated within this earlier discourse, often (again) through what Zola's texts seek to disown. While Zola's allegiance is to the integral body, whole in itself, the figurative language with which he characterizes the naturalist revolution images a different body – fragmented, recombined (the old formulas were based on "the rearrangement and systematic amputation of the truth" [22]), and agitated (Romanticism, as we have seen, was "racked by a dangerous fever" [19]). In these figural margins, one encounters the seeds of later conceptions of the "modern" in medicine and theatre: the agitated machine-body of Marinetti's Futurist theatre; the contagious body of Artaud's plague theatre; the prosthetic body of the technologized Bauhaus stage; and the fragmented body of a play like Tristan Tzara's *The Gas Heart*, shadowed as it clearly is by the spectacle of disfigurement during and after World War I and the development of cosmetic surgery. In modernism, as in naturalism, one sees the theatre responding to medical discourse and practice, exploring the interfaces between the human body and its technologies of visibility. Modernist theatre, like the naturalist theatre from which it emerged, often conceives its modernity in terms of the medicalized body and the environments – inner and outer, somatic and mechanistic – that offer themselves to our gaze.

NOTES

1 Anton Chekhov's *The Seagull* also stands as a parable of the modern's emergence, though its modernity derives from different sources and takes a decidedly different form. Treplev's onstage play in Act One stands out against the backdrop of Chekhov's own play, but its indulgent expressionism throws into relief the understated, "non-dramatic" newness of Chekhov's own refusal of grand theatrical gestures. Playing out the theatrical implications of what John Jervis sees as the modernity of ordinary experience, the true modern in Chekhov's plays is the dramaturgical backdrop of the everyday against which fashion, novelty, and the dramatic occur. Jervis's characterization of this form of modernity could serve as an epigraph to Chekhov's theatre: "there is modernity as an experience, of change and continuity, of ever-shifting, ever-altering frameworks and episodes of everyday life, manifested

in 'humble' narratives, the stories of fortune and misfortune, drama and triviality, the love and pain of ordinary relationships, among ordinary people, in a secular and individualist age" (331).

2 Zola's main theatrical writings can be found in the Preface to *Thérèse Raquin* (1878), *Le Roman expérimental* (1880), *Le Naturalisme au théâtre* (1881), and *Nos Auteurs dramatiques* (1881). Translations from Zola's French are my own; when possible, I have consulted Albert Bermel's translation of excerpts from *Le naturalisme au théâtre* (Zola, "From *Naturalism*").

3 See, for example, *1956 and All That*, Dan Rebellato's revisionist reading of the Royal Court revolution of 1956.

4 On links between naturalism and nationalism, see Osborne (9). In the field of experimental medicine, nationalistic competition became particularly acute after the Franco-Prussian War. Colonial rivalries, too, played themselves out in the field of medical research; these rivalries were particularly acute in tropical medicine (Bynum 142–52).

5 Nietzsche served as a medic during the Franco-Prussian War and was discharged after one week when he caught dysentery and diphtheria from the patients he treated (Krell xiii).

Making Sense of Sensation: Enlightenment, Embodiment, and the End(s) of Modern Drama

LOREN KRUGER

The end of the twentieth century may have postponed millennial fever, but it gives us a good opportunity to revisit prophecies for the end of drama, which, like those for the end of humanism or the end of modernity, have yet to be completely dispatched by any post-al delivery. We may be witnessing a post-dramatic theatre, as Hans-Thies Lehmann argues in a recent magisterial study entitled *Postdramatisches Theater,* but, as he concedes, the post-dramatic, like the postmodern and the post-structuralist, performs a double act, hedging its bets, as it were, in an ongoing engagement with the dramatic, the modern, the structure and form of the aesthetic object it deconstructs (11).[1] I am not going to imitate the Hegelian gesture of *Aufhebung* (summary, but also supersession) borrowed by Lehmann, a gesture that is modern as well as magisterial in its claim to master its subject, but, rather, will press a little on the genealogy as well as the current and future implications of this double-talk. Before we declare drama dead and modernity *passé,* we ought to conduct a genealogical investigation of "drama," to track its modernity, and perhaps its obsolescence. If, as Raymond Williams suggested more than twenty years ago, "modern drama" has migrated to "fiction" and "non-fiction" television, is performance still dramatic? Or is the order of the day a "post-dramatic theatre" or a polymorphously metaphorizing performance, in which both "modern" and "drama" can expect only supernumerary appearances in antiquarian costume?

Genealogies of drama in the West habitually begin with Aristotle, or at least take Aristotle as the source for habitual assumptions about drama, even if only as a prelude to dismissing them. But Aristotle's conception of tragic action marginalizes elements whose central place in drama is still taken for granted: conflict, character, and the suspense and resolution of conflict that capture, sustain, and satisfy audience involvement in a plot. Aristotle's tragedy is "a representation ($\mu\iota\mu\eta\sigma\iota\zeta$) of a serious, complete action which has magnitude [...] by people acting and not by narration" (Aristotle 49b25–29), but it can

nonetheless exist without character (50a25) and without performance
(50b19).[2] Drama appears only on the margins of this definition – as the noun,
το δράμα, meaning deed or act or "doing" (48a28), derived from the verb,
δραμειν (Janko 204) – and is associated not with any playwright but with the
epic poet Homer (48b36). Aristotle's text subordinates character to action –
"tragedy is a representation not of human beings but of action and life"
(50a16–17) – and treats conflict not as collision of protagonist and antagonist
but as elements of a logical structure, "parts of plot," whose reversals (perip-
eteia) and recognitions (anagnorisis) (50a34) drive the action to an already
determined goal.

Despite Aristotle's authority, however, it is to Hegel's *Aesthetics* (and, in
English, to his readers, from Coleridge and Carlyle on) that we owe the commonplace but pervasive idea of drama as the representation of human characters and passions in conflict. For Hegel, tragedy involves not only "actual or
current human actions and relationships [*gegenwärtige menschliche Handlungen und Verhältnisse*]" but also "persons expressing their actions" (*Vorlesungen* 3: 475; *Aesthetics* 2: 1159).[3] The emphasis on persons and their
relationships (not "affairs," as the standard translation has it) – in short, on *subjectivity* as well as agency against the constraints of state and tradition – is distinctively modern and quite different from Aristotle's famous emphasis on plot
over persons. It is to Hegel that we owe the idea of drama as such as the product
of modernity, of "those epochs in which individual [*subjektive*] self-consciousness has reached a high stage of development" (3: 501; 2: 1179) and the
modernity *of* drama as the expression of this subjectivity in collision with the
complexity of this world as opposed to that of the ancients – as elaborated by
Peter Szondi, student of Hegel and theorist of modern drama ("Theorie" 11–
15; *Theory* 3–6). Against Aristotle, drama for Hegel is less "the accomplish-
ment of a specific aim" than the "*collision* of circumstances, passions, and
characters" leading dialectically to "actions and reactions that require a *resolution* or *settlement [Schlichtung]* of conflict and discord" (3: 575; 2: 1159). It is
thus against *Hegel's* defense of the dramatic conflict between subject and
object and the resolution of this conflict through the expression of and identification with passion that Brecht launched his polemic for an epic, "non-Aris-
totelian" as opposed to a dramatic theatre, for the critical interruption and
analysis rather than the puathos and resolution of the action. And, finally, it is
against Hegel as well as against Brecht that post-Brechtians – playwrights like
Heiner Müller or David Greenspan, directors like Peter Zadek or Ann Bogart,
production/performance teams such as the Wooster Group or Goat Island who
combine writing and reworking textual, bodily, and scenographic repertoires,
and critics writing texts like *The Death of Character* (Fuchs), *Presence and
Resistance* (Auslander), or *Unmaking Mimesis* (Diamond), as well as *Postdramatisches Theater* – have continued to act. As these titles attest, the targets for
contemporary attacks remain the key concepts of Hegel's modern drama.

Before examining the modernity of drama in an era of purportedly post-modern performance art, we ought therefore to return to Hegel, whose ideas of drama have become so much second nature that we no longer see them as the source. It is Hegel who first theorized, if he did not invent, the collocation of modern and drama, in the conflict between self and society and its logical res-olution (*Schlichtung*), which connotes rational, worldly, even legalistic settle-ment rather than the metaphysical "reconciliation [*Versöhnung*]" of tragedy (*Vorlesungen* 3: 526; *Aesthetics* 2: 1198). In this article, I propose not to offer a full exegesis, genealogy, or necrology of the term "modern drama" but, rather, to investigate both the tenacity and the limits of these terms. I intend first to show how Hegel's terms and dialectical theory still pervade, if they do not fully dictate, current views of "modern" and "drama"; second, to probe the aporia in this theory of dramatic modernity and its antagonists to suggest that even the most emphatically postmodern post-dramatic performance has yet to shake the shadow of modern drama; and, finally but by no means conclusively, to explore performances that straddle the boundary between modern drama and postmodern performance and so challenge emphatic claims for this rup-ture.

Situating this investigation theoretically between Enlightenment concep-tions of modernity and drama in the sensible as well as sensuous representa-tion of conflict rationally resolved, at one end, and contemporary speculation and spectacle that pit sense and sensation (rather than sensibility) against rea-son, at the other, I will take as my examples in this final section the perfor-mance and re-presentation of pain, which, as the most unshareable of sensations, resists the language of communication that we associate with the modern, rational, enlightened interpretation and redress of suffering but, at the same time, challenges performers and audiences to find new ways of making sense of this sensation. My examples – performances of sensation and pain by the ordeal artist Ron Athey and dramatic representations of the Truth and Rec-onciliation Commission in South Africa – may appear at first to have nothing in common except a rather general association with pain and sensation, but their very differences may provide the links between sense and sensation that the exemplary theory of modern drama, the theory we inherit from Hegel, with or (more often) without acknowledgment, is unwilling to accommodate.

DIALECTICS OF "MODERN" AND "DRAMA"

Before looking at the gaps between sense and sensation, theory and matter, in Hegel's modern drama, we should begin by looking at the theoretical structure that defines these gaps by excluding sensation at crucial points from the idea of theory as well as the idea of drama. Although Hegel defends an Idealist notion of high tragedy, whose reconciliation (*Versöhnung*) of conflict "affords [a] glimpse of eternal justice" (3: 526; 2: 1198) and thus of the Absolute Idea of the Deity (2: 257; 2: 623), his theory of drama is essentially modern and sometimes even materialist. The modernity of his theory is clear in the claim that the individual protagonist drives the action, that "drama must display situations [...] as determined by the character of an individual" (3: 478; 2: 1161), rather than, as Aristotle asserts, the action driving – or discarding – the character (50a25). Lest there be any doubt that a modern preoccupation with individual self-consciousness drives the theory, Hegel goes on to argue that dramatic poetry "owes its origin *only* to those epochs in which individual self-consciousness has reached a high stage of development" (3: 501; 2: 1179, emphasis added). Although he shifts emphasis later, when he highlights the innovation and timeliness of modern drama and asserts, in contrast, that characters in classical tragedy are "a purely individual embodiment [or animation (*Verlebendigung*)] of ethical powers" (3: 555; 2: 1223), as, for instance, the conflict between Creon and Antigone embodies the struggle between "state power" (*Staatsgewalt*) and the "tie of blood" (3: 549; 2: 1217), Hegel argues at the outset of his discussion of drama that "truly *tragic* action necessarily presupposes [...] a live conception of *individual* freedom and independence" (3: 534; 2: 1205).

In this light, the deepening subjectivity of modern drama, its representation of an individual's "sufferings [*Leiden*] and passions [*Leidenschaften*]" (3: 556; 2: 1223) – represented for Hegel by the modern classics Shakespeare and Schiller, and embodied above all in Hamlet – constitutes not a radical departure from but an intensification of the essential attributes of dramatic poetry, especially the embodiment of individual freedom in the protagonist acting in and against the norms of society and custom. While one might say that this attribution of individualized subjectivity to an essentialized original form evacuates the historicity and thus, as it were, the *modernity* of modernity, Hegel argues that the individual's passion emerges in human actions and reactions to "specific ends drawn from the concrete spheres of family, state, church, etc." (3: 556; 2: 1223) and, therefore, emerges out of specific customs and conditions and a reflexive, that is, *modern,* attitude to the historical moment. Highlighting the paradox of modernity as a historical, perhaps past or *passé,* moment and the characteristic attitude of contemporary reflection, Hegel offers readers in the present, perhaps postmodern, moment an understanding of the ways in which the term *modern drama* encapsulates and enacts the dialectic of modernity, alternately a temporal and an epistemological category, a moment of crisis or opportunity, and a critical reflection on that moment.

IDEALISM, MATERIALISM, AND THE PROBLEM OF TASTE

Hegel's argument for dramatic modernity takes him closer to an acknowledgment of the historical and material conditions of dramatic poetry, performance, and audience response than conventional readings of his Idealist philosophy might allow. Despite reiterating Aristotle's claim for the more philosophical and universal character of poetry, especially dramatic poetry, over the more prosaic, contingent writing of history (Aristotle 51b6–12; Hegel, *Vorlesungen* 2: 257–61; *Aesthetics* 2: 986–89) and thus drama's representation of an Ideal action rather than contingent events (3: 256; 2: 985–86), Hegel departs from Aristotle's strict anti-theatricality. He argues instead that the dramatic work is fully dramatic only through "live performance for *viewers*" (*Aesthetics* 2: 1184, my translation and emphasis; "*lebendige Aufführung vor Augen*," *Vorlesungen* 3: 508) and that the playwright is responsible to a particular audience (*Aesthetics* 1175) or *Publikum* (*Vorlesungen* 476). This acknowledgment of the sensuous present-ness of dramatic action (*gegenwärtige Handlung*) in performance, the contingent responses of particular audiences at specific times and places, decisively shaped by an "organized national life" (*Vorlesungen* 3: 476; *Aesthetics* 2: 1159) and by the subordinate but significant influence of "practical stage know-how" (*Bühnenkenntnisse*, *Vorlesungen* 509; *not* merely "stagecraft," *Aesthetics* 1183) bespeaks a certain recognition of the historical, phenomenological, and material, if not an explicitly material*ist* determination of dramatic meaning and impact.

But Hegel's phenomenological turn to the performance of meaning and the meaning of performance takes his theory only partly beyond the Idealist disdain for the transience and decay of material phenomena. To be sure, he challenges the Idealist dismissal of theatre as ephemeral and therefore superfluous to the essential work of art, arguing in the pages on drama near the end of the *Aesthetics* that the sensuous immediacy of dramatic representation (*Darstellung*) in performance (*Aufführung*) fundamentally determines the meaning of drama and the epistemological value of performance. Nonetheless, at the beginning of the lectures on art, he follows classical Idealism in granting the status of art only to objects of hearing and, especially, sight. Following the derivation of sight, theatre, *and* theory from the Greek θέομαι (to gaze upon), which, as a verb in the middle as opposed to the active or passive voice, highlights the reflexive legitimation of the act, Hegel treats sight as the most theoretical of the senses (*Vorlesungen* 2: 255–56; *Aesthetics* 2: 622–23). Whereas sight and hearing are supposed to be theoretical because their action occurs at a reflective distance from the intact object, touch, and especially smell and taste, "dissolve and consume [or waste – *verzehrt*]" objects, which are in turn objects of appetite rather than art. Only an object not so consumed but, rather, contemplated intact in its "autonomous objecthood [*selbständige Objektivität*]" is eligible for the status of art, and, in corollary, only the disinterested gaze, which Hegel glosses in thoroughly Kantian terms as "desireless seeing [*das begierdelose Sehen*]," allows the work of art to remain autonomous and thus to transcend the realms of utility or appetite (2: 255; 2: 622).

The desireless gaze disinterestedly contemplating the autonomous work clearly occupies a position of authority in Hegel's theory, as it does in the Idealist tradition from Kant to Adorno, but it can only uneasily inhabit the body of the discerning (male) spectator, who, as the taste-maker of the modern theatrical scene, is *interested* in the performance, in that he is both attentive to and invested in the performance, even if he does not betray that interest in visible feeling. Unlike his classical forebears, Hegel places his discerning audience in a defining social context, "the organized national life," as well as against the mass of spectators who lack aesthetic judgment. Ideally, this discerning audience will exercise the desireless eye of judgment, but he nonetheless risks contamination from the sentimental weeping and spectacular suffering of those whom Hegel dismisses as "small-town females [*kleinstädtische Weiber*]" (3: 525; 2: 1198) but whose characteristic responses – sympathy and sentimentality – nonetheless affect the performance. While he does not explicitly invoke Diderot's ironic characterization of sensibility as a loss of control of the diaphragm (*Paradoxe* 99; "Paradox" 144), Hegel's contrast between sentimental weeping and dialectical logic suggests that the latter depends, like Diderot's paradox, on physiological as well as dialogical regulation.[4]

Hegel's epithet for the discerning public, "*das kunstreife Publikum*" (3: 508), "the audience ripe for art," captures more precisely than the disembodied neutralized translation, the "educated public" (2: 1184), the tension between these modes of spectatorship – sympathetic suffering as opposed to rational discernment – and, I would argue, captures as well the constitutive contradiction between the Idea of drama, the complete action of magnitude, and the contingent, messy materiality of the theatre event and its consumption. The contradiction is constitutive because it lies at the foundation of the theory it deconstructs: Hegel's theory of drama, or, indeed, any theory of drama that seeks an essence of dramatic action behind the contingency of "mere stage know-how" but wants nonetheless to see performance as central to meaning. In this case, the contradiction is enacted in the paradox of *taste* or *Geschmack*, which, in Hegel's German as in the equivalent English, struggles to hold both appetite and discernment, ripeness and autonomy, and thus to transcend the tension between the consuming, immediate senses and their decaying objects, and the supposedly discriminating theoretical senses and their eternal, autonomous works, with which the *Aesthetics* – and aesthetics as a discipline – begins and ends.

This constitutive contradiction in Hegel's text matters not because it topples the idealist architecture of Hegel's theory but because it re-enacts in a precise, compelling, and instructive way the fundamental dramatic collision in modern theatre theory between the idea of a coherent, legible, instructive dramatic action and the contingent, messy materiality of theatre events and their unpredictable audiences. It is dramatic because, despite the familiar sound of this collision or the blasé response of post-dramatists, the problem still engages our attention; it is fundamental because the problem remains a central, if paradoxical, attribute *of* the theory as well as of the practice; finally, it is modern,

in both temporal and epistemological senses, in that it precedes the decon-
struction of the coherence of plot, character, and dramatic representation usually attributed to *post*modernism and in that it continues to set the terms, if not
the outcomes, of current debates. The dialectic that troubled Hegel between
word and flesh, between desireless eye and desiring organs, between the logic
of representation and the risks of performance, continues to structure the theatrical and theoretical practice of what might be called post-dramatic performance or the post-dramatic in performance, from Brecht's thoroughly modern
attempt to recreate theatrical and theoretical legibility in non-dramatic theatre
to more recent challenges to this project as an outdated legacy of Enlightenment modernity or as an imposition of coherence and closure on a world possessed of neither, including much of the performance art and anti-art called
variously "postmodern" (Fuchs), "post-dramatic" (Lehmann), or, less apoca-
lyptically, "contemporary" (Auslander).

WHEN AND WHAT WAS POST-DRAMATIC?

I ask this question in the past tense because the phenomenon is, as Lehmann
suggests, already partly history (47–48). Brecht's early-twentieth-century call
to *"liquidate"* aesthetics (Brecht, *Werke* 21: 202, my translation, emphasis
added) – not, as in the current English translation, merely to "abolish" it
(*Brecht on Theater* 20) – may appear to subject idealist theory to materialist
condemnation, and his notorious polemic against "dramatic" as opposed to
"epic theater" may challenge the logic of classical dramaturgy, but his attachment to the logic of the plot (*Fabel*) and to the legible event it represents, as
well as to the discerning spectator who makes sense of the event, end up
renewing rather than overturning dramaturgy and dramatic aesthetics.
Although Brecht challenges the Hegelian investment in integrated plots,
subjective characterization, and final reconciliation in favor of montage, "disillusion" effects in acting (*verfremdete Schauspielkunst*, *Werke* 22: 960), and
other techniques that separate the elements of theatre from each other and the
audience from its attachments (*Werke* 24: 78–79; *Brecht on Theater* 37),[5] he
shares with Hegel an argument for the cool observation of the (masculine)
"desireless" eye, purged of the (feminine) sentimentality of the matinee audience, and with both Hegel and his Enlightenment predecessor (and Brecht's
acknowledged mentor) Diderot an interest in the coolly detached actor. But
whereas the cool actor in Hegel's text dispenses with his own feeling so as to
transform his body into the author's character (*Vorlesungen* 3: 513; *Aesthetics*
2: 1188), Brecht's actor, like Diderot's, resists complete transformation into
character (*Werke* 22: 643; *Brecht on Theater* 137). However, while Diderot's
comédiens are actor's actors, virtuoso performers in control of their doubling
– at once "la petite Clairon" and "la grande Agrippine" (Diderot, *Paradoxe* 41;
"Paradox" 105), Brecht's actors, including the exemplary Helene Weigel, hold

off from "total [or, literally, 'unremaindered'] transformation [*restlose Verwandlung*]" the better to represent the whole of the action (*Fabel*) (*Werke* 23: 83; *Brecht on Theater* 193). And while Brecht the director appears to embrace the appetite and physicality of theatre (especially in his early writings on theatre spectatorship as a kind of sport) of the kind that would make Hegel uneasy, the theorist's formulation of pleasure in the theatre migrates steadily away from fun (*Spaß*) to a thoroughly classical version of aesthetic pleasure (*Vergnügen*), the exercise of which requires an art of the audience (*Zuschauerkunst*) just as discriminating as Hegel's *Kunstreife*.

Brecht's hesitation on the threshold between a classical chamber for disinterested "theoretical" senses and "desireless eyes" and a plebeian public space for embodied performance and unpredictably desiring organs helps to focus attention on the multiple bodies of performers and spectators on contemporary stages as well as on their disembodiment through mediatization. The sites, cites, and repertoires of contemporary performance share only a negative commonality in a certain distance from the developed plot, rounded character, and illusionist (not necessarily naturalist) staging that still dominate most Western theatre, with formal features that range from collages of elements from multiple narratives and media that deconstruct the logic of plot, the affect of character, and the authority of stage presence, to renewed attachment to the stories and persons hitherto marginalized from center stage, to institutional practices that challenge middlebrow sentiment or Enlightenment projects from both the lofty precincts of high-art and high-subsidy experiment and the lowly realms of guerrilla street action. This range of practices is, in a broad sense, both post-dramatic and postmodern, as a series of uneven responses to the much vaunted collapse of critical distance and master narratives, although only a subset might, as Philip Auslander suggests, be called postmodern*ist,* performance shaped by mediatization, by commoditization, and perhaps also by cybernetic disembodiment (5–34) – represented, for instance, by Robert Wilson's *Monsters of Grace* (1999) – rather than the still modern, still dramatic forms that dominate broadcast media, more than twenty years after Williams's announcement of the dramatized society. The programming of Wilson's cybernetic post-drama may erase the human(ist) interest, passion, and plot of the Hegelian modern and even, in *Monsters,* of bodies in the flesh from the field of vision (in this case, it is no longer a stage), but the images so generated still pay homage to Hegel's theoretical sight emanating from a desireless eye, even as they sever the connection between the eyes and bodies of performer and spectator, agent and witness.

MAKING SENSE OF SENSATION

While acknowledging the presence (or only mediation?) of cybernetic postmodern post-drama, I want to open up discussion on the bodies, the feelings, *and* the ideas that animate enactment and response in performances that may critique both "modern" and "drama" without prematurely dismissing either. I claim no primal, pre-textual truth for such bodies, for to do so would merely invert the modern, Enlightenment rejection of illegitimate senses in favor of a *theory* of untheoretical, unmediated flesh, not the thing itself. Nor does my critique of the *desireless* eye attempt to escape the regime of the visible per se. As Peggy Phelan rightly points out, performance "disappears into memory" even as it "plunges into visibility" (148), but this dis-appearance is *marked;* spectators are invited to make sense of it by conjuring a (not yet visible) meaning for the spectacle or by following the visible into an invisible but visually marked realm in their own minds' eye. Or, as Maurice Merleau-Ponty reminds us, the phenomenology of perception operates against the Idealist separation of Idea and expression, essence and representation, vision and experience. There is no separating experienced phenomenon and -ology or discourse theorizing the experience: "if we try to seize 'sensation' within the perspective of the bodily phenomena which pave the way to it, we find [...] a formation already [...] endowed with a meaning" (9). In other words, rather than merely opposing reflex to reflection, material to ideal, sensation to sense, we should find a way to encompass the reflection in the reflex, while negotiating the difficulty of doing so.

Recognizing that the reflection in the reflex may not lend itself to display and that display might betray rather than reveal it, I would like to probe not only the political limits of visibility but also its political potential. "Representational visibility" as a mode of potential empowerment certainly risks the "traps" of "surveillance, fetishism, voyeurism, and sometimes, death" (Phelan 10–11), but this is surely a risk worth running, if the reflex is to have any *communicable* meaning. The scripts of emancipation through visibility, scripts which have laid the foundation of Enlightenment modernity, may risk fetishizing or commodifying the subjects they seek to write in to the scene of freedom, but they do not *inevitably* succumb to this logic. As even T.W. Adorno concedes, as one whose lament of the commodification of visibility and the project of emancipation in the wake of the Holocaust half a century ago has its *locus classicus* in *The Dialectic of Enlightenment* (1947) and who famously accused Brecht and other political writers of "preaching to the converted" and thus of turning critique into advertising (*Ästhetische Theorie* 359–67, my translation; *Aesthetic Theory* 242–47), Brecht's notion of the "thinking comportment" (242) (*denkendes Verhalten* [360]) that animates critique makes of commitment the *embodiment* of the "critical reflective tendency" (365; 246), which cannot be reduced to dictation of a transparent political solution. Combating both Adorno's underemphasis of the communicative value of art and Brecht's possible overemphasis of the gest that transparently communicates meaning to the eye of the critical spectator, we could suggest that the performative as well as political dimension of "comportment" in the dialectic between commodification and critique allows us to *re-organ-ize* and *re-embody* as well as to re-view the bounds and boundaries of the dialectic of Enlightenment and the drama of modernity.

At stake in my in-corporation of the disinterested eye in an interested and organ-ized phenomenology of performance is thus not merely the redemption of the hitherto illegitimate senses of taste, smell, and touch in and of the leaky body and its organs, although an often unspoken theory of fleshy redemption animates the pain in the performing bodies of artists from Carolee Schnee-mann to Karen Finley and Annie Sprinkle, Chris Burden to Bob Flanagan and Ron Athey, and the witnessing bodies of their audiences. Nor is it the repudia-tion of the power of images or of the eye as the organ of meaning, which a strictly defined *iconoclastic* – image-destroying, and therefore theoretically impossible – theatre might proclaim.[6] It is, rather, to highlight the opportunity that iconoclastic performances provide for theorizing multiple corporeal scripts animating audiences as well as performers and, especially, for thinking through the limits of these scripts in conveying – embodying and deciphering – pain. As Elaine Scarry reminds us, pain "resists objectification in language" (5): "whatever pain achieves, it achieves in part through its unsharability, and it ensures this unsharability through its resistance to language" (4) and, I would add, to communication through performance as well. For, while perfor-mance theory has developed a repertoire of terms and discourses to describe and inscribe theatrical and social scripts for behavior that we can therefore recognize as scripted, including, as Elin Diamond has noted, the retrospec-tively scripted shudders of an actor like Weigel ("Shudder" 162–63), it is often at a loss to theorize the audience's shudder, taste, or smell, or, indeed, the spectator's reflexes, from the most unthought (but not quite unconscious) mimicry of an actor's gesture to perhaps the more sensational, such as flinch-ing at the pierced, suspended, or otherwise wounded bodies of Fakir Mustafa, Angelika Festa, or Ron Athey.

By highlighting flesh and sensation in the performance space, I am forget-ting neither the sociocultural determination of sense and sensation nor "the cultural conditions that make theatre and an audience member's experience of it possible," as Susan Bennett stresses in *Theatre Audiences* (vii) but, rather, noting the need as well as the difficulty of theorizing sympathetic (or, indeed, antipathetic) sensations *as* legible instances of production or reception and thus as intelligible parts of social, cultural, historical representations of perfor-mance. As David Graver writes of Phelan's reading of Festa's bound and sus-pended body in her work *Untitled Dance* (1987), there can be "a troubling gap" between the critic's "acute observations on the importance of the human body in ordeal art and her attempt to give significance to this bodily presence" ("Violent Theatricality" 48). In the attempt to give voice to the "grammar of the body" and its metonymic relationship to other bodies in the space and on the ground, including the observers', the critic is often tempted to resort, as

Phelan does against her own grain (152–58), to the "grammar of words," the flight of metaphor, and the lofty perch of the allegorical reading, particularly the reading that claims for the performance the power of political resistance. I claim no special immunity to this temptation, but, struck by the promiscuous political allegorizing at the conference that provided the impetus for the current issue of *Modern Drama,* in which all manner of performances were found to dramatize the inequities of late modern globalization or its surrogates and the pain of its victims, I suggest a tactical return to sensation as a kind of ground zero. The sensation that receives the flinch in the instant before the take and double-take that might claim the reflex for political action and reflection is ground zero not in the sense that it is degree zero or pre-political but in that it marks the act of political appropriation in the moment of its apparent absence.

To begin to map the tracks between reflex and reflection that cross the gap between sense and sensation and thus inhabit but do not close the constitutive aporia of modern drama outlined in the introduction to this article, I will be moving between two very different ways of making sense of sensation in performance. The first is the public display of sensation whose cause and motivation remain private, exemplified here by the ordeal performances of Ron Athey, gay, HIV positive, (ex-?) Pentecostal Christian, especially his recent solo *The Solar Anus* (Athey), which may be regarded as post-dramatic in that it abandons the dramatic conflict between characters in favor of an individual's performance of his own intense and immediate sensation, which exceeds or eludes representation or interpretation by an autobiographical narrative. The second is the public mediation of past and present suffering that attempts to avoid the fetishization of private pain while interpreting the social and individual causes and consequences of that pain in two projects to render legible the South African Truth and Reconciliation Commission's attempt to document collective and individual violence and suffering during the apartheid years and thus to transform past pain into present meaning through its re-presentation. *The Story I Am About to Tell,* a collaboration among the Centre for the Study of Violence and Reconciliation (Johannesburg), the Khulumani Survivors Support Network, and the Market Theatre Laboratory in 1998, in which actual survivors tell actors and the audience of their suffering within the frame of a fictional story, and *Ubu and the Truth Commission* (Taylor), a play about perpetrators, victims, and the TRC process for actors, puppets, and animation, staged by William Kentridge and the Handspring Puppet Company (Weimar, Germany, then Johannesburg, 1997; North American premiere in the Public Theater, New York, 1999) are both dramatic and modern in that they take their power from a belief in the possibility of healing survivors and educating audiences through representing and interpreting pain that defies but also compels representation, but they take diametrically opposed positions on the ethics of representing the suffering of others: *Ubu* uses puppets to represent victims and survivors to acknowledge the contingency of representing the unrepresentable and thus to highlight the risk of inauthenticity (Kentridge xi), while *The Story* attempts to avoid the charges of inauthenticity or aestheticization by bringing survivors themselves onto the stage to express and to represent their experiences in dialogue with actors and audiences.

My comments on these performances and the very different kinds of enactment that they exemplify are intended to indicate points on a map rather than the fully realized simulacra that exhaustive coverage might claim to provide. But these points on the map are not willfully connected. Despite their manifest differences, the ordeal artist representing his own sensation and the dramatist representing the perpetrators, victims, and survivors of apartheid state violence share a commitment to a project we can now recognize as Hegelian. Both attempt to use the vivid presentness of the "live performance for viewers," which Hegel, *contra* Aristotle, introduced as the foundation of drama, to represent the subject who experiences pain and the passion to overcome it; both struggle with the tension, which Hegel raised but could not resolve, between the theoretical eye theoretically coolly remote from this suffering and the organs and reflexes experiencing the representation on stage and in the house, which cannot attain the state of desirelessness that Hegel proposes as the ideal condition of the knowing spectator. While Athey and the drama of the TRC are certainly not the only avenues for exploring the theoretical and theatrical aporia between sense and sensation, their very difference highlights the point of common query and so points the way both to further theoretical investigation and to questions that might be posed and answered in in-depth analyses of these and many other examples.

REFLEX AND REFLECTION IN RON ATHEY'S ORDEALS

Ron Athey's solo performance supplement to his video, *The Solar Anus,* at the Hot House bar/"center for international performance and exhibition" in Chicago in February 1999 is an illuminating point of departure for investigating the oscillation of reflex and reflection, sensation and sense, because it is an untitled performance that presents acts – piercing and penetration – in a manner that is as low-key in this format as such acts are sensational(ized) in Athey's better-known large-scale spectacles. *Martyrs and Saints* (1993) or *Four Scenes in a Harsh Life* (1994), for instance, have an array of performers attending, aiding, and duplicating Athey's enactments of ordeals made familiar by biblical representation, including the lurid Technicolor of the illustrated Book, and radically defamiliarized not only by the evident pain and threat of infection presented (rather than *re*presented) by the blood streaming off the bodies but also by the throbbing techno-rock, miked harangues (through sewn-up lips) and trashy drag acts and paraphernalia that precede the ordeals, such as Athey's butch nurse ministering to the ill bodies in the act before he strips to receive the crown of needles and ritual whipping that is the heart of *Martyrs and Saints* (see McGrath, esp. 24–31). Bringing together elements and individuals whose acts may be "blatantly badly done and clichéd" (McGrath 27), professional sex workers with practitioners *(non*-actors?) of sado-masochism and Athey himself re-presenting his youth experiences in ecstatic Pentecostalist ritual (in his account, possession, speaking in tongues, faith-healing), this *mise en scène* juxtaposes to vivid effect, if not to coherent argument, images of evangelical charlatans, the truly transported, sado-masochistic (non-)actors and AIDS activists (Graver, "Actor's Bodies" 232), which fill the spectators' eyes and ears with sensations rather than representations or reflections.

Athey's solo performance *The Solar Anus,* by contrast, probes the gap in a manner that seems subdued, even surgical, between the spectator's reflex flinching and the critical reflection that might give it meaning (Athey). The show, if it is a show, follows a rather static video of the same title, which documents the application of a tattoo radiating from Athey's anus like the sun in Georges Bataille's text and begins with his explicit but low-key reflection on the source of his acts in the Pentecostal faith healing ordeals – whether felt or faked – that marked his childhood and on his current engagement with a body affected by the incurable but as yet invisible disease and with the body of political activism around it. It ends with a gesture that enacts a self-reflexive return to the body, but not with any explicitly collective political turn. The crown of needles that he applies or inserts on his head may well quote the suffering of Christ, but neither the citation of the crown of thorns nor the autobiographical narrative deciphers the staring, depersonalized look of the performer's eyes, caused – but not explained – by the needles that prevent him from blinking. This look has the effect not only of arresting the spectators' attention but also of arresting their thinking. The act of staring appears not to be an act of seeing; rather, the needles prevent the performer's visible acknowledgment of the spectators' gaze and, in this way, interrupt the meaning that flows from the convention by which theatrical visibility is supposed to translate into theoretical coherence.[7] While the religious spectator who leaves abruptly at the outset may find the mere idea of the spectacle blasphemous and its meaning therefore clear, if abhorrent, those who remain are less likely to have a clear discursive framework that might support an equally clear counter-interpretation. The performer's final act, turning his back to the audience to insert dildo-shaped high heels into his own anus, mimics the gest of demonstration rather than pleasure. It remains self-reflexive rather than transitive and seems, to judge by the response of gay companions, to deflect the audience's gaze as surely as the staring eyes. Despite his autobiographical explanation, Athey's meaning "remains locked in the body of the performer" (Graver, "Actor's Bodies" 232) who is and is not himself. The provocation of sensation in performer and spectator may occur in the same space and be felt by both, but the sensations in question remain separate and the link between them as inchoate as it is powerful.

Whereas the power of sensation in Athey's performance and in the spectator's struggle to comprehend depends in part on its opacity to comprehension, the force of dramatically representing the impact of the TRC depends fundamentally on the execution and comprehension of a model dramatic conflict and reconciliation that is strikingly Hegelian in form. At the same time, the drama of reconciliation represented by the TRC hearings risks being swamped by too much communication and explanation. Rather than wresting meaning "locked in the body of the performer" into the public eye, theatrical representations of the Truth and Reconciliation Commission (TRC) have had to contend with a *surfeit* of contending interpretations, which have flowed from the mouths of survivors, perpetrators, commissioners, and commentators since 1996, when the TRC's Human Rights Violation Committee began the first of more than fifty public hearings into more than 20,000 reports into human rights violations between 1 March 1960 (the banning of independent political organizations such as the African National Congress [ANC], now the ruling party in government) and 10 May 1994 (the inauguration of President Nelson Mandela and the official end of apartheid) and which continue to flow, albeit more slowly, even after the TRC's Amnesty Committee concluded its work on amnesty applications by perpetrators in May 2001, many of them ex-members of the Security Police currently serving long sentences for murder, illegal arms possession, and fraud, while maintaining that these acts were committed with the complicity, if not the proven approval, of apartheid leaders in pursuit of alleged enemies of the state.

The contention has focused on the unresolved tension between, on the one hand, the TRC's mandate, according to the Promotion of National Unity and Reconciliation Act of 1995, "to enable South Africans to come to terms with their past on a morally acceptable basis and to advance the cause of reconciliation" through the public acknowledgment of victims' suffering (but not, as yet, reparation for that suffering), and, on the other, the charge that amnesty, in response to the public confessions of perpetrators applying for amnesty for any individual "act, omission or offence associated with a political objective," whether that objective was the security of the apartheid state and its police apparatus or the overthrow of that state, could obscure the distinction between those who fought for apartheid and those who struggled against it and thus impede the implementation of justice through the condemnation of the former in the name of the latter.[8] Although only 849 out of 7112 amnesty applications were granted (TRC, Amnesty Hearings Index), a little over 10 percent, key players in the anti-apartheid movement, such as the family of Stephen Biko, the student activist who was killed under torture in 1977, maintained that the procedure let criminals go free. When key players like these reject the dramatic closure of reconciliation in the name of unresolved injustice, they also reject the theology of forgiveness that, in the formulation of TRC Chair Archbishop Desmond Tutu, claims that confession and forgiveness will heal both survivor and perpetrator.[9]

The problem of resolving authentic acts, if not truthful accounts, out of multiple interpretations is compounded in theatrical performance by the problematic link between representation and impersonation. As Antjie Krog, South African Broadcasting Company (SABC) radio commentator for the TRC hearings and TRC consultant for *Ubu and the Truth Commission*, points out, testimony from survivors and perpetrators was mediated representation rather than direct expression (Krog 50). In the first place, the institution, setting, and script of the TRC mandated reconciliation rather than confrontation, crying rather than expressions of rage (Krog 212). In the second place, translation, even in the first person, makes of self-expression a kind of impersonation; even if they sit in a glass booth at some distance from their subjects, interpreters play survivors, speaking in the first person, and are aware that they are acting, even as they are possessed by the testimony. As interpreter Lebohang Matibela noted, "It is quite interesting to sit in that booth. You're aware that you are becoming an actor, but [...] unconsciously you end up throwing up your hands as he throws his, you end up nodding your head when he nods [...]" (Krog 290). Lapses and recovery of memory highlighted the performative aspect of this self-expression as well as its fundamental incompleteness. This last aspect was further complicated, in the testimony of the perpetrators, by the possibility of omission, if not outright lying, and by attempts to play confession as a sinister replay of torture techniques. In one striking case, Tony Yengeni, black activist turned Member of Parliament, had ex-torturer Jeffrey Benzien demonstrate the "wet bag method" of near-suffocation to an audience scrambling to watch the white man pin down the black on the floor of the chamber, only to have Benzien retaliate by telling the assembly that, during the actual interrogation in detention, it took only "thirty minutes" of this treatment to get Yengeni to talk (Krog 93–94). Finally, the officially separate realms of testifiers and listeners, TRC participants and reporters, bled together as all were compelled to witness both suffering and unrepentant manipulation. Participants, including reporters, suffered symptoms of trauma, "breaking down, packing up, or freaking out" (Krog 221), experiences that some observers, especially black men, were initially unwilling to confront (221–25). Translators, especially, felt overwhelmed by the incompatible demands of warring impersonations, of "switch[ing] identities" between victim and perpetrator (Tutu 286).[10]

The challenge for a theatrical representation of TRC testimony is thus not simply to convey sensation or to generate emotion but to interpret their media-tion. The translators, compelled to embody the words and personas of both victim and perpetrator, become the exemplary figures of the difficult necessity of this interpretation. If, on the one hand, the unmediated expression of the survivors' sorrow overwhelms the audiences, from translators to commission-ers to reporters to the public, and, on the other, the perpetrators' confessions remain unreadable to listeners who cannot be sure that they are telling the truth, both threaten to repeat rather than re-present the pain that destroys lan-guage (Scarry 5; Krog 57). Representing painful testimony without merely repeating it painfully on stage thus raises ethical and epistemological ques-tions as well as aesthetic issues: can actors know their subjects' pain? do they have a right to represent them? how can they do justice to the truth by being both theatrically compelling and ethically persuasive?

William Kentridge, director and designer of *Ubu and the Truth Commis-sion,* argues that using puppets as a "medium through which the testimony can be heard" relieves the audience of the tension between "believ[ing] the actor for the sake of the story" and "not believ[ing] the actor for the sake of the actual witness," who is not present (Kentridge xi). Although he claims that this medium provided "an answer to the ethical question: what is our responsi-bility to the people whose stories we are using as raw fodder?" (xi), he admits that this "ethical route was primarily a justification after the event" or perhaps an ethical consequence of the artistic decision to combine two projects: pup-pets as medium for testimony from the Angolan civil war and human actors for a dance/animation of the Ubu figure (ix–x).[11] Ubu and his mate, Ma Ubu, culled from Alfred Jarry's *Ubu Roi,* perpetrate violent acts in the name of the state with apparent impunity. The cruel burlesque of Jarry's plot has the poten-tial to highlight the capricious and often arbitrary violence of state operatives, but the adolescent excesses of Jarry's text also runs the risk of trivializing the suffering of those testifying against such acts of cruelty. Kentridge acknowl-edges the fragile balance between the realm of cruel burlesque, occupied by Pa and Ma Ubu, and the space of the wooden witness-puppets, who occupy the same stage but a completely separate realm characterized at its best by qui-etly moving dignity, but he does not fully examine the risk that the dignity embodied by the puppets might turn into a kind of spectral haunting, over-shadowed by the aggressive stage presence and stage noise of the fleshy perpetrators.

The moral power of this haunting against the amoral appeal of the actors deserves more attention, however. The witness-puppets, in rough-hewn brown wood whose grooves catch the light in ways that highlight expressions of sor-row, are animated no further away than arm's length (and usually closer) by two puppeteers. They appear as witnesses proper only in the second act, after a brief appearance at the start of the play when an ordinary householder cook-ing soup is summarily offed by Ubu to cartoonish music (Taylor 1); the cartoonish suddenness of the deed leaves the audience no time to react before the rest of the act is taken over by the Ubus and their puppet accomplices: Brutus, three-headed dog of war, attached to a suitcase filled with incriminating documents, and Niles, a crocodile with a mouth big enough to swallow them.[12] Animated by a visible puppeteer (Louis Seboko), who also speaks the Xhosa text of the witness's report (from the earliest hearings about mass killings by the police in the Eastern Cape), the silent puppet provides a subdued but intense contrast to the violence of the report and the lurid caption on the animation screen: "Bath [morphing into] Bloodbath" (Taylor 11).[13] Here, as in a later, much-quoted moment when a witness-puppet appears to lay a forgiving hand on a recumbent Ubu twitching through a nightmare memory of the day's torture (Taylor 46; Kentridge xi–xii; Coetzee 44), the symbiosis of puppet and puppeteer encourages the audience to feel with the witness and to find signs of sympathy in the puppeteer's handling of his charge. Despite the strong desire of audiences to see and feel this sympathy (Coetzee 39; informal corroboration with spectators in South Africa and the United States), however, the producers remain at odds on the fact and value of this symbiosis. Puppeteers Jones and Kohler suggest, from their place behind the puppet, that "the fact that the manipulators are present ... allows us to use the emotions visible in the puppeteer's face to inform our understanding of the emotions of the puppet character" even if its features remain "immobile" (Jones and Kohler xvii), but director Kentridge apparently encouraged the puppeteers to handle the puppets in a less overtly "sensitive" manner so as to focus audience attention on the evidence (qtd. in Coetzee 45). If this effort to deflect audience emotion was successful, it was not because of stubborn sentimentality on their part but, rather, because the audience's attribution of sympathy to the puppeteers made sense of this sensation, made feeling a necessary sign of the meaning and meaningfulness of the representation of pain. It is this attribution of meaning through sense and sensation, and not just the aesthetic symbiosis of puppets and puppeteers, that becomes a point of resistance to the ever-present threat that the realm of burlesque and the bodies of the Ubus would swamp this meaning.

Played with farcical malice by Dawid Minaar as a satyr in dirty underwear and Busi Zokufa as a regal African queen – but in burlesque whiteface – Pa and Ma Ubu, the security officer and his bully-wife, are charismatic villains whose malevolent charm threatens to tip this balance. Their quarrels about Pa Ubu's "nocturnal activities" (Taylor 3) and his conspiratorial meetings with his henchmen, represented by Brutus (the three-headed dog of war attached to a suitcase full of incriminating documents) dominate the first act, in which victims and witnesses appear only once momentarily. Even after the survivors have given their testimony and the screen has displayed images of now well-known methods of torture and their alibis, such as the notorious "he slipped on soap in the shower and died," literalized on the screen by an animated bar of soap apparently attacking a penciled figure in a shower and reiterated on stage by Ubu's shower, which doubles as the translator's booth, it is the perpetrators and their human interpreters who rule the stage. When Zokufa, still in Ma Ubu whiteface, steps into the interpreter's booth to speak the English translation of the first witness's speech, the audience cannot but see the notorious shower and the bully, even as they hear the testimony against violence. More ambiguously, by appearing throughout in dirty underwear, whether he is repeating verbatim testimony of the torturer describing the "tubing method" of suffocation, pulling the victim's tongue through an inner-tube otherwise covering the face (43), or arguing that he and his kind were loyal soldiers of a discredited government that left them in the lurch ("such loyalty is no longer fashionable" 67]), Minaar invites – and received – audience acknowledgment of, if not sympathy with, his predicament; as one critic wrote, "he seems at times to colonise the terrain of both perpetrator and victim [...] He is not an entirely reviled character" (Friedman). At his final hearing, "Ubu Tells the Truth," the protagonist borrows the words and the manner, an uneasy but compelling fusion of anger and abjectness, of Eugene de Kock, a.k.a. Prime Evil, leader of the most notorious torture and death squad, who argued at his 1995 trial for murder, fraud, and illegal arms possession, and at his 1999 TRC hearing, that he committed crimes in the name of the state, with the tacit approval of former President de Klerk, who was, he claimed, too cowardly to admit it (Meredith 46–54) but who, once in prison, came to a certain truce with the surviving daughter of one of his better-known victims.[14] Faced not by visible witnesses, who have apparently vanished by the final act, but by microphones that seem to flinch at his touch (as they are manipulated by invisible hands beneath the podium: Taylor 67), Minaar's Ubu was not Prime Evil but Banal Evil, whose confession – "Remorse, I can assure you, a lot, a helluva lot" (69) – turns what had been an ambiguous persona into a cliché, a provocateur of ambivalent audience responses, which might have led to a moment of Brechtian "thinking comportment" to show the "not-but" of both character and action, into an inert puppet. Instead of a provocateur, Pa Ubu, at this crucial moment in *Ubu and the Truth Commission*, is merely a "statue" wheeled off the stage as the familiar images of the Struggle and the sound of the national anthem sweep away not only the ambiguity of the perpetrator but also the delicate, rather than massive or mass, resistance of the individual witnesses.[15]

Rather than the narrative certainties of the Struggle, *The Story I Am About to Tell* returns to the awkward individual struggles of the survivors themselves, in secluded support groups, in the glare of TRC publicity, and on the theatrical stage as their own interpreters. Aided by seasoned actors playing interlocutors, whether friendly or skeptical, in a minibus taxi, they retell their stories in a process that began as group therapy before it became a performance for strangers abroad as well as family at home. But even if the performance began as a series of autobiographical narratives told by members of the

Khulumani ("Talk!") Survivors Support Group – including Duma Khumalo, who spent three years on death row for a "necklacing" he did not commit, and Thandi Shezi, tortured and raped in prison – to Bobby Rodwell, workshop facilitator at the Market Theater Laboratory, and became a play whose title invokes – with doubtless *un*intended irony – the convention of TV docudrama, "The story I am about to tell is true; only names have been changed …," the status of the performance as re-presentation remained precarious.[16] However, the very instability of representation and the awkwardness of its interpreters, as well as the uncertain relationship between past and present pain, is what moves the action and illuminates the play's meaning – the difficult necessity of making sense of unrepresentable and unbearable sensation. While veteran actors, such as Ramalao Makhene as the taxi driver and *raisonneur,* or "reasonable man," narrator of the connecting action, played their roles smoothly, survivors like Khumalo forgot their lines, suffering from lapses of memory – or perhaps from the burden of the kind of memory that suppresses speech. The responses of spectators in Munich and in Johannesburg, from a Munich woman married to a "disappeared" black South African, who found a measure of reconciliation in the performance, to local audiences who argued themselves about the acts of perpetrators and survivors in their area, suggest that the sense, and perhaps also the truth, of these representations emerges in the sensation of the pain and healing of such lapses. As in the official hearings, it may be that the truth of the witness, over and above (but not necessarily opposed to) the facts of the testimony, emerges in the silences, the memory lapses, the tears of both speaker and listeners, and the *struggles* (plural, small *s*) of all to make sense out of sensation, rather than in their final word.

RIPENESS IS ALL

It is thus at the conjunction of the moment when pain resolves into words, sensation into sense, and when words dissolve into silence that can be healing but may be flinching, that the possibility emerges that pain may *dissolve* (disappear, be healed and contained by) words. This is not quite what the rationalist Brecht meant by "thinking comportment" or "critical bearing" (*kritische Haltung*), but this moment of embodied sense (feeling and meaning) may be the (e)utopia (good rather than non-place) where meaning moves by touch as well as sight and where the interpreter's ability to make that meaning becomes not merely discernment but the full-bodied and mindful ripeness that Hegel's modern drama allowed only theoretically, not in the flesh. This (e)utopia is elusive but not atopia (nowhere); as my brief account of the re-presentation of pain suggests, audiences do make sense of sensation and, in so doing, sustain the process of theorized and felt embodiment and enlightenment that is the drama of modernity.

NOTES

1 As this paraphrase implies, Lehmann resists a clear-cut definition of the post-dramatic, or, at least, a definition that would produce a clear cut between the dramatic and the post-dramatic or between the modern and the postmodern. Indeed, one could argue that this very hedging gesture reflects a certain skepticism about modernist prescriptions for the utterly new, including the prescription that the postmodern is the new.

2 References to Aristotle's *Poetics* are by paragraph and line number rather than page.

3 References to Hegel's *Aesthetics* cite the German original, *Vorlesungen über die Ästhetik* (3 vols.), and then the English translation, *Aesthetics* (2 vols.); I have occasionally modified Knox's translation for greater accuracy.

4 In *Syncope,* Catherine Clément reads this triumph of reason over the diaphragm symptomatically; she uses Hegel's comment that his hypochondria (literally, "contraction of the ribs") forced him to turn inward to a "more noble existence" as the basis for the claim that "Hegelian dialectic is caused by a depressive spasm" (62). Whether or not we take this literally, the notion that the logical discernment of taste depends on a certain physiological contraction even as it disavows physiology in the name of logic is suggestive.

5 Although John Willett's mistranslation of Brecht's *Verfremdung* as "alienation" has stuck, the first English translation of Brecht's first usage of the term in "Verfremdungseffekte in der chinesischen Schauspielkunst" ("An Essay on the Effect of *Disillusion* in the Chinese Theatre" [1936, emphasis added], *Werke* 22: 960) better captures the original sense: undoing theatrical illusion so as to encourage the audience to understand and thus critique the world off- as well as onstage (22: 401). I have occasionally modified Willett's translation with my own.

6 Several articles on the Iconoclastic Theatre Season at Chapter Arts, Cardiff, Wales, published in *Frakcija*'s special issue explore the paradox of iconoclastic theater, the "impossible task of rendering the invisible visible" (Kruger, "Goat Island" 70), of representation "without the disclosure characteristic of traditional theatre"(Buljan 13); see also Blažević, Roden.

7 Comments about the arresting of meaning are drawn from conversations with graduate students and colleagues who watched the performance with me or, in one case, left abruptly at the beginning.

8 Citations are from the TRC Report, chapter 4, "The Mandate," paras. 1–10, which reiterate the Act's definition of the mandates of the TRC and its three committees, without, however, noting, as one prominent critic has pointed out, that the Reparations and Rehabilitation Committee has not proceeded beyond "policy documents" and "workshops" to implement even the modest goal of R1000 (a little more than $100 in 2002) for access to medical care (Krog 218–21). My primary focus in this article is on the modest field of the sense and sensation of theatrical representations

of the TRC process rather than on the wider investigation of its political and social impact. Those interested in the TRC should consult the Web site; the TRC's *Report*; the account of its chairman, Desmond Tutu; and critiques of the TRC's reliance on the theology of forgiveness, whether from the perspective of the ANC (Asmal, Asmal, and Roberts) or from that of philosophical skepticism (Holiday), as well as accounts by observers both critical and engaged (Krog; Meredith).

9 The abstract (and secular) English term "reconciliation" is also abstract in Afrikaans (*versoening* is close to the Hegelian German *Versöhnung*), but translates into African languages, like the Xhosa term *uxolelwano*, in terms closer to "coming to peace," which suggests resolution of conflict in the name of common humanity (*ubuntu*).

10 Kentridge suggests (xiv) that the TRC initially encouraged translators to mimic the emotions of the witnesses, but the accounts of both Tutu and Krog suggest that this mimicry was both inadvertent and painful, rather than deliberate impersonation.

11 *Ubu and the Truth Commission* emerged out of an initially serendipitous combination of a project using puppets as interpreters of the survivors of human rights violations (developed by Kentridge and the Handspring Puppet Company, who had collaborated on *Woyzeck on the Highveld* [1993] and *Faustus in Africa* [1995]) and a plan to produce a dance/animation version of Jarry's *Ubu Roi* (proposed by Kentridge and choreographer Robyn Orlin). Jane Taylor, who had curated *Fault Lines* (1996), an exhibition that linked the 1976 uprising in Soweto and beyond with the TRC's investigations twenty years later, was commissioned to produce a text that juxtaposed a local adaptation of *Ubu Roi* with TRC testimony. For comment on this collaboration, see Jones and Kohler; Kentridge; and Taylor; for a brief account of the previous work of Kentridge and Handspring Puppets, see Kruger, *Drama of South Africa* (195–97).

12 Kentridge argues (viii) that a crocodile rather than a dog was chosen as a shredder simply because the former has a bigger, more visible mouth, but South African audiences would find it hard to avoid the association of this beast with "die groot Krokodil," the epithet applied to P.W. Botha (the president responsible for the militarization of South Africa during the period of unrestrained state violence and guerrilla resistance he called the "total onslaught") so named because he was known to twist his mouth and nose into a shape resembling those of a crocodile, especially when angered.

13 In the play as in the TRC hearings, witnesses give evidence in South Africa's major indigenous languages, Xhosa, Sotho, Tswana, and Zulu, not merely in Zulu (*contra* Coetzee 43), while Ubu speaks Afrikaans when giving evidence, English otherwise. The play follows the TRC in beginning with testimony in Xhosa, the language of the Eastern Cape, for three centuries the site of the most sustained resistance to Dutch and British colonialism, and later apartheid, and therefore the site of the opening hearings. Despite being the language with the most speakers in South Africa, Zulu appears only once in the play, in keeping with the limited cooperation of the Zulu-dominant party, Inkatha, with the TRC.

14 From 1986 to 1993, de Kock ran the death squad based at Vlakplaas. The squad tortured and killed not only known ANC guerrillas but also their own black subordinates who knew of the white officers' fraudulent deals and assaults on bystanders in the conflict. De Kock was sentenced initially to 212 years and later received partial amnesty for conspiring to bomb the South African Communist Party headquarters in London (see Amnesty Decisions 1999b) and for the Parker Pen Bomb Incident (see Amnesty Hearings 2001) but not for the torture, executions, and gun running out of Vlakplaas. Once in prison, de Kock agreed to meet with Jann Turner, daughter of the academic activist Professor Richard Turner, killed before her eyes. Jann Turner wrote after several visits with him not only of the tension between his acts of violence and his charm but also of his unanswered challenge to his superiors, who have not been indicted.

15 The play does not end with this collective crescendo but with a return to *Ubu Roi,* as Pa and Ma sail away to a "bright future" (Taylor 73), but this staging of their escape scot-free ducks the questions about future individual and collective relations between perpetrators and victims in South Africa that are thrown up every time Ubu, the witnesses, and the animated evidence are juxtaposed on stage. It is this sense of an ending deflected or deferred that leaves some critics with the feeling that this "ambitious multimedia production" may have missed its mark, not so much because the South African (as opposed to overseas) audience has been anesthetized to horror or desires a cathartic "fairy-tale ending" that the play denies them (Friedman) but, rather, because this escape, in combination with the quotation of the Struggle, *is* a fairy-tale ending that dodges the complexities raised by the action.

16 "Necklacing," public assassination by throwing a burning tire over the victim's head, was performed as summary punishment during the "emergency years" of 1984–1990, usually by young "comrades" identified loosely with the then-banned ANC or the smaller Azanian Peoples Organization (AZAPO), on people, including children, accused of being informers or sell-outs. Khulumani, meaning "talk" in the plural imperative, highlights the community dimension of this and other survivor support groups. For comment on reactions to the performance, see Dodd; for video records see Segal and Hahn; for documentation of Khulumani's work in the context of its primary sponsor, the Centre for the Study of Violence and Reconciliation, see the Centre's web site.

Luminous Writing, Embodiment, and Modern Drama: Mme Blavatsky and Bertolt Brecht

SUE-ELLEN CASE

In the fall of 1875, Helena Blavatsky, founder of the Theosophical Society, accessed the Astral Light for her writing. Mme Blavatsky was beginning the first volume of her erudite and complex work on the occult sciences entitled *Isis Unveiled*. Writing in Ithaca, New York, at the home of Hiram Corson, a professor of English at Cornell University, Mme Blavatsky produced twenty-five pages a day. Professor Corson reported that she was

quoting long verbatim paragraphs from dozens of books of which I am perfectly certain there were no copies at that time in America, translating easily from several languages [...]. She herself told me that she wrote them down as they appeared in her eyes on another plane of objective existence, that she clearly saw the page of the book, and the quotation she needed [...]. (qtd. in Cranston 154)

The Astral Light provided a luminous text base for Mme Blavatsky roughly a century before the digital script of the Internet began to appear to many others. Although Mme Blavatsky put the astral script to the use of print, she perceived it as a source of knowledge, accurate and sustained by physical and psychic properties "beyond" those practiced within print culture. Moreover, this fund of knowledge, like the World Wide Web of electronic technology, could be accessed from anywhere, including Ithaca, to be written into rigorous and scholarly accounts, without the warranty that print culture, or actual books, were constituted as bestowing. Even a professor of English at Cornell could be convinced of an astral accuracy that did not reside in a local print library. It could be said that Mme Blavatsky revealed a worldwide web of information outside of modern modes of production and access.[1]

Mme Blavatsky's perception of the astral source did not appear to her as part of a "new" or "modern" regime, as the digital script announces itself to be; instead, her access to the luminous source renewed encounters with the ancient and eternal. The "modern," in Mme Blavatsky's day, and perhaps lingering on in ours, had to do with Western incursions into the Asian subcontinent through partnerships among Christian missionaries and colonial agents. Mme Blavatsky and her Theosophical Society, against the tide of this "modern," pursued an access to the indigenous ancient scripts, and, for that pursuit, were honored by many, including the fourteenth Dalai Lama, for reviving access to texts that Christianity sought to overwrite (Cranston 85). Mme Blavatsky revealed how ancient texts and practices, deemed superstitious and detrimental to the processes of modernization, could be perceived as accurate and useful. The ancient figures of mantras and hieroglyphs were set against the emerging, arcane symbols of physics. Of course, Mme Blavatsky was also a part of her times in staking these claims in the ancient. Other Russian artists and cultural thinkers were embracing exotic images of ancient worlds and earlier so-called primitive societies, such as Goncharova. In fact, there was even a movement called "the Wanderers," whose members, like Mme Blavatsky, sought ancient truths through nomadic practices. Yet, in so doing, this Russian movement was pulling away from Western European modernist tendencies, resisting the rise of science and the "modern." As Alexandre Benois put it,

> For us the world – despite triumphant Americanism, railroads, telegraphs, telephones, all this modern brutality and vulgarity, all this despicable transformation of the earth – for us the world still contains great charm and promise. (qtd. in Bowlt 60)

The image and influence of Mme Blavatsky, from the mid-nineteenth century through the twentieth, helps to organize the tension between a sense of the modern and an impulse toward the ancient that has accompanied the development of "new" technologies and imperialist dreams. This tension around the technological claim of the "new" and the indigenous association with the "ancient" has generated conflicting social, epistemological, and performative claims that continue to proceed into the twenty-first century. By setting the familiar figures of Mme Blavatsky and Bertolt Brecht against one another, we can character-ize this tension, animating the competing practices of scripting, embodiment, and performance as they partner competing constructions of gender, nationhood, and the global.

FLESHING OUT

In addition to scripting the astral light Mme. Blavatsky practiced a particular form of embodiment, or corporeal performance, that accompanied her access to the astral plane. Several months before she began writing *Isis Unveiled,* she underwent a physiological change. In her memoirs, she describes the events that took place in the spring of 1875:

And just about this time I [began] to feel a very strange duality. [...] I never lose the consciousness of my personality; what I feel is as if I were keeping silent and the other one – the lodger who is in me – were speaking with my tongue. [...] I know that I have never been in the places which are described by my "other me," but this other one – the second me – does not lie when he tells me about places and things unknown to me, because he has actually seen them and known them well. [...] In the night, when I am alone in my bed, the whole life of my No. 2 passes before my eyes, and I do not see myself at all, but quite a different person – different in race and different in feelings. (qtd. in Cranston 149)

This man of "another race" is referred to as a "Hindu man" who often appears outside of her: "I see [him] every day, just as I might see any other living person [...]. Formerly I kept silent about these appearances, thinking that they were hallucinations. But now they have become visible to other people as well." Yet at other times, Mme Blavatsky notes, "he overshadows the whole of me, simply entering me like a kind of volatile essence penetrating my pores and dissolving in me. Then [...] I begin to understand and remember sciences and languages – everything he instructs me in, even when he is not with me any more" (qtd. in Cranston 150). Mme Blavatsky's transgender, transracial performance of the "Hindu man" did not overcome her continued performance of her self. She could embody both personae at once, transferring new data across the gender and race divide. This "man" could appear entirely separate from her, accompanying her journeys, or could be embodied within her, as a "lodger" who had traveled from afar.

The "Hindu man" was considered to be a link to the circle of "masters," as Mme Blavatsky called them, who existed in different parts of the world but whose wisdom and being proceeded from Tibet. As an appellation, "Hindu" seemed to connote more a spiritual locus somewhere in the region of the Himalayas than a religious tradition.[2] In her younger days, Mme Blavatsky's transgender role-playing accompanied a pursuit of occult knowledge through travel to distant and exoticized lands. In later years, she embodied the distant and the masculine in her own, ample body.[3] Her sense of Tibet as the remote spiritual center of the world was in keeping with her times, for Tibet was emerging as the mythical center of occultism and exoticism in the late nineteenth century. She would even claim that she had served a secret seven-year apprenticeship into mystical matters high in the Himalayas, though there seems to be little evidence of such a journey. Nevertheless, the desire to make that journey would inspire many cartographers, adventurers, adepts, and even Hollywood movies, from the late nineteenth century to the present, with signature works such as James Hilton's *Lost Horizon* in 1933 and the current spate of books written by the Dalai Lama in the 1990s. Orville Schell's recent publication *Virtual Tibet* traces these various historical and pop records of Tibet, illustrating its signifying power of the ancient amidst the "new." Mme Blavatsky's dual perfor-

mance, then, was not only of the "other" gender and race, but also an embodiment of an "elsewhere." While she aimed at reviving the ancient, she did so by
transgressing the boundaries of geography and gender. Mme Blavatsky's
worldwide web of luminous script and masters lent her an agency and relief
from discipleship that other women who were attracted to the subcontinent
would not find.[4] She remained an independent woman and the leader of a
movement, without assuming any subordinate relationship to a guru.

Mme Blavatsky's penchant for cross-gender roles was not limited to these
"possessions"; it began much earlier, with her first world travels. At age sev-
enteen, she escaped from her husband by riding alone on horseback through
the mountains of Russia, rather than submit to his "conjugal rights," as they
were termed. She made it to Odessa, where she sneaked aboard a ship, sailed
to Constantinople, and began traveling as a companion to Countess Kisselev
(Cranston 37–38). Mme Blavatsky reported, when preparing her memoirs,
"Suppose I was to tell you that [in India] *I was in man's clothes* [...] I was in
Egypt with the old countess K[isselev] who liked to see me dressed as a *man
student*" (qtd. in Cranston 42–43). These images of the young, cross-dressed
Mme Blavatsky, traveling through countries redolent with mystic wisdom,
evoke subversive practices of gender in the midst of occult transcendence. In
fact, if her male student drag was designed to please Countess Kisselev, evo-
cations of same-sex desire might also emanate from the image. Given her penchant for cross-gender drag and her flight from conjugal rights, Mme
Blavatsky's Hindu male "lodger" takes on a different affect than if she were
prone, so to speak, to seek male attention. It is as if "crossing the bar" of gender also morphed geography and wisdom into a fleshly form.

This combination of strategies that would ally a resistance to dominant
practices of gender and sexual orientation with an attachment to the ancient is
familiar to a wide range of feminist critiques. For example, in "The Forgotten
Mystery of Female Ancestry," Luce Irigaray proposes a return to Greek myths
of embodiment, in order to imagine an alternate vision of the structuring of
women's libidinal drives. Arguing that the contemporary cultural structuring
of women's libidinal drives results from the abstracting processes of psychoanalytic narratives, Irigaray calls for a return to Greek narratives of embodiment, which "retained a special relationship to space, time and the
manifestation of the forms of incarnation" (101). These ancient myths, which
tied the symbolic order to material conditions through embodiment, scripted
different possibilities for women's libido. Irigaray thus abandons the modernist psycho-scientistic approach of understanding desire as an affect lodged in
some abstracted interiority in order to take up myths of embodiment as re-
imagining women's libidinal processes. She claims ancient texts against modern practices for a reformation of the relationship between women and desire.

Mme Blavatsky's interest in the ancient, however, is not a recuperation of
classical Western traditions but a way of inhabiting, through being inhab-

ited, the uncharted, mystical region of Tibet. The "Hindu man" appeared in her at about the same time that Europeans were discovering the lure of the Himalayas. High mountains were beginning to inspire the European cultural imaginary through the growth of mountaineering, as a sport of conquest, combined with a new sense of their heights as divine (Schell 149–61). Tibet brought together several different desires of the time: it offered the promise of physical challenge; a sense of divine heights, both in its elevations and in its theocratic culture; and a realm of secrets to be discovered, long closed to the West. Mme Blavatsky cannily reinterpreted the notions of reincarnation she found in both Hindu and Buddhist beliefs in the region to house the region in her. In fact, the Tibetan notion of the *tulku,* one who houses the reincarnation of a master, is recreated through her practice as the housing of the living "lodger" rather than as the reincarnation of one who lived earlier.[5] So Mme Blavatsky's technique of embodiment is a reinvention of traditional notions from the region, used to allow her to access its secrets. While she would later travel to India to set up Theosophical sites that would play an important role in its future, her practice of embodiment actually warranted her right to do so.

Her displacement through corporeal practice could be understood as a particular version of Roger Caillois's definition of mimesis as "being tempted by space" (qtd. in Taussig 34). In *Mimesis and Alterity,* Michael Taussig reads beyond Caillois to postulate that "mimesis is not only a matter of one being another being, but with this tense yet fluid theatrical relation of form and space with which Caillois would tempt us. I am especially struck by the notion of 'presence' as an invented space [...]" (34). As Mme Blavatsky performed the "presence" of the distant master, she reinvented the distant space of Tibet and India as situated within her own body. Thus mimesis and alterity form a dual subject position for the other and the self through an imagined space of special knowledge.

There is some logic in regarding Mme Blavatsky's practice through Taussig's work, for Taussig developed his sense of mimesis by observing practices of possession and sympathetic magic. Taussig, in studying people in contact with colonial and postcolonial projects, regards the invention of the spiritual, often associated with the ancient, as an embodied relationship to knowledge that operates as a foil to colonialist, modernist, scientistic discourses. Taussig argues that modernity, in its division of labor, began to produce knowledge and skills in isolated units, while the development of communication technologies isolated visual and aural experiences from tactile ones. In other words, modernity shredded knowledge into bits (or, we might say, bytes) that could be communicated exclusively through images and sound, without the practice of embodiment. Quoting Hegel, Taussig insists on an epistemology that sinks "into the material in hand, and following the course that such material takes," produces knowledge (36).

So, for both Mme Blavatsky and Taussig, performances of possession produce a tactile, experiential, epistemological effect – an embodied knowledge in contrast to the practices of modern technologies that offer bytes of data. While Mme Blavatsky may have accessed a luminous script through a worldwide web of masters, she did not participate in the shredding and redistribution of abstracted data. Instead, she deployed the notion of ancient wisdom against Darwin's project of de-animating the past through empiricism. *Isis Unveiled*, brought to her through the luminous script, attempts to bring together what the binary of the modern sciences would divide: science and religion. In fact, she kept a stuffed baboon in her parlor, as an icon of Darwin's limited, and fallen, project that would insist upon only one form of knowing.[6] Taussig describes performances of possession as sensuous moments of knowing, through "yielding [...] in contrast to Enlightenment science's aggressive compulsion to dominate nature" (46). Now, while Mme Blavatsky did set possession against science, her performances were not of the "yielding" sort. As Washington suggests, Mme Blavatsky was a dominant, not a submissive, medium. She "constituted the medium as a power in her own right, not a mere channel of communication" (42).

Mme Blavatsky offers a compelling model of a popular nineteenth-century performance for women: one that directly challenged Darwinists, and the other emerging discourse of science and technology, with an embodied knowing, which she somewhat controlled, through a reanimation of the ancient and a compaction of space and alterity. Her cross-racial, cross-gender performances sought to animate the ancient through practices of embodiment. On the other side of the binary, the baboon of modern drama rose up against Mme Blavatsky's project of embodiment. The notion of a "modern drama" organized the other side of the binary, arguing for the deployment of a "modern" form of theatre as a correction of the ancient and the traditional. Perhaps a brief review of the strategies of one of the most influential practitioners and theorists of the power of a "modern drama," Bertolt Brecht, could help to situate the project of modern performance practices. For Brecht, a new scientific theatre promised to correct the errors of nineteenth-century practices. The "modern" presaged societal change. The classics required a new approach, and the practices of performances needed to be brought into line with the "new" scientism.

BRECHT'S FORK

What relationship exists between such calls to ancient performances and the notion of specifically modern dramatic practices? First, we might turn to Bertolt Brecht's "modern" acting technique, where we find, again, a dual performance practice, but one that was solidly on the side of scientism. Like Mme Blavatsky, Brecht invented the notion of a dual performance. Indeed, situating

Brecht's conception of theatre proximate to Mme Blavatsky's offers a seminal model of how a dramaturgy dedicated to the invention of a "modern drama" might appear when compared to one dedicated to the revival of the ancient and unchanging.

For Brecht, "new" was a concept shared across social, economic, and aesthetic spheres, signifying a kind of interactive radical change. In various places, Brecht argues for his epic reforms by referring to the "*new human type*" ("Radio Speech" 18) and a new "audience of the scientific age" ("Dialogue" 26). "New" subjects for the theatre, such as petroleum, along with new technologies of the stage, would drive dramaturgical change, while new information technologies would change the relation between representation and reception. Brecht celebrated film for its "splendid inductive method" ("Film" 48).

As part of his sense of the modern, Brecht turned to the practice of acting, seeking to achieve a more "scientific" approach to character. If Mme Blavatsky worked against new sciences, Brecht worked with them, against any process that suggested the values of spiritualism. In his notes on acting, he wrote literally against the "séance" ("Dialogue" 26) and the "un-technical, anti-technical 'glowing' art, with its religious links" ("Film" 48). These were effects produced by what he referred to as "trance" acting, by which he meant Stanislavky's method of identification ("Dialogue" 26). Brecht's sense of the trance was actually opposed to Taussig's notion, for Brecht regarded the trance as an anti-epistemological state of social stasis. The audience is not encouraged to make decisions but is "plunged" into the trance of a static "self-identification" (28). In one place, he dismissed trance-type acting precisely because "nobody learn[s] any lessons" (26). To counter this effect, Brecht created a notion of the actor's dual presentation of character and actor to work in the service of a critical, rational, and empirical epistemology dedicated to social change. The Brechtian actor would perform a dual role, performing a character while also maintaining a critical attitude toward that character. Working in combination with other techniques created through the epic plays, the mechanics of the *Lehrstück,* and the construction of the model books, Brecht sought to create what he termed a *Kunstübung,* or a practice of the social through art, in which the cultural workers could imagine a new society. In part, the cultural worker would employ the inductive method, searching for answers through the doing of theatre. But what of the character – the other – who appeared within the dual performance?

The Measures Taken offers an apt example of both Brecht's innovative strategies of character assignment and his fascination with Asia – specifically, China. Like Mme Blavatsky, Brecht turned to the East for his setting and his playing of the "other" in this play, as well as in *The Good Person of Setzuan.* He seemed to find, in China, a distant ground for the character as "other." *The Measures Taken* is set in China. The actors take on the masks of the different characters: the underground Communist agitators, the Chinese coolies, the owner, and the Party's Control Chorus. The use of masks heightens the sense of the dual portrayal, as the character is formalized and distanced from the actor's body. Brecht also suggested an exchange of masks, during the rehearsal period, to further distance the actor from the perspective of any one character. Moreover, in the narrative, the agitators are disguised as Chinese in order to organize the coolies into an uprising against the owner. Thus a transracial performance guides the method of acting, both as actor and as agitator. Toward the end of his life, Brecht made it clear that this play was to be performed without an audience. It was designed purely as a *Kunstübung,* an "art/social exercise for the actors themselves" (Steinweg 87–88). Thus, in the play, the cross-racial signification is essentially barren, as it is in his other parable plays. There is nothing from China that brings knowledge or drama to the performance. Unlike Mme Blavatsky, Brecht's method in no way yields to the "other" as part of the pedagogy. Unlike Mme Blavatky's enlightened Hindu man, Brecht's Chinese coolies are simply the fertile ground for the spread of Communism.

Brecht's transracial performance is set up to embody the contradictions involved in the advance of a Western modernist ideology through a notion of the international. As the agitators tell us in *The Measures Taken,* the aim is to teach the "ABC of communism," so we may observe the vanguardist dramaturgy at its most literal (Brecht, *The Measures Taken* 79). Brecht's use of a cross-racial performance in *The Measures Taken,* as well as in *The Good Person,* where cross-racial joins cross-gender, is set up as a feedback loop to the practice of a critical discourse among the actors themselves, or among audience members, who could use the sign of China (or, in Shen-Te's case, a Chinese man) to examine their own socio-political processes. But even though Shen-Te offers a cross-gender performance, the borders between the two genders are strictly patrolled. Her "male" role is strictly fictional and functional; her "female" role, with all of its gendered narrative elements as mother and lover, remains naturalized.

Brecht's cross-gender and cross-racial performance carefully maintains his dual acting technique, which lends agency to the actor and the spectator by patrolling borders rather than crossing them. The "other" merely stands in as an embodiment of an ideological struggle, which inspires rational consideration. Returning to Mme Blavatsky's techniques, we can see how these two traditions bring contrasting notions of agency to the representation of the "other." Even if Mme Blavatsky is a dominant, rather than submissive, medium, her "Hindu man" still provides her with new knowledge and experience through possession. New realizations "come" to her through him. In Brecht, the "other" serves more as a social cipher, a demonstration of possibilities, scrutinized through critical thinking under the secure guidance of an ideological system. Moreover, Mme Blavatsky does not privilege the masculine over the feminine in her embodiments. They remain in a balanced tandem with one another, the one never instrumentalized in the service of the other.

Mme Blavatsky's receptive relation to processes of embodiment also marks her relation to writing. The luminous script, without authorial ownership and agency, was accessible to all, able to be "downloaded" in many geographical locations, and able to guide processes of knowing. In Brecht's work, the organization of embodiment is firmly guided by the operations of print culture. In his "modern drama," writing precedes performance. Brecht himself is set up as the source of scripting (or so he would have the world believe, in spite of the creative work of women on his dramaturgical team). His strategies for the stage were basically devices located in the production of the script. In spite of his notion of a cultural exercise, improvisation was strictly guided by the stability of the script, produced prior to the production. In other words, for Brecht, the print text warrants production and improvisation, just as a stable ideology warrants the writing of it. Brecht's understanding of theatre proceeded from the role of the playwright as part of a vanguard that could teach, or model, or distance. Brecht's theatrical practices reveal how "modern drama," or a sense of the new as catalytic, combined with the stability and authority inherent in print culture. In fact, the term "modern drama" signifies the privileging of the written text over performance. It bears the same values of distribution that *The Measures Taken* acts out: a stable, print source is prior to all theatrical production. No matter the distance the production takes from the source, it remains the playwright's theatre.

The structural role of print culture encouraged Brecht, and others in his tradition, to regard new technologies as transmissions of information. It is as if a discrete unit could be transmitted, like a byte of information. Brecht's *Lehrstück, The Flight of Lindbergh,* celebrated the radio as just such a technology. Yet Brecht foresaw the role of an interactive listener as in keeping with his sense of how modern drama could inspire discussion, writing that "[t]he radio would be the finest possible communication apparatus in public life [...] if it knew how to receive as well as to transmit, how to let the listener speak as well as hear, how to bring him into a relationship instead of isolating him" ("Radio as an Apparatus" 52). Brecht foresaw interactive technologies as a form of representation that would suit his sense of a critical forum for modern drama. Meaning could be transmitted, or distributed, then, through the dialectic, refashioned. Rational processes would move the dialectic toward a certain kind of conclusion. Interestingly, Brecht's ideological practices led him to participate in the organization of a new state, the German Democratic Republic, where his sense of the model was received as formalist. The notion that meaning could be transmitted in an abstracted form, such as the parable, was perceived as formalist, in contrast to the literal and local signification socialist realism organized.

Using Brechtian terminology, we could perceive Mme Blavatsky as performing the social *gest* of the troubled intersection between the new, modern West and ancient, indigenous practices. For Mme Blavatsky, the ancient knowledge was always already "there," a potential to be scripted through different practices. The astral plane, or astral light, implied no authorship. Moreover, the occult nature of this knowledge was against the enlightenment notion of "teaching," or information. On the contrary, it was secret, imparted only to those who were already "in the know." Several kinds of practices could perform the relation between the ephemeral condition of this knowledge and material properties. The performance of the "Hindu man" practiced embodiment, while certain other practices, associated with séances or the transformation of objects, were designed to reveal the constitution of matter. While it could not be said that Mme Blavatsky's performances prefigured an interactive information technology, as Brecht's might have done, they were working with the principles of physics. Rather than transmission, her performances participated in circulation.

In addition to her dual performance of the "Hindu man," Mme Blavatsky performed "phenomena." She garnered much attention for making objects appear or disappear. Calculating how to convince those believers in the modern uses of science and reason, such as Thomas Edison, to join the Theosophical Society, and before Einstein's famous equation or Robert Wilson's *Einstein on the Beach,* Mme Blavatsky staged the relative transformations of matter and energy. These performances remain untheorized by Mme Blavatsky, but another woman who, through her own transgender and transracial performances, made her way to Lhasa in 1924 records the physics behind the appearances. Alexandra David-Neel, the first European woman and possibly the first European to reach the sacred Tibetan city of Lhasa, wrote numerous manuscripts translating Sanskrit texts into Western languages. In the years between 1921 and 1924, when she was in her fifties, David-Neel walked over 1,000 miles through Mongolia and Western China to Lhasa. In the tradition of Mme Blavatsky, David-Neel disguised herself sometimes as a man and sometimes as a possessed old Tibetan woman by smearing burnt cork on her face, braiding black yak hair into her own, and darkening her face and body with Chinese ink and crushed charcoal (Foster and Foster 205). In one of her books, *The Secret Oral Teachings in Tibetan Buddhist Sects,* David-Neel reveals the Tibetan Buddhist understanding of matter. She illustrates the theory with an imagined situation: you are on a large plain and see a fleck of green in the distance. The green fleck is the size, say, of your finger. However, memory creates meaning, so, through the memory of other green spots you have seen, "ratiocinations," as she calls them, not information from the senses, you translate the green fleck into the image of a distant tree. Probability joins memory to convince you of your image. So, basically, you assign attributes to sensations (17–18). However, as David-Neel explains it, Tibetan Buddhist physics offers a kind of particle theory, arguing that there are no objects per se but only movement, which, through repetition, constitutes sensations construed as objects (19). Thus what seems to be an object is really what David-Neel terms an "event," meaning a confluence of dependencies caught temporally and translated, through memory and learned rational processes, into an object (20–21).

Although Mme Blavatsky provides no such cogent explanation, she does perform these principles in order to convince others of their accuracy. Claiming to grasp the essentials of the construction of matter, Mme Blavatsky made things appear and disappear at will. She explained that, often, these appearances were simply "mesmeric hallucination," or powerful suggestions that others took for real (Cranston 174). At other times, it seemed, she grasped the cohesive power that attracted atoms into forming objects, however unstable. As one of her fellow theosophists wrote, "The profound art is to be able to interrupt at will and again restore the atomic relations in a given substance" (qtd. in Cranston 176). Mme Blavatsky gave public performances of her adept strategies in her parlor and in the homes of others. These were invited performances, in which she exemplified the particle nature of matter and its instability. Obviously, these performances drew the most attention to Mme Blavatasky's occult abilities, as well as supplying most of the material for doubt. Attacks upon her as a charlatan were prompted primarily by her manipulation of "phenomena." Those looking for scientific proof claimed to discover that her transformations were mere tricks. The status of "fake" provided the greatest breach with the modernist dictum, based on the enlightenment principles of documenting and warranting. Science had become inextricably linked to reason. The status of metaphor did not resurface within science until Einstein's falling elevators created the understanding of even more distant space.

While Brecht's performance theories suit a consideration of a now dated modern drama, Mme Blavatsky's practices prefigure a postmodern, Internet performance. Mme Blavatsky already performed through a device that is now emerging in the practices of the World Wide Web: an avatar. Making a visual appearance on the Web relies upon what are called, in Web-speak, "avatars." Interestingly, this new techno-term is derived from the Hindu meaning of an avatar as a manifestation of a deity, much as the appearance of Mme Blavatsky's "Hindu man." Jennifer Gonzalez aptly describes the dual relationship between an avatar and a user on the Internet. In her article "The Appended Subject," Gonzalez situates the avatar as "an object constituted by electronic elements serving as a psychic or bodily appendage, an artificial subjectivity that is attached to a supposed original or unitary being, an online persona understood as somehow appended to a real person who resides elsewhere, in front of a keyboard" (27–28). These avatars do not necessarily relate mimetically to the user. In fact, cross-gender relations between user and avatar are heralded as one of the great revelries of the Net. As Tim Jordan exclaims in *Cyberpower,* "The ability to play with identity gives rise to some of the most spectacular, and so most discussed, instances of difference between online and offline life" (65). His examples are the familiar ones of the popular and sought-after "Julie," who turned out to be a man, and Dorian Sagan, who signed on, variously, as a young man, then a young woman, and so forth. Typically, as Gonzalez and others have noted, these avatars are composed of the most stereotypical elements of gender identification. While they may not emulate Mme Blavatsky's balance of power between genders, avatars do structure a dual performance technique.

This avatar exists in a global realm, shared across natural divides. As avatars meet, they play together in a realm, a plane of light – astral, if you wish – accessible from anywhere and existing nowhere. Cyber-bodies, new cultural life forms, are being organized in this luminous realm, whose appearances are not warranted by any iconic signified or signifier behind them. As AIs, or Artificial Intelligences, begin to appear on the Web, the avatars are not even necessarily warranted by a human body at some "terminal." Nevertheless, in the main, a kind of dual performance is now being practiced, one in which the "experience" – if such a term may be borrowed from the realm of the real – or something resembling experience belongs to the avatar, not to the presence behind it. In other words, the equation of actor to character set up by Brecht is reversed, implying something more like what Mme Blavatsky records. The avatar provides new experience and knowledge, as it behaves out in the wide world, through which the actor learns, or doesn't. It is the theatre of masks, which may, or may not, inform actors.

"Phenomena," as Mme Blavatsky called them, represent the physics of the Net. Creatures of light, those representations that resemble objects appear and disappear through channels of the electronic flow. And morphing is the mode of change, rather than a sequenced inductive, deductive, or developmental process. The capricious nature of Net composition has unsettled truth claims, or, indeed, any claims of intellectual property, including the ownership of ideas or the warranting of proof. The accusations leveled against Mme Blavatsky as a "fake" also haunt Internet processes: How can anyone believe what is found there? What process tests its proof? The luminous script does not proceed from a hierarchical source, but is playfully and randomly composed. Both Mme Blavatsky and the players on the Internet use such "fakery" to achieve their representational goals. Unlike the earnest and seemingly forthright drama of empirical truth, they revel in slippages of signification and bastard notions with no claim to strict, genealogical roots.

Today, in the popular imagination, China and Tibet continue to signify the dialectic that Brecht and Mme Blavatsky represent here. The modernist revolution is pitted against the occult spiritualism of Tibet. *The Measures Taken* meets *Isis Unveiled.* Economic plans are set against mandalas etched in sand.

Should the situation be perceived as Marx's famous prognostication that, in the future, there will only be barbarism or Communism? This modernism has evacuated the occult Tibet, driving it into a diasporic mode. Instead of pilgrims making their way to the distant Lhasa, the head of state, the Dalai Lama, is traveling in exile through the West. This diaspora has gained much of its momentum and global attention during the same years as the expansion of the World Wide Web. Bumper stickers about the relationship of China to Tibet abound. Movie stars, such as Richard Gere, organize performances around it. The circulation of the conflict between China and Tibet inspires various kinds of performances that do not distinguish between religion and politics. What is at issue are competing forms of embodiment and epistemology.

However, the World Wide Web enters as the third term in this paradigm. Performances scripted through statehood still rely upon the citizen body to warrant the existence of the state (Stone 41). Yet, on the Internet, representation overcomes any sense of the represented. It can provide a realm of signs without referents. Drama, now, could be reinstated as a script, but it would be a script without actors. Rather than preceding production, depending on modernist notions of development, it would be preceded by production. After all, this is the sense of acting that the constructionist critique offers, with Judith Butler's performative subject constituted as a devolution of institutional processes. Scripting the effects of institutions, the masks without actors, one could reinstate drama.

But what of "modern?" Is there any way to redeem that term? I think the sense of the modern resides in the machinic nature of this World Wide Web that does pronounce itself daily as "new." The technology, rather than the order of representation, fulfills Brecht's sense of how the interactive form of transmission in itself brought promise to a new world order. Even if the "ghost in the machine" can be imagined through the tradition of occult possession and performance of "phenomena," it is the machine itself that hails the new subject, to borrow from Althusser, or so it is signified. So the new machine technology claims the avatar and the luminous as modern and as the barren signifiers of script.

OTHER WORLD-LY

As we know, the majority of producers and users of this new technology are men. Logocentrism reigns through the deployment of the new luminous script, or phallogocentrism, as Lacan appended it. So, apparently, it still remains for women to insist upon some way of imagining or performing the "other" online, since they share its status. Is there any way to take a cue from the strategies of Mme Blavatsky for an entrance onto the Internet stage? Karen Wendy Gilbert offers a manifesto toward such a performance in her "Urban Cyborg Sha(wo)man Manifesto." Filtering terms from ethnography and technospeak through feminist critical theory, Gilbert combines ancient practices, such as shamanism, with prosthetics and a critique of gender to create an avatar for online performance. Gilbert insists that this "cyborg sha(wo)man" is "a technological subject, a being who metabolizes information" (104). A subject constituted *through* technology, this avatar does not set up polar oppositions between technology and human, or between machinic and subjective; rather, she appears only through cyborgean fusions.

This "cyborg sha(wo)man" compounds the ancient with the new by imagining the shaman's rattle, or even the hand itself, as a prosthesis of power similar to the extension of cyberspace. Rather than perceiving technology as a "new" corrective to older, enmired processes, Gilbert situates the cyber within a spectrum of the most immediate and the most ancient of adjuncts. Even the notion of space itself gives up its "elsewhere," as Mme Blavatsky imagined it. Using Haraway's notion of "location" to fuse space with difference, Gilbert argues against ontological differences in favor of relational, patterning effects: "Location is always partial, always finite, always the fraught play of foreground and background, text and context ... not self-evident or transparent" (110). Cyberspace is not of a different ontological order, then, from "real" space, nor are the imaginaries of space, the "virtual Tibets," of a different order from the "real" one. They are relational locations marking difference through cultural, economic, and social practices. Donna Haraway, in exploring ancient, indigenous practices of negotiating distance and geography as virtual, turns not to Tibet but to Australian aboriginal practices. Noting that cartography is a particular practice of spatializing, specific to certain cultures, Haraway describes "spatialization practices [that] involve recursive layers of stories and metaphors that tie land and people together in interconnected networks" (139). We can imagine, then, those cartographers who marched through Tibet with their instruments and native bearers, "opening" Tibet to the West, as part of a modernist understanding of spatial relationships that would later inform how we perceive cyberspace.

Seeking, as Mme Blavatsky and Irigaray have done, a different practice of inhabiting space, Gilbert, through Haraway, indeed, by now, a line of women, may perform in space, cyber- or otherwise, within quite different parameters. Interestingly, although Gilbert is working within some of the most contemporary critical traditions of feminist cyborgs, she evokes some of the same Buddhist structures that David-Neel and Mme Blavatsky sought to perform in their physics. Imagining this new Internet persona, Gilbert writes, "like algae-within-the-fungus which are lichens, like the ghost within the machine that are computer networks, patterns are the sequence whose symbiotic structure is 'Sha(wo)man.'" Then Gilbert adds, "Buddha identified five skandas, or aggregates that structure being. The cyborg is herself an aggregate" (110). Thus we can locate a tradition, of sorts, that proceeds from the earlier women scholar/adventurers, who devised independent and transgressive performances of self, to the luminous Net performances of patterned morphings and cyborgean fusions, grasped and mandated through feminist redefinitions of technology.

As shifting, local patterns overcome ontology, the molding of performance accretes rather than acts. Attempting to upload earlier definitions of performance onto the Web may clarify certain modes of appearing there, but it may also prevent us from understanding the fuller implications of a construction of "space," or of spatializing processes. Looking to the alternative practices of embodiment and "phenomena" Mme Blavatsky and others have explored, women may inhabit and perform within an "outer" space.

NOTES

1 In *Madame Blavatsky's Baboon,* Peter Washington identifies "the astral light" as a common nineteenth-century term for the source of divine dictation. He compares it to Joseph Smith's claims about the source of the *Book of Mormon* (50–51).

2 In the nineteenth century, it was common practice to subsume various sects under the rubric of "Hindu," as Parama Roy discusses in "As the Master Saw Her" (113–14).

3 Washington reports that she was "massively stout" (33). By some reports, she weighed 17½ stone (245 lb, or 111 kg).

4 See Parama Roy's study of heterosexist, masculinist discipleship of religion and nationhood, in her fine study of Margaret Noble and Vivekananda.

5 Alexandra David-Neel briefly explains *tulkus* in *Secret Oral Teachings,* 104. She takes up the subject at length in her *Mystics and Magicians in Tibet.*

6 See Washington 44–45.

The Haunted Houses of Modernity

DAVID SAVRAN

Despite having survived a fin-de-siècle anxiety attack, the industrialized world has come more and more to resemble a spook-house. With the emergence of new media and new industrial and social technologies, it has developed ever more subtle ways of creating virtual realities, inspiring fear, and offering intimations of the sublime. Although these achievements of the so-called information age may seem unprecedented, they are far less novel, I want to argue, than they at first appear. These new technologies represent instead the fulfillment of a particular historical logic, a kind of monstrous repetition of the past. And despite a widespread (and arguably premature) disillusionment with Marxism, Marx himself can hardly be accused of over-dramatization when he rather famously writes that "[t]he tradition of all the dead generations weighs like a nightmare on the brain of the living" (15). For the 150 years since he penned those words have witnessed a proliferation of nightmares that I hardly need enumerate. Beginning in the 1960s, however, with the emergence of what passes for postmodernism, the weight of these nightmares has produced a curious side effect that Marx could not have anticipated: it has functioned increasingly to make time seem to have stopped dead in its tracks. Have not theorists, politicians, media celebrities, and the other arbiters of culture ever more incessantly proclaimed the end – the end of man, of liberalism, of the welfare state, of modernity itself? And all the while proclaiming the end, and seeing its signs in everything from the fall of historical Communism to the miraculous appearance of the Virgin Mary on a window pane in New Jersey, these same prognosticators seem intent on killing history off as well. On the one hand, most U.S. politicians, from George W. to Bill Clinton, have taken the knife to history because the millennial new age, they insist, has already arrived. Standing, in Francis Fukuyama's words, at "the end of history," "we cannot picture to ourselves a world that is *essentially* different from the present one, and at the same time better" (qtd. in Kumar 77–78).

For these neo-liberals obsessed with maintaining "free markets and private property," progress will result automatically from simply fine-tuning the status quo (Friedman 21). Most theorists on the academic left, on the other hand, have become born-again postmodernists who dismiss Marxist historiography as hopelessly outmoded and idealist. For them, the construction of a universal history – or, for that matter, the attempt to critique capitalism as a world system – amounts to little more, in Aijaz Ahmad's mocking words, than "a contemptible attempt" to construct "grand narratives" and "(totalitarian?) knowledges" (69).

But modernity is not so easily killed off. Like a zombie, it is coming back to stalk us, and perhaps nowhere as insistently as on the stage. For the plays that have filled U.S. theatres during the past ten years are full of ghosts. From the surprisingly placable apparition of Ethel Rosenberg in Tony Kushner's *Angels in America*, to the unquiet spirit of Uncle Peck in Paula Vogel's *How I Learned to Drive*, to Sarah Brown Eyes in Terrence McNally's stage version of E.L. Doctorow's *Ragtime*, the American theatre has become a truly haunted stage.

Yet the recent proliferation of ghosts is hardly a unique occurrence. From its beginnings, the modernist theatre – understood as a self-consciously revolutionary insurgency – has set itself apart from the dramas of the past. Yet time and again it has been haunted by that which it believes it has displaced, that "tradition of all the dead generations." For by defining itself in relation to the past, it betrays a secret link to history. And this dependence on the past is no less true of that theatre that some would call postmodernist than of its explicitly modernist precursors. For the return of the living dead is, I believe, symptomatic of the contemporary stage's debt to modernism and a sign of its continuity with the modernist insurgency that began more than 100 years ago. I want first to analyze the haunted American stage of the past ten years and then to link it with two other historical moments during which the Western stage was similarly invaded by ghosts.

Unlike mass culture, with its addiction to novelty and its embrace of the commodity form, the theatre remains slightly antique. Not only is it one of the oldest performing arts, but its legacy – alas – seems far grander than its somewhat precarious present state. Most regional theatre companies in the U.S. anchor their seasons on the classics – from Shakespeare to Tennessee Williams, Ibsen to Rodgers and Hammerstein – while Broadway has been deluged over the past decade by so many revivals that the Tony Awards have had to invent new categories for them. At the same time, the emergence of the talkie in the late 1920s has allowed, and indeed encouraged, theatre to develop as a relatively elitist and critical form. At least since the 1930s, with the Federal Theatre Project and the Group Theatre, and continuing with the development of off-off-Broadway in the 1960s, the American stage has been positioned as a relatively oppositional cultural formation.

But theatre is distinguished from mass cultural forms by more than its penchant for social critique. It is also the most literary of the performing arts, and plays have long (and misleadingly) been considered a branch of literature. Despite the high profiles of certain directors and designers, playwrights and their plays are usually taken to be the generative forces behind most productions on what Derrida calls the theological stage, that physical – and metaphysical – space in which "a primary logos" is not literally present on "the theatrical site" but "governs it from a distance." Performances on the theological stage – which is to say, the modern stage – will always be evanescent, but the written word of the "author-creator" is imagined both as a divine injunction and as a kind of time capsule, a tomb in which are interred both his or her own ideas, predilections, and emotions and the remains of a vanished time and culture ("Theater of Cruelty" 235). (It is little wonder that the citizens of Grover's Corners include a copy of Thornton Wilder's *Our Town*, that most celebrated of ghost plays and the very text in which they appear, in the cornerstone of their new bank.) If the playtext is indeed a kind of memorial, then theatrical performance must be akin to awakening the dead. For both performing and reading are ways of remembering; they jog the memory and help restore what has been lost. But if performance is an act of remembering, it must also remember what, in effect, was never there. For in bringing a written text to life, performance always reveals that the text is incomplete, that it is composed of what are, in effect, dead words. Yet as a form of resuscitation, it must revivify this incompletely realized artifact in relation to the desires, fantasies, and beliefs of the absent playwright – which can be endlessly hypothesized but never fully known – and to those of the living actors, designers, and director. Performance based on a written text thus always (and uneasily) occupies two historical moments, the moments in which it was written and in which it is performed. Negotiating between past and present, the theological stage always dramatizes not the coincidence but the gap between written text and performance, writer and director, character and actor. Theatre, in short, is always about the impossibility of representing what was never fully there in the first place. For performance is always in thrall to a written text that is not quite alive yet not quite dead. Film may be haunted by the absent actor whose luminous reincarnation fills the screen, but theatre is haunted by the absent author-creator whose text functions as a kind of ghost, mediating between death and life.

Given the status of the dramatic text as a memorial, an incomplete project, a specter, it is little wonder that the theatre, from Greek and Renaissance tragedy to Japanese Noh, has long been linked to the occult and populated by ghosts. Actors may be passing before our eyes, but they are of necessity only standing in for those imaginary beings who, like the ghost of King Hamlet, vanish before we can touch them. As Mac Wellman's *Crowbar* so vividly suggests, every performance, like every theatre building, is haunted by what has come before, by the ghosts of characters and actors who have trod the boards. Entering a suburban multiplex, whose walls are inevitably plastered with posters announcing ever more glorious coming attractions, we are swept into the future, dazzled by technology, computer animation, digital sound, or, at the least, the play of light on a brilliantly blank screen. But entering a theatre, either a Broadway house or a repertory theatre whose walls are invariably dotted with posters and photographs of previous productions, we walk into a past that is haunted by the spirits of dedicated, hard-working, and sometimes inspired artists. Theatre, despite recent advances in sound and lighting technologies, remains curiously anti-technological, a place for those who do and those who act – in the broadest sense – a site for re-imagining and remaking the self. For if film is about technology, fantasy, and plotting, then theatre is about character, about the richness of a human subject about whom one fact is indisputable: he or she is going to die. Yet, as Joseph Roach notes, it is the very mortality of the actor that allows him or her to stake a claim for a kind of immortality:

Even in death actors' roles tend to stay with them. They gather in the memory of audiences, like ghosts, as each new interpretation of a role sustains or upsets expectations derived from the previous ones. This is the sense in which audiences may come to regard the performer as an eccentric but meticulous curator of cultural memory, a medium for speaking with the dead. (78)

In the act of curating cultural memory, the performer not only conserves the theatrical past but also, and ironically, commemorates both his or her own mortality and the mortality of the performance itself. For all performance, as Peggy Phelan reminds us, "becomes itself through disappearance" (146). It silently acknowledges its evanescence, the fact that it is a unique and fleeting occasion that can never be preserved or reiterated. Like Prince Hamlet, it always dies at the end of the last act.

During the last decade of the twentieth century, as the American theatre tried yet again to carve out a space for itself distinct from film and television, it became a privileged site for confronting the past. For it is my contention that ghosts are so important on contemporary stages because they function as a point of intersection between memory and history, two processes, Pierre Nora argues, that now "appear" – in this age of identity politics – "to be in fundamental opposition" to each other. Memory, as Nora explains, is usually understood to be spontaneous, a part of lived experience. Connecting us with the past, it fills us out. It gives us an identity. It is alive, immediate, and concrete. It is communicated through the body, through gesture, words, and rituals. Memory is in our blood, in our genes; it is "a bond tying us to the eternal present." History, on the other hand, is assumed always to be second-hand, to come to us from outside. It is reconstructed through cultural narratives we read or watch or listen to. It "belongs to everyone and to no one, whence its claim to universal authority" (8–9). Even our own memories become history only when, in effect, they are no longer ours, when we meet them again in someone else's representations. For no matter how vibrant or how densely populated by the sweating, teeming masses, history always has something vaguely abstract about it.

The theatrical ghost is a figure uniquely positioned in relation to both memory and history. As a token of memory, the ghost is usually intensely personalized, emanating from and materializing characters' fears and desires (and playing off our own as well). For, like Uncle Peck or Sarah Brown Eyes, the ghost returns almost ritualistically to tell characters (and audiences) what they know but would rather forget. It is thus a concrete manifestation of fears and desires that, because they have never been resolved, literally haunt a character. For the ghost has historically been imagined as a tortured soul who has not yet found peace but who walks the earth seeking satisfaction. The ghost, in short, is unfulfilled and appears only to those figures who are themselves unfulfilled. It is a token of an intensely personal loss, a loss so great or so painful that one is loath to acknowledge it. And coming to peace with the ghost means coming to terms with this disavowed loss in such a way that it is both internalized and transformed, as if by magic, into a kind of profit. Thus, *How I Learned to Drive* is about learning that what has been lost can never be struck from one's memory, that Li'l Bit must live always with the unexpectedly comforting reflection of Uncle Peck in her rearview mirror. It demonstrates that Peck is also her own reflection, a double, a shadow self, a figure who has taken root inside her and yet stands apart, watching her from a distance.

Like Peck, virtually every ghost in the contemporary theatre signals a crisis in the constitution of the subject, for whom the ghost represents an other who has been lost and yet is imagined to inhere both inside and outside the self. For these bereaved subjects, the ghost functions as a symptom of a melancholic process whereby the subject attempts to incorporate that which he or she has lost. Freud, in his essay "Mourning and Melancholia," describes both of these conditions as "the reaction to the loss of a loved person, or to the loss of some abstraction" (153). The difference between the two consists in the fact that "melancholia is in some way related to an unconscious loss," unlike "mourning, in which there is nothing unconscious about" it (155). In both cases, however, the experience of loss compels the subject, as Judith Butler explains, "to incorporate that other into the very structure of the ego, taking on attributes of the other and 'sustaining' the other through magical acts of imitation" (57). But because the melancholic (unlike the mourner) refuses to relinquish the love-object, "internalization becomes a strategy of magically resuscitating the lost object, not only because the loss is painful, but because the ambivalence felt toward the object requires that the object be retained until the differences are settled" (61–62). It is precisely this act of melancholic sustenance that is dramatized in *How I Learned to Drive* and *Ragtime*. Yet these plays also suggest that the very act of calling up theatrical ghosts and letting them tell their stories allows for the transformation of melancholia into mourning, unconscious into conscious. It is little wonder, then, that both *How I Learned to Drive* and *Ragtime* should end with gestures of putting the past to rest in what counts as something of a triumph for the characters who survive.

But the theatrical ghost is more than just an illustration of Freud's theories of loss and subject formation. It is also symptomatic of the persistence of history during a period when it is fashionable to deride it, whether history be understood in Marxian terms, as a chronicle of struggle among classes, peoples, and nations, or more broadly, as Nora explains, as that which "binds itself strictly to temporal continuities, to progressions and to relations between things" (9). For the ghost is not only a product of highly subjective, personal memories but also an embodiment of social, political, and economic forces. The ghost need not be that of a public figure like Ethel Rosenberg, but it nonetheless serves as a representative and reminder of the skirmishes that constitute history, skirmishes, for example, between Reagan's cocky henchmen and guilty liberals or between African Americans and a racist fire chief in New Rochelle. Insofar as each skirmish has a winner and a loser, then the ghost usually represents a casualty of history, for it is almost always numbered among the losers. It may not imagine itself a victim, but its refusal to die, to disappear, leads one to suspect that it has in some way been wronged or oppressed. Thus, for example, the spectral figures of Ethel Rosenberg and Sarah Brown Eyes are the spirits whom the victors would rather forget. *Angels in America* resurrects Ethel Rosenberg to incite both Roy Cohn and the audience to remember the injustices perpetrated by McCarthyism in the name of national security. And *Ragtime* calls up Sarah as a reminder of the racialized violence that remains a legacy of slavery and continues to ravage American society. One of these figures is historical, while the other may be a product of fantasy, but both roam the earth because they cannot be consigned neatly to another time and another place. Rather, they function as the sign of the haunting of the present by the past, the living by the dead.

Insofar as the theatrical ghost functions as a historical referent, as a representative of what Marx calls the "tradition of all the dead generations," this ghost is less an incorporeal essence than that which Derrida (following Marx) designates a specter, an impossible conjunction of spirit and flesh whose persistence on the stage (and off) testifies to the fact that we still live with the ghosts of those persons and social institutions we thought we had put behind us. Located on the threshold between two worlds, two orders of being, and two temporalities, the specter is proof that society lives in all of us and that we are both its products and its makers. It is the sign, as Derrida notes, glancing at Marx and at *Hamlet*, that "*[t]o be* [...] means [...] to inherit" (*Specters of Marx* 54). For the specter is "a paradoxical incorporation, the becoming-body, a certain phenomenal and carnal form of the spirit. It becomes [...] some 'thing' that remains difficult to name: neither soul nor body, and both one and the other" (6). As a figure endlessly undoing the opposition between flesh and spirit, the carnal and the abstract, this almost nameless "thing" ends up deconstructing the opposition between memory and history. Or, more precisely, it represents the site and the occasion for the transformation of memory into history, the individual into the collective, the particular into the universal. It represents the persistence of the past, the intractability of the other, "the furtive and ungraspable visibility of the invisible" (7). It demonstrates that what is memory one moment can be history the next. For as we watch the spectacle, in a darkened auditorium, of other people remembering, we see memory changed into history as the struggles in which they participate and the society in which they (are forced to) play their parts are illuminated. We see memory and experience suddenly problematized, dematerialized, rendered untrustworthy, a kind of phantom limb produced by an individual consciousness unaware that it is a historical construction.

In a culture obsessively foreseeing the end, a uniquely forgetful culture that regards last month's headlines as a dusty chronicle – Monica who? – the theatre sometimes becomes a site for *re-membering*, literally piecing together what has been lost. As a marginalized and endangered form of cultural production, the American theatre in particular is haunted in so many ways: by its own more glorious past, by the culture that it both critiques and helps prop up, by the written texts of vanished author-creators, and by characters who are in turn stricken with memory. It is haunted by the fact that it is no longer a central feature of U.S. culture. It is haunted by the 1960s, the last truly progressive era – one in which so many prominent theatre artists came of age and to whose utopian promises they continue to hearken. Yet a mere glance at recent U.S. history reveals that these promises have been consistently and brutally betrayed. For America itself is haunted by the disillusionment and the losses of the past twenty-five years: by the ever-widening disparity between rich and poor, black and white; by the backlash against feminism and affirmative action; by the increasing power of social and fiscal conservatives; and by the gradual whittling away of possibilities for and incitements to change.

It seems to me that theatre, because of its history as a sometimes oppositional formation, has attempted more conscientiously than most other forms of cultural production to keep utopian impulses alive. And this has become a particularly difficult – and important – project during a period when alternatives to capitalism and commodity culture seem increasingly foreclosed. For it is the specter, as *Angels in America* so clearly suggests, that, in keeping the past alive, also announces the promise of a radically different future. As Derrida emphasizes, the spectral – and utopian – character of the promise "will always keep within it ... this absolutely undetermined messianic hope at its heart," this hope for "an alterity that cannot be anticipated." "[T]he very place of spectrality," therefore, must always be left empty "in memory of the hope," in memory of an unimaginable future (*Specters of Marx* 65). Following in the footsteps of those peerless tragedians, Hamlet, Marx, and Walter Benjamin, Derrida envisions history itself as a kind of theatre in which one forever awaits the appearance of a ghost and in which memory functions to keep both past and future alive. History is always incomplete, a site of absence, loss, horror, betrayal. Taking up these betrayals, the real theatre, as *Angels in America* so compellingly demonstrates, can become a site of "infinite promise," a place for "awaiting what one does not expect [...] any longer," for re-membering what has never happened (65).

Despite their undeniable spectral and spectacular power, Ethel Rosenberg, Sarah Brown Eyes, and Uncle Peck are in the end only ghosts, that is, a sign of the increasing inaccessibility of a living past in an era that is profoundly anti-historicist. As analysis of the past has, in recent years, given way more and more to a fetishization of experience, as history has been displaced more and more by nostalgia (a whiff of the past from which social struggles have been conveniently excised), we can now imagine history only as an intervention from without, a kind of *Invasion of the Body Snatchers*, or as a specter that suddenly materializes to confront a frightened and amnesiac population. As if to acknowledge and treat this amnesia, the theatre has, in the hands of at least a few practitioners, become a space in which to remember what we have forgotten. Yet even in commemorating the utopianism of the 1960s, in valorizing the revolutionary praxis that has historically been inscribed in the very idea of America, the American theatre – like the culture of which it is a part – has been ill disposed to confront the imperial posturing of the U.S. as the last remaining superpower. With the exception of a handful of playwrights, American writers have been curiously insular, even isolationist, in their concerns. This isolationism has many correlations and causes. It seems linked in part to a refusal on the part of the major media outlets to critique the U.S. role on the world stage. Few American writers are committed to investigating the increasingly globalized post–Cold War economy and the relationship between the First and Third Worlds. For the displacement of the proletariat of the First World to the sweatshops of the Third may have set the class struggle out of our line of vision, but it has by no means erased it. And it may well be that the specter haunting the American theatre, the ghost that most writers cannot see, is this new proletariat, which cannot even be represented directly but instead makes itself known through surrogates, through those abjected ones on the fringes of plays that happen to have the word "America" in their titles, persons of color with names of countries like Belize (in *Angels in America*) or Brazil (in Suzan-Lori Parks's *The America Play*), that so provocatively reference this unseen presence.

Although it might appear that I am criticizing already marginalized producers for their refusal to acknowledge those more marginalized than themselves,

I am more concerned with drawing attention to the economic and cultural logic that produces these marginalizations. Convincing playwrights to critique the new international division of labor is not likely to alter the latter's structure. And I believe it is a mistake to look to even a sometimes dissident theatre as a way of producing social and economic change. Indeed, when I hear critics and artists calling – always with the best intentions – for an aggressively feminist or antiracist or anti-homophobic theatre, I wonder, "Why do we want the theatre to redeem us?" I don't particularly enjoy watching reactionary art. But I think it is a mistake to look to theatre to solve problems that can be solved only in the political arena. Might it not be that the agitation for a redemptive theatre is a symptom of a profound disillusionment with electoral politics, coupled with the virtual extinction of mass movement politics since the end of the Cold War? We cultural producers, whom Bourdieu rightly dubs a "dominated fraction of the dominant class," feel disempowered because we are (15). But storming the barricades at Berkeley Rep, or the Modern:Drama conference, for that matter, can lead to real political and economic change only through the most impossibly tortuous of routes.

I want to return to examine further the displacement of imperial relations in recent American plays because this displacement marks the sign, I believe, not of a break but of a continuity with the canons of modern drama. For contemporary plays are hardly the only texts in which one discovers ghosts. As Derrida suggests, modernity itself, as inaugurated and instantiated by *Hamlet*, represents a kind of spectral drama. And there is no question but that the stage, from the Early Modern through the Romantic periods, often called up the spirits of the dead. But beginning in the late nineteenth century, with the development of a modernist drama that explicitly interrogates and sets itself apart from tradition, the theatre became a far more ambiguously and disturbingly spectral site. In the experimental dramas of Maeterlinck, Wedekind, Strindberg, Cocteau, O'Neill, and many others, the early modernist stage defined itself as a space in which to problematize presence, which is to say, to interrogate and deconstruct the oppositions between past and present, here and there, self and other, spirit and flesh, text and performance, the real and the hallucinatory, the living and the dead. If, throughout the twentieth century, this tradition – and I think that is the correct word to describe it – has remained the dominant strain of what passes for modern drama, its hegemony testifies to what surely must be seen as an aestheticizing and theologizing tendency within modernism and within theatre. Brecht's historicist and materialist theatre, in contrast, could be described as, if not exactly a theatre without ghosts, then at least a theatre that goes to great lengths both to illuminate and to debunk the claims of the undead.

Yet early modernist plays are not the only spectral dramas that fill play anthologies and modern drama classes. For within the dominant, aestheticizing strain of Western theatrical modernism, there is a second prominent collection of ghost plays that is the product of what has misleadingly been branded the Theatre of the Absurd. The characters who people the plays of Beckett, Genet, and Ionesco are invariably haunted by the desires of and for others who remain either unseen or inaccessible, others who are neither altogether present nor altogether absent but who represent the promise of an impossible return, like the Orator in *Les chaises* or, of course, Godot. Beckett, in particular, is so central to the modernist canon in part because he problematizes theatrical presence in a way that both recapitulates and defamiliarizes the achievements of early modernism. He is like Maeterlinck without all the fog and veils.

If I am correct, the canon of modern drama is in fact marked by a triple efflorescence of ghost plays. The first dates from the years between 1885 and, say, 1925; the second from the 1950s and early 1960s; and the third from the 1990s. And I want to argue, moreover, that this latest flowering represents not only the repetition of a distinctive formal logic but, more importantly, the fulfillment of a certain globalizing imperative. For the three periods of ghost plays – all of these plays, it must be noted, the products of metropolitan cultures – also correspond to three distinct phases of Western imperialism. The first phase marks European imperialism's triumph after the Berlin Conference of 1884, when, as Fredric Jameson notes, "a significant structural segment of the economic system as a whole is now located elsewhere," in colonies in Africa or Asia. As a result, "daily life [...] in the metropolis [...] can now no longer be grasped immanently; it no longer has its meaning, its deeper reason for being, within itself." And "artistic content," in its turn, "will now henceforth always have something missing about it." Metropolitan modernism, with its formal disjunctions and constitutive absences, must then quite precisely "[live] this formal dilemma," a dilemma it can neither compass nor solve, through a ritual decorporealization (50–51). How else, for example, is one to interpret the long-distance murder of The General in Cocteau's *Les mariés de la Tour Eiffel*, who is devoured on the eponymous Tower by a lion that "is actually in Africa" and, hence, only a mirage (109)?

The second phase, the so-called Theatre of the Absurd, should more accurately be described as the theatre of decolonization, or the theatre that emerges when the violence of anticolonial struggle is sublimated as metaphysics. This is the drama of disorientation that resulted when Europe's relations with its former colonies were radically altered and the metropolitan capitals suffered an unprecedented identity crisis, which is to say, a crisis of economic and military power, of memory, and of place. How else, for example, is one to make sense of the obsessive attempts of Ionesco's blundering bourgeois in *Rhinoceros* to determine whether a rioting rhinoceros is, in their words, "African" or "Asiatic"? Why else would their frustration lead them to a furious and finally unresolved dispute over whether "Asiatics" are "bright yellow" or "white ... like us" (499–500)?

The third phase, and arguably the most monstrous repetition, is the drama of neocolonialism that signals the replacement of occupying armies by the pinstriped brigades of the World Bank, the International Monetary Fund, and the World Trade Organization. While the first two phases focus on relations between Europe and its colonies, the last marks a geographical shift. For with the fall of the Soviet Union and the increasing mobility and internationalization of capital, there is no question but that the U.S. has become the new imperial hub, whose bankers and CEOs structure relations of domination on a global scale on the American plan. Yet this neocolonialism, I believe, no more marks a radical break with the past, and with imperialism, than postmodernism does with the discourses of modernism, or the new ghost play does with the old. I would argue, in fact, that postmodernism – and the huge mass-mediated apparatus that trumpets its achievements – represents less a momentous epistemological shift than an attempt to divert attention away from increasingly uneven patterns of capital accumulation toward the social and the cultural. Within this global context, the ghost plays of both the 1990s and the 1890s emblematize what might be called, with a nod to George Lucas, the dark side of imperial triumphalism, the repressed anxieties that return unwelcomed to haunt the metropolitan conscience.

If I am correct that the very category "modern drama" is in fact a product of imperialism, then its very existence is predicated upon a certain disavowal, a certain refusal to credit the corporeal existence and the labor power of those nearly invisible others who haunt its margins. Is it any wonder, then, that in all these modern dramas the ghost remains an enigma? For, like the category "native," which, Fanon reminds us, is also a product of imperialism, the ghost is both utterly material and utterly disposable, a nearly invisible producer who is at the beck and call of the prosperous few and yet whose realm, language, and social relations remain mysterious and mystified. The continuing power of disavowal, the continuing failure to recognize the vital – and exploitative – interconnections between the First and Third Worlds, remains a sign that time has not stopped dead in its tracks and that the final curtain has not yet lowered on the spectacle of modern drama – and the drama of modernity.

Hauntings: Anxiety, Technology, and Gender in *Peter Pan*[1]

ANN WILSON

J.M. Barrie's *Peter Pan* (1904) circulates in the popular imagination as a happy tale for children that, through the adventures of Peter and the other children in Never Land, celebrates playfulness. As Mark Twain commented, "It is my belief that *Peter Pan* is a great and refining and uplifting benefaction to this sordid and money-mad age; and the next best play is a long way behind" (qtd. in Jack 158). Tellingly, Twain's comment that *Peter Pan* is uplifting seems to depend on ignoring the fact that each of the "lost" boys is a baby who has fallen out of his pram "when the nurse is looking the other way" and who, if not claimed within seven days, is "sent far away to the Never Land" (Barrie 101). The boys of Never Land are dead, and so Peter Pan, arriving at the window of the Darling family, is a ghost. As the stage direction before Peter's arrival indicates, "*the nursery darkens [...]. Something uncanny is going to happen, we expect, for a quiver has passed through the room, just sufficient to touch the night-lights*" (97). As Freud suggests in his 1919 essay, the "uncanny" arouses an experience of "dread and horror," partially because the familiar (*heimlich*) evokes the unfamiliar (*unheimlich*), rendering the comfortable and "homey" uncomfortable and alien (224). The familiar, now both familiar and unfamiliar, generates anxiety.

Peter Pan, as a ghost whose first appearance is announced as "uncanny," is the sign of anxiety within the play. Beneath the familiarity of middle-class life, in the opening and closing scenes, and the culture of children's play evident in the adventures in Never Land is the anxiety aroused by the shifts in masculine identity in relation to modern life, including the new technologies of the workplace and the demise of Empire. Barrie's response is anxious and nostalgic, the desire to return to an imagined past of stability that, if it ever existed, is impossible to recuperate, a point marked by the setting of the play in "Never Land."

The "modern," as the experience of recent times, involves the memory of the past and anticipates a future. Thus, the experience of the "modern" is change. In the flux, the familiar may be lost or altered. If change is a characteristic of the modern, then *heimlich* and *unheimlich* – the familiar and the unfamiliar – with the resulting dread and anxiety produced by change are important features. One of the implications of this understanding of "modern" is that as capitalism emerges as the economic ethos of Western countries, the changing technologies of industry that buttress capitalism become key to understanding the "modern." Industrial technologies are not simply tools within the workplace; because they change the terms of work, they inevitably have an impact on the relation of workers to their labour and, hence, on the identities of workers, particularly in terms of redefining class and gender. As industrial technologies evolve, they effect radical change, which generates anxiety, particularly for the middle class, which, located between the upper and working classes, is in a site of negotiation and inherent instability.

Industry and its technologies opened a set of social relations that gave rise to the middle class. It is relatively easy to define the upper class as those who enjoy social privilege by virtue of aristocratic birth and those with established fortunes – either made or inherited – that allow access to social institutions of power. In contrast, as Ed Cohen notes in *Talk on the Wilde Side*, "agricultural labourers and the industrial working classes [...] were largely determined by the material constraints circumscribing their lives" (19), which is to say that the work in which they engaged was mainly physical, intellectually disengaged, and under-waged, so that there was little possibility of accruing excess capital. Members of the working class did not have the luxury of imagining that their financial circumstances would improve significantly.

The middle class seems more difficult to define. Cohen, synthesizing a wide range of commentary on class formation, suggests that understanding the middle class depends partially on the empirical and partially on understanding the epistemological underpinnings of the concept (19). As its name implies, the middle class falls between the upper and working classes as an unstable site of mediation between the two. The instability of the middle class means that arriving at a definition is difficult, but a point of departure might be the consideration of the broad terms of work for the middle class, which requires a degree of intellectual engagement and is remunerated at a level above subsistence; in these two ways it differs from the work performed by the working class. The accumulation of savings, frequently resulting in members of the middle class buying property, results in a horizon of expectation and imagined possibilities: affluence brings the promise of a better life, which seemed a consequence of the economics of Empire. As Cohen comments,

Without too much quibbling [...] we might say that the denizens of the Victorian middle class were those who had been able to advance themselves financially and socially in the accelerating, expanding, and industrializing British economy. Hence it included

a wide array of individuals from merchant princes and entrepreneurial wizards, to an
ever-growing number of professionals, bankers, bureaucrats, and civil servants, to
local shopkeepers, artisans, teachers, clergy, and clerks, along with their families. (19,
20)

The broad range of individuals who make up the middle class means that,
given the differing social locations of these individuals, it is relatively difficult
for this class to coalesce around common interests: the aspirations of a curate
serving in a rural parish are not those of a shopkeeper in an urban setting,
although both are "middle class." The lack of commonality contributes to the
instability of the middle class. Further, its instability is an effect of the cycles
of capitalism, which means that being middle class is not secure. In times of
affluence, some members of the middle class acquire savings. But the margin
of comfort afforded by such savings tends to be limited, and so an economic
depression can lead to financial demise for those in the middle class. Hence,
as Cohen notes, the spectre of failure haunts the middle class even as it anticipates a better life (19–21). Put another way, to be middle class is to be located
within a social sphere of inherent instability marked by the lack of homoge-
nous interests amongst members of the class and by the reality that the defining economic location is precariously uninsulated from vacillations in the
economy. The optimistic investment – psychological and fiscal – that the
future brings possibilities of affluence and a better life is the underlying anxiety that the conditions of capital generate in the middle class. A valence of the
"uncanny" that renders the comfort of the "homey" uncomfortable may well
stem from the fundamental instability of the middle class, which, given its
investments, cannot acknowledge that "instability" is its condition. It is a class
that, as Cohen suggests, is haunted by the possibility of failure.

The strain of having limited and insecure affluence is the context of *Peter
Pan*, which opens in the nursery of a house "at the top of a rather depressed
street in Bloomsbury" (87). The house is so nondescript that Barrie advises,
"you may dump it down anywhere you like, and if you think it was your house
you are very probably right" (87). While this is a particular house, belonging
to the Darling family, Barrie assumes that members of his audience recognize
and identify with it because they, like the Darlings, are middle class: if they
don't live in a house like the Darlings', they know of people who do.

The opening scene of *Peter Pan* continues to offer a glimpse of the middle
class, particularly in terms of the negotiation of gender. The action of the play
begins with the Darling children pretending to be their parents. Says John to
his mother, "We are doing an act; we are playing at being you and father"
(89), as if gender roles are performed. John and Wendy's rehearsal of their
parents seems like a recurring part of the dynamic of the family, so that Mr
Darling's entrance and his petulant demand that his wife fix his tie read like an
extension of the role playing: as the children play their parents, so the father

plays his child. Says Mr Darling to his wife, "I warn you, Mary, that unless this tie is round my neck we don't go out to dinner to-night, and if I don't go out to dinner to-night I never go to the office again, and if I don't go to the office again you and I starve, and our children will be thrown into the streets" (91). Given that the audience does not have access to the stage directions while they watch the play, and given that Mr Darling does later self-consciously play his son, the audience might be forgiven for seeing Mr Darling as entering the spirit of the domestic scene by "playing along." The stage directions suggest that it would be a misreading to see Mr Darling as naturally given to the sulks and resentful of others being the centre of attention:

> *Mr Darling arrives, in no mood unfortunately to gloat over this domestic scene. He is really a good man as breadwinners go, and it is hard luck for him to be propelled into the room now, when if we had brought him in a few minutes earlier or later he might have made a fairer impression. In the city where he sits on a stool all day, as fixed as a postage stamp, he is so like all the others on stools that you recognise him not by his face but by his stool, but at home the way to gratify him is to say that he has a distinct personality. He is very conscientious, and in the days when Mrs Darling gave up keeping the house books correctly and drew pictures instead (which he called her guesses), he did all the totting up for her, holding her hand while he calculated whether they could have Wendy or not, and coming down on the right side.* (90)

This stage direction is extraordinary in a number of ways, not the least of which is that Barrie includes important information in a stage direction that an actor would have difficulty conveying in performance. The information amounts to a curious recognition and, given that the information is unplayable, suppression by Barrie of the effect of the economic on the lives of individuals. In a moment that one might expect to find in a play by Ibsen in which characters are anxious about their finances (such as *A Doll's House*), Barrie tells us that the Darlings are not flush and had to calculate whether they could afford to have a child (with the interesting implication that they must have been practising contraception). As well, the stage direction establishes a tension between Mr Darling's identity at work, where he is anonymous, and his demeanour at home, where he is the protective husband who, as the master of his house, takes responsibility for reconciling the household finances. Barrie establishes the beginnings of a critique of masculinity in which there is a separation between the identity of a man in the workplace and his identity at home. Work alienates and dehumanizes the labourer, whereas within the sphere of home, his humanity is restored within the codes of manhood that make him the first element of the dyad man/woman. At home, he is ostensibly the breadwinner, provider, and protector of his family.

This scene seems to suggest two types of instability: the instability of mas-

culine identity as a man moves between work and home; and financial instability or insecurity. Given the Mr Darling to whom the audience is introduced
in the opening act, the strain seems too much. "George, not so loud, the servants will hear you," instructs Mrs Darling after Mr Darling has petulantly
compared his situation to that of Nana, the governess of his children, who,
because the family is in economic straits, is a Newfoundland dog.[2] When, in
this moment, his daughter, Wendy, tells her father that he has made Nana cry,
he responds, "Coddle her; nobody coddles me. Oh dear no. I am only the
breadwinner, why should I be coddled? Why, why, why?" (95). It is then that
Mrs Darling tries to regulate her husband, to insist that he lower his voice, presumably in order to maintain the illusion of middle-class decorum, and financial solvency, before the servants. Mr Darling responds, "Let them hear me;
bring in the whole world," because he is *The desperate man, who has not
been in fresh air for days, [and] has now lost all self-control*" (96). Mr Darling's desperation, it is implied, is a consequence of his being cooped up at
work, where he is denied a sense of individuality and autonomy, a cipher in
the workings of the office.

Mr Darling is faceless, known by his stool, and is likened to a postage
stamp, which dehumanizes him in a particular way. By being made into a
piece of furniture in the workplace and a postage stamp, which marks that the
cost of sending a piece of mail has been paid, he is rendered a part of the technology of industrial capital. Given that postage stamps were introduced in
England in 1839, Mr Darling seems not even to be a part of current technologies. What is at stake here is more than a rhetorical figure of synecdoche in
which a stool or a stamp stands for Mr Darling. Barrie suggests that under
capitalism, human identity becomes a technology. The social codes of masculinity are thrown into crisis because notions of "mastery" that were key to
middle-class masculinity are impossible for men like Mr Darling in the context of their work, which shapes a significant aspect of their identity. Rendered less than fully human in the workplace, Mr Darling is not even the
"master" within his own home, where the terms of his livelihood as a clerk
mean that his ability to provide for his family is uncertain; and, given the
shabbiness of the house and the fact that the family has a dog as its governess,
Mr Darling's inadequacies as a provider seem to announce his "failed"
manhood.

Part of this sense of "failure" is a consequence of the shifting demographics
of the workforce. The expansion of industrial capital involved the expansion
of the business end of the operations. With this expansion, women entered the
labour force as clerks, which, in the early part of the nineteenth century, had
been a male occupation. As the offices of industry enlarged, the nature of clerical work shifted, creating a "dual labour market": "highly trained, trusted and
well rewarded employees [undertook] the demanding and responsible work,
while the routine work was performed by a shifting group of low-paid, easily

replaced workers who could be hired and fired as pressure of work demanded" (Jordan 12). As Elizabeth Roberts notes in her study *Women's Work, 1840–1940*, "In 1914 about 20 per cent of clerical workers were women. Between 1861 and 1911 the number of male clerks had increased fivefold while the number of women clerks had risen by 400 per cent" (28). From the description of Mr Darling on his stool, it is clear that he does not hold a senior position of responsibility but performs "routine" work that offers little job security and is increasingly becoming the domain of women. As routine clerical work became feminized and devalued, the sense of failure for men like Mr Darling became pronounced. The workplace is a site of emasculation that denies men performing clerical work the sense that they can provide assuredly for their families. As a result, failure is the condition of masculinity for Mr Darling and men like him, who, under the changing terms of work in industrial capital, can never be "masterful" men.

The emasculation of Mr Darling is emphasized in the final scene of the play, in which Mr Darling is, literally, in the doghouse. As he emerges from the kennel, the stage direction indicates that "*It ought to melt us when we see how humbly grateful he is for a kiss from his wife, so much more than he feels he deserves*" (148). The play suggests that Mr Darling is being punished for losing his temper. As I have argued, however, his outbursts are not symptomatic of his limitations as an individual but, rather, are socially produced through the irreconcilable codes of masculinity that he has to negotiate. The anger and the feeling of impotence, which lead to childish outbursts, become modes of social regulation that ensure that middle-class men will not enjoy consistent identities within the public and domestic spheres. Put another way, the full title of the play is *Peter Pan or the Boy Who Would Not Grow Up*. "Would" suggests agency and choice. In Mr Darling's case, the contradictions of masculinity may amount to the man who could not grow up. Faced with the impossibility of coming to terms with the eroding sense of masculinity as the demographics of the workplace shift and women perform clerical tasks but the imperative remains for middle-class men to be the "bread winners" of the family, Mr Darling "plays" the child at home. The play rehearses this regression when it moves to Never Land, the world of childish adventure that is an escape from the pressures of adult life.

In Never Land, the parental figures – Mr and Mrs Darling – are left behind, and so Barrie abandons the critique of the middle class that he seemed to offer in the first act. Never Land, as its name implies, doesn't exist, save in its imaginative rendering within the constraints of the proscenium arch. It is a place of play within a play. The terms of Never Land are nostalgic and gendered. Never Land is a boy's world, "very compact, not large and sprawly with tedious distances between one adventure and another, but nicely crammed" (105).

Act Two introduces Never Land and begins while Peter Pan is still off in London, where he is trying to recover his shadow, which he lost in the Darlings' house, which Mrs Darling found and Mr Darling is keen to sell: "There is money in this, my love. I shall take it to the British Museum to-morrow and have it priced" (93). Without Peter Pan, their leader, the other boys in Never Land are "lost," trying to imagine the mothers from whom they were separated as small children (107). Enter the pirates, led by Captain Hook, who, in the context of the adventure, are the enemy. Barrie provides a long and detailed description of Hook, who, among his other features, is described as having his hair *"dressed in long curls which look like black candles about to melt, his eyes blue as the forget-me-not"* (108). Further, he is described as having elegant diction, which, along with *"the distinction of his demeanour, show him one of a different class from his crew, a solitary among uncultured companions. [...] At his public school they said of him that he 'bled yellow.' In dress he apes the dandiacal associated with Charles II"* (108).

The identification of Captain Hook as a "dandy," in the wake of the trials of Oscar Wilde in 1895, is significant inasmuch as it opens the complex issue of Hook's sexuality. As Ed Cohen (in *Talk on the Wilde Side*) and Alan Sinfield (in *The Wilde Century*) argue, the trials (which were widely reported in the popular press in England and, indeed, throughout Europe and the United States) were crucial in the construction of the homosexual as a recognizable social identity. As Sinfield notes, "The dominant twentieth-century queer identity [...] has been constructed [...] mainly out of elements that came together at the Wilde trials: effeminacy, leisure, idleness, immorality, luxury, insouciance, decadence and aestheticism" (*Wilde Century* 12). Sinfield's point is that while these characteristics have since become associated with homosexuality, Wilde's public personae of aesthete and, later, dandy were not read by his contemporaries as obvious signs of his homosexuality. While Wilde's dandyism was recognized, celebrated, and reviled, his self-staging did not lead "either his friends or strangers to regard him as obviously, even probably, queer" (2).

With the case of Wilde serving as the cautionary note, a reading of Captain Hook as "queer" is problematic. Certainly, that he is the only adult in Never Land, engaged in "play" with the boys, does suggest a latent anxiety about the homosexual as arrested in his development, invested in the culture of youth, inclined to pederasty. Given that the "lost boys" are dead, a sexuality that eroticizes death could be added to the list of anxieties about the homosexual. Captain Hook, rather than being obviously homosexual, is a dandy. As Sinfield suggests in "'Effeminacy' and 'Femininity': Sexual Politics in Wilde's Comedies,"

Dandy effeminacy signalled class, far more than sexuality. The newly dominant middle class justified itself by claiming manly purity, purpose, and responsibility, and identified the leisure class, correspondingly, with effeminate idleness and immorality. In the face of this manoeuvre, there were two alternatives for the wealthy and those who sought to seem wealthy. One was to attempt to appear useful and good; the other was to repudiate middle-class authority by displaying conspicuous idleness, immortality, and effeminacy; in other words, by being a dandy. (38)

Given that a theatrical convention is to have the role of Captain Hook played by the actor performing the role of Mr Darling, and given that middle-class masculinity has failed Mr Darling, Captain Hook can been seen as Barrie's inscription of what amounts to a fantasy, for Mr Darling, of his having access to the privilege of leisure and luxury associated with the upper classes. This is not to discount the idea that there is a homoerotic undercurrent in *Peter Pan*; this is another mode of haunting in the play because at issue is masculinity, related to issues of class, rather than simply sexuality. The interrelation between sexuality and class is complex, and, as Sinfield's comments imply, adopting the guise of a dandy may signal more than homosexual inclinations. In some sense, Mr Darling might be read as a figure in Never Land who escapes the pressures of being an adult by donning the guise of Captain Hook, a dandy – leisured and effeminate – who has the time (which is to say, financial security) to indulge in play and is free of the necessity to work. Further, playing an effeminate male figure offers Mr Darling the fantasy of recuperating a sense of masculinity that is eroded in his working life, in which the role of clerk increasingly is becoming the domain of women. If a cause of Mr. Darling's anxiety about his masculinity is the feminization of clerical work, playing the dandy – the feminized man of wealth – is a way of managing that anxiety because the dandy is a figure of financial means; Mr Darling is anxious about his ability to provide for his family. Never Land is a haunted world, not just because the boys are "dead" but because it is not free of the spectre of social and economic pressures on the middle class.

It seems impossible for Barrie to imagine a place without class, perhaps because Never Land is the nostalgic response to the conditions of the middle class that Barrie established in Act One. The fantasy circulating around the ethos of Never Land rehearses that of the public schools, which were, as Jonathan Rutherford has suggested, implicated in establishing codes of manliness associated with a virtuous Englishness that justified imperialism. He suggests that "public schools sought to inculcate four qualities in their boys": "sport," "readiness," "character," and "religion" (15). While the last, "religion," is not particularly evident in *Peter Pan*, the others are. In Never Land, the culture of the public school is rehearsed in the separation of the boys from family and, particularly, the influence of mother. In the face of the loss of family, the boys become a "family" and forge close, intense bonds that are homosocial and, inasmuch as these affective relations are "between boys" (to borrow and adapt Eve Kosofsky Sedgwick's phrase), open an emotional terrain that allows the intimacy to become homosexual. Through their "games" or adventures, they learn not only about readiness in responding to the surprise attacks by Hook but about submitting to enforced regimes, and so they become obedient. As the opening of Act Two suggests, without Peter Pan as their leader, the other boys flounder, remembering mother but, as the stage direction reminds us, "*not that they are really worrying about their mothers*" (107).

Codes of manliness involve physicality through the games/adventures but a pronounced avoidance of the body as sexual. When Wendy reaches out to touch Peter in their initial encounter, he recoils and says, "You mustn't touch me" (98). As the stage directions note, "*He is never touched by any one in the play*" (98). Indeed, the play establishes a curious economy of desire in which Wendy, Tinker Bell (the fairy) and Tiger Lily (the Indian maid) are all attracted to Peter Pan, who doesn't reciprocate their interest. Wendy, in Act One, offers herself to receive a kiss from Peter Pan, who "*offers her the thimble*" (101). "Thimble" becomes a means for negotiating the awkwardness of the moment as Wendy leans forward to kiss Peter, who seems perplexed and doesn't recognize her attraction to him. Their faces don't meet; Wendy screams, saying that she felt as if someone were pulling her hair (101). "That must have been Tink," explains Peter. By Act Four, when Wendy has established a household where she plays mother and Peter plays father to the boys, Wendy asks, "What are your exact feelings for me, Peter?" (130). "Those of a devoted son, Wendy," he replies. Apparently disappointed, Wendy turns away, causing Peter to comment, "You are so puzzling. Tiger Lily is just the same; there is something or other she wants to be to me, but she says it is not my mother" (130.) "No, indeed it isn't," retorts Wendy (130).

Each of the three female figures attracted to Peter Pan recognizes the other's desire for him, even if he is oblivious. Tinker Bell reacts with obvious jealousy, pulling at Wendy's hair and, when Wendy is arriving in Never Land, telling the boys that Peter has ordered them to shoot her. Given that they have been trained to obediently follow the orders of their Captain, they shoot arrows at her until she falls to earth, which Tootles believes will make Peter proud of him (112). Wendy recognizes Tiger Lily's desire for Peter because it parallels her own. The terms under which Barrie represents female desire are worth considering because they suggests how class and ethnicity are elements in producing codes of middle-class femininity.

When Wendy offers to give Peter a kiss, and he reveals that he doesn't know what a kiss is, she gives him a thimble. Peter then asks if he should give her a kiss, and then offers her an acorn (99). The scene, played between a young boy and girl, seems innocuous enough but, even so, provides cues about middle-class perceptions of female sexuality. Wendy has the opportunity to take the lead and give Peter a kiss, but instead offers him a thimble. His reciprocating by offering her an acorn creates an economy in which the exchange of tokens of affection substitutes for the expression of affection itself. A few moments later, Wendy seems to feel that the opportunity might be right for a kiss, but this time, rather than offering to kiss Peter, she offers herself: "Peter, you may give me a kiss" (101). It is as if the codes of middle-class femininity prevent Wendy from expressing sexual agency; her role is to make herself passively available, despite her own desires.

The play hints at a logic behind the suppression of sexuality. Never Land, rehearsing the culture of public school, is homosocial, a site for establishing relations between men in which women, if they figure at all, do so as currency in the exchange.[3] While the homosocial is not homoerotic, the spectre of the homoerotic, lurking as the unspoken possibility, haunts the scene. The negative connotations of "lurking" are deliberate, because by the time Barrie wrote *Peter Pan* the dissident figure of the homosexual as pathological and criminal was established in the cultural imaginary of England through press accounts of the trials of Oscar Wilde. The castigation of Wilde in the popular press speaks to an already established anxiety about homosexuality and, indeed, about sexuality in general. To gesture to this anxiety, it is worth remembering that in 1864 Britain implemented the Contagious Diseases Acts, which allowed the police to apprehend any woman who *appeared* to be infected with venereal disease and subject her to medical examinations in hospital, where she was held for three (and later nine) months. The women who appeared to be infected were prostitutes, and the cultural context of prostitution is important. Prostitution was a mode of casual employment for working-class women employed in the three major occupations which were available to them (laundry, needlework, and domestic service), none of which paid adequate wages (Clark 642). Occasional stints as prostitutes supplemented the income of these women. Prostitution came to be seen as a threat to the nation in the aftermath of the Crimean Wars, in which men in the military had high rates of infection from sexually transmitted diseases.

There is little evidence to suggest that the castigation of working-class women who supplemented their incomes through prostitution had any effect on rates of venereal disease infection amongst the military. My reference to this moment of history is intended to serve as a reminder of the terms of the Acts: sexually engaged women were cited as contaminating men. Because the women were from the working class, the measures against them were severe. Women were apprehended on the basis of appearing to be infected, held for months in hospitals, segregated from their families and communities, and subjected to the regulation of being put on a register. Further, the police, having identified the women, patrolled the areas where they lived, and so all women within those communities became suspect (Clark 644). This hyper-vigilance gave rise to suspicion about female desire. Wrote Henry Mayhew in *London Labour and the London Poor* in 1862, "'Literally, every woman who yields to her passions and loses her virtue is a prostitute'" (qtd. in Clark 642). The mid-nineteenth-century concern over sexuality transmitted disease was understandable, but it became a panicked response that made manifest fears of

female sexuality as dangerous and needing regulation. While men were the
agents of the Empire that fuelled the economy and the commensurate sense of
nation, they somehow were not responsible for their own sexual conduct or
for availing themselves of prostitutes, apparently rendered powerless by the
allure of female sexuality. Socially engaged women responded to the Contagious Diseases Acts with an evangelical fervour, but part of the movement
involved notions of purity and eschewing sex outside marriage because it was
dangerous and sinful. Further, the purity movement, with its distrust of the
body as sexual, included the regulation of homosexuality, which, like prostitution, was seen as undermining a "manliness" that was crucial to the project of
Empire, even if the ethos of Empire seems to have depended on the
homosocial. The result of the anxiety around homosexuality was the 1885
Labouchère amendment, which made homosexual acts, whether in public or
in private, criminal. As Sinfield notes, the title of the amendment is "Outrages
on public decency" (*Wilde Century* 9). These references to the regulation of
sexuality in Victorian England speak not only to the public anxiety about sexuality but to the recognition of the body as sexual, even if that body is reviled.
This history of sexual regulation is another mode of haunting in *Peter Pan* in
which Peter, forever the boy, panics and avoids the advances of the three
female figures in Never Land.

Although Wendy desires Peter, she is reticent about acting; not Tinker Bell,
who tries to cut Wendy from Peter's affections so she can have him to herself.
Tinker Bell is brazen and, as Peter remarks, "not very polite. [...] She is quite
a common girl, you know. She is called Tinker Bell because she mends the
fairy pots and kettles" (100). It would seem that even the fairy world is
marked by class and that Tinker Bell, who is working-class, is impure and suspect in ways that are consistent with the middle class's imagining of the working class. Later on in the play, at the opening of Act Four (titled "The Home
Under the Ground"), Barrie establishes a contrast between Tinker Bell, who
has retreated to her unseen bedchamber, where she "is probably wasting valu-
able time just now wondering whether to put on the smoky blue or the apple
blossom" (126), and Wendy. While Tinker Bell indulges in attiring herself,
presumably for the pleasure of Peter, who isn't home, Wendy presides over
the dinner as if she were mother of the boys (126). It would seem that the role
envisioned for middle-class women is that of mother, evacuated of any sexuality – which, because it contaminates, is displaced onto the working class,
becoming another reason to sanction the regulation and containment of that
class.

There are other implications to rendering the figure of mother as pure and
asexual: as I mentioned earlier in commenting on Mr Darling, middle-class
masculinity, produced within industrial capital, may militate against men
growing up. As well, the fear of female sexuality as diseased and the resulting
celebration of the middle-class woman as "pure" and "chaste," occurring

within the context of a homosocial ethos haunted by fear of homosexuality, which is seen also as diseased, leads to suspicion of the sexualized body. This point is made by Barrie's depiction of the sexualized female as Tinker Bell, the fairy who is a coloured light and so without a body.

In mapping the construction of middle-class sexuality through *Peter Pan*, I want to draw attention to another aspect of the contrast between Tinker Bell and Wendy. Tinker Bell is a light, but one that is coloured, while Wendy – in keeping with tropes of purity – is associated with white. As Wendy and her brothers approach Never Land, Tinker Bell offers a feigned alert and tells the boys in fairy language that Peter wants Wendy shot (111). The boys shoot at Wendy, who has been *"fluttering among the tree-tops in her white night-gown,"* almost like a ghost. As if to emphasize the visual cue of the fluttering figure, one of the boys comments, "How white it is!" (111). Wendy is "it" and not "she," the feminine denied gender, looking ghostly but representing such a threat to the boyish culture of Never Land that she has to be shot down on the instruction of Tinker Bell, who pretends that the instruction comes from Peter. Women (or, at least, female figures – Tinker Bell is hardly a woman) are key to the regulation of sexuality, as evinced historically by the involvement of middle-class women in social purity movements; Tinker Bell's wanting Wendy shot is a mode of regulation, but one motivated by her selfish desire to have Peter to herself, and so she makes no pretence about serving the social good.

Multiple anxieties are at work in this scene, beginning with the implications of "whiteness." "Whiteness" is a crucial critical category in the production of discourse around race because, as Henry Louis Gates, Jr., reminds his readers in the introduction to *"Race," Writing, and Difference*, "Race, as a meaning-ful criterion within the biological sciences, has long been recognized to be a fiction. When we speak of 'the white race' or 'the black race,' 'the Jewish race' or 'the Aryan race,' we speak in biological misnomers and, more gener-ally, in metaphors" (4). Wendy's "whiteness" marks her purity and effectively announces visually that she is sexually pure. As we have noted, the legacy of the Contagious Diseases Acts was to mark working-class women as licentious and dangerous, carriers of disease that threatened to exceed the working class and infect the middle class. Taking my cue from Gates's comments, the force of the metaphoric deployment of whiteness in *Peter Pan* is a referent to the set of social understandings around the relation of feminine sexuality to class. Perhaps the latent anxiety around female sexuality resonates most strongly in Tinker Bell being a fairy, and so having desire but no body that might unleash that dangerous working-class desire.

The purity of whiteness figures strongly on another valence in *Peter Pan*. Through the figure of Tiger Lily, the stereotype of the over-sexed aboriginal figure is introduced. Like Tinker Bell, Tiger Lily desires Peter Pan. In an early manuscript, that desire is articulated through a rape fantasy:

TIGER LILY	Suppose Tiger Lily runs into the wood – Peter Paleface attack her – what then?
PETER	(*bewildered*) Paleface can never catch Indian girl, they run so fast.
TIGER LILY	If Peter Paleface chase Tiger Lily – she no run very fast – she tumble into a heap what then? (*Peter puzzled. She addresses Indians.*) What then?
ALL INDIANS	She him's squaw. (qtd. in Jack 169)

In a play marked by the negotiation of anxiety and filled with the play-wright's self-censoring (including the displacement to the stage directions of concerns about how industrial technologies impact on Mr Darling), *Peter Pan* starts to seem to be a play with an unconscious. Lurking in that unconscious is an anxiety about female sexuality as dangerous and, in the case of aboriginal populations subjugated in the colonizing enterprise of imperialism, wanting to be raped. To the contemporary reader, Barrie's depiction of the aboriginal is embarrassing, for, while the play depends on stereotypes of femininity – of the middle-class Wendy as the figure of mother, of the working-class Tinker Bell as self-absorbed in her desire for Peter – the early manuscripts, which feature a stronger presence of Tiger Lily, are horrific in their suggestion that aboriginal women so strongly desire white men that they want to be violently conquered through rape. While the rape fantasy does not figure in the version of *Peter Pan* that was finally staged, Barrie depicts the aboriginals as stereotypes of the primal and pre-social, so that the braves can say little beyond "Ugh, ugh, wah!" and Tiger Lily's command of language is only slightly better: "The Great White Father save me from pirates. Me his velly nice friend now; no let pirates hurt him" (129). Indeed, the use of "velly" sounds like a racist stage depiction of a Chinese person, suggesting that all who are not white meld into an undifferientiated "other." The deployment of the phrase "The Great White Father," mimicking the nineteenth-century appellations of Queen Victoria as the Great White Mother, signals that Never Land is not just a re-creation of the public school ethic – although it is that – but an invocation of Empire that ties the public school ethic to imperialism.

Jacqueline Rose, in *The Case of Peter Pan or The Impossibility of Children's Fiction*, devotes a chapter to issues of language. The chapter titled "Peter Pan, Language and the State," with the subtitle "Captain Hook Goes to Eton," offers a useful reminder that in Barrie's short story "Jas Hook at Eton," Hook's final words before jumping overboard are "Floreat Etona" (115). Given that the story was written in 1925, the contrast with the "plain" language of the play, written just over twenty years earlier, serves as another useful index of Barrie's anxiety about the changing world brought about by the industrial technologies of capitalism. The specifics of Rose's argument about the tension of various levels of language in Barrie's iterations of the Peter Pan story, at a time when there were state initiatives around literacy and more accessible education based on the deployment of a standardized vernacular, have limited applicability to the concerns of this paper. But her comments do draw attention to the use of language and its implications for maintaining class distinctions. Barrie has Tinker Bell's utterances unheard by the audience but clearly marked as being in a foreign tongue – that of the fairies – that needs translation and is ungrammatical (136). The figure of Tinker Bell, so innocuously presented as a disembodied fairy, is Barrie's management not just of the working class but of the working-class immigrant for whom English was not a first language. Similarly, Tiger Lily and her braves seem to have limited abilities in English, marking the xenophobia of the English middle class to the "other." It is Wendy, that figure of purity and the virtues of English womanhood, who has full command of English. To return to the earlier scene in which a "kiss" was interpreted by Peter Pan as a "thimble," R.D.S. Jack reminds readers that the issue is one of understanding referentiality: Wendy knows the referent to "kiss" and Peter Pan doesn't (232). The middle-class English woman is figured as the sign of purity, a repository of Englishness marked by her command of language.

To state what at this juncture must be patently obvious, *Peter Pan* is a fable of modernity, anxiously negotiating industrial technologies that produced a middle class predicated on instability and which encoded impossible roles for men and women. Given the circulating ideologies of manliness that involved notions of their agency, of being patriarchal masters in their immediate households and in that enterprise of nation predicated on a lexis of "family," middle-class men at the turn of the twentieth century seem to have been denied any actual way of becoming "real" men. The evolution of industrial capital inscribed their failure. But no less did it regulate middle-class women by locating them as asexual, pure figures whose "natural" inclinations to maternity became the sign of the inherent virtue of whiteness. Mr Darling may be *"really a good man as breadwinners go,"* but the implication is that "goodness" is accessible only to a middle-class woman like Mrs Darling.

The experience of the modern is that of the present or the very recent past, which is marked as different from the more distant past. This difference is, in effect, change, which, since the Enlightenment, Western culture has understood as cumulatively amounting to "progress" and, ultimately, to social betterment. Given that the various aspects of society do not function as discrete entities but are interrelated, change in one aspect has some degree of impact on others, including gender and sexual identities. Barrie's strategy for managing the anxiety is a nostalgic retreat to Never Land, the fantasy of boyish adventure, which rehearses the ethos of the public school and Empire. Never Land, as its very name suggests, is an impossibility, an idealization of what never was, because part of the strategy of managing anxiety about the changes that the modern brings is nostalgia for a (mis)remembered past now gone.

Selective remembering is not restricted to *Peter Pan*; it also characterizes the response to the play, as Twain's comment about it being an "uplifting benefaction" suggests. Twain forgets that Never Land is inhabited by dead boys who are ghosts. For the most part, the play's reception has been marked by its being read as a play for children, a jolly fantasy of fun-filled adventure. As a consequence, it is not included in the canon of modern drama, as if a work for children cannot tackle issues with the gravity of a writer like Ibsen. So, for example, Elaine Showalter writes,

New Women and male aesthetes redefined the meanings of femininity and masculinity. There were fears that emancipated women would bear children outside of marriage in the free union, or worse, that they would not have children at all. In the wake of Ibsen, women's oppression became the theme of successful plays by Arthur Pinero, Oscar Wilde, Harley Granville-Barker, and George Bernard Shaw.... (3)

Showalter's comment is instructive inasmuch as her list of playwrights who address issues relating to the shifts in gender and sexual identities celebrates those whose works anticipate, and are compatible with, changing roles for women and a greater social acceptance of homosexuality in the late twentieth century. In the move to inscribe a genealogy for the social movements of the present, Showalter and others ignore plays that do not seem politically "progressive." The remarkable longevity of *Peter Pan*, which receives more productions today than do the works of Pinero or Granville-Barker, suggests that it appeals to audiences. While much of the appeal is, no doubt, the highly theatrical fantasy of the play, this fantasy is a means of managing the anxiety of loss. It may well be that Barrie's anxieties resonate with audiences who are haunted by the loss that change brings and seek escape in fantasy.

NOTES

1 My thanks to Alan Filewod for his careful reading of an early draft of this paper. I owe a tremendous debt of thanks to the students in a senior seminar on dramatic literature that I taught at the University of Guelph in winter 2000. The course focused on ideologies of gender and sexuality in relation to nation in the late nineteenth and early twentieth centuries. The students' enthusiastic, thoughtful engagement did much to shape my thinking.
2 Bendure notes, "In addition to being something of a status symbol, Newfoundlands were also employed as canine nannies and personal companions, and saw great popularity as gun dogs. There is even a story from the last century of a husband trading his wife for a Newfoundland dog" (70).

3 Sedgwick notes in her introduction to *Between Men* that "'Homosocial' is a word occasionally used in history and the social sciences, where it describes social bonds between persons of the same sex; it is a neologism, obviously formed by analogy with 'homosexual,' and just as obviously meant to be distinguished from 'homosexual'" (1).

Bodies, Revolutions, and Magic: Cultural Nationalism and Racial Fetishism

Now, being in the movement was about change
Changing the injustices in our society
Changing the system that ignored our history in this country
But the movement changed something else ...
my wardrobe....
CHANGE ... TALK ABOUT CHANGE
[...] first you had an army jacket with lots of buttons on it
then to complete the look ... a beret
now blacks had black berets, Latino – brown berets
maroon was our color ... better with our complexion
[...] we were remaking ourselves
creating our own images and expressions
             – Nobuko Miyamoto, *A Grain of Sand*[1]

We might consider race in accordance with Judith Butler's useful conception of gender as constructed in terms of *a corporeal style*; in this sense the racialized body is also made meaningful through "the legacy of sedimented acts rather than a predetermined or foreclosed structure, essence or fact, whether natural, cultural, or linguistic" (Butler 274). The particular ways in which we perceive, interpret, and value racial difference in the United States today can be understood as a kind of 'performance' that takes its significance from not one but, in fact, many layers of social meaning that history has deposited on bodies. Some of these meanings are determined by racist ideologies disguised as "natural" or "biological" hierarchies of difference, "punitively regulated cultural fictions that are alternately embodied and disguised under duress" (273); others present somewhat more optimistic possibilities for racial performance.

Such a conception of racial performance is consistent with Michael Omi and Howard Winant's figuring of race as "an unstable and 'decentered' complex of social meanings constantly being transformed by political struggle" (55). Within Omi and Winant's terms of "racial formation," the civil rights period of the 1950s and 1960s figures prominently as the period of "the great transformation,"[2] where new social movements would "expand the concerns of politics to the social, to the terrain of everyday life" (96). The excerpt that opens this essay, from Nobuko Miyamoto's *A Grain of Sand,* a theatrical recollection of Miyamoto's experiences in the civil rights movements, recalls the quest for a 'new look' to accompany a nascent Asian American movement's pan-ethnic, diasporic, and collective politics. Miyamoto's playful reminiscence marks but one of the many new kinds of racial performance that emerged from this period. For her and others, such 'looks' went hand in hand with distinctive modes of thought and action; bodily style was inextricably linked to activism and revolutionary sensibility. For instance, Kobena Mercer notes that the wearing of Afros, the urban guerilla look of the Black Panthers, and elements of 'traditional' African dress such as the dashiki or the headwrap did indeed delineate "massive shifts in popular aspirations among black people," thus furthering "a populist logic of rupture" (107).

These bodily performances have clearly left their mark on how race is understood today. However, the particular cultural legacy of this period, like its political legacy, is still uncertain. Celebration of uniquely "black" or "Chicano" or "Asian American" modes of cultural expression has given way to a questioning of these often overburdened identity categories. In a recent essay on Asian American theatre, Karen Shimakawa describes her students' less than enthusiastic responses to a revival of Frank Chin's *The Chickencoop Chinaman* (originally produced in 1972):

For while, in keeping with the "retro" style currently popular, many of these young people affected the idioms (clothes and musical tastes) of the 1970s, they were utterly baffled by this artifact of the era; and post-play discussions revealed that, to their eyes, this play had very little to do with "Asian American identity" as they understood that concept (or even a hetero-masculinist version of it). Certainly, protagonist Tam Lum's jazzy, beat-poetic/stream-of-consciousness style of oration was part of their difficulty ("why can't he just talk like *regular people?*!" one student asked in exasperation) but their discomfort and bewilderment went far beyond their unfamiliarity with a particular aesthetic: the critique centered primarily on the appropriation of (stereotypes of) African American culture and discourse (Tam's childhood friend goes by "Blackjap Kenji," for example), heterosexist gender roles and simplistic, problematic renderings of multi-racial identity. Surely we had progressed beyond this level of identity politics, the students proclaimed; the Asian America represented in Chin's play, they insisted, was unrecognizable to them, discontinuous with the world they inhabited. (283–84)

It is not only Shimakawa's students who have difficulty seeing connections between "now" and "then." Current scholarly and critical work sometimes also tends to avoid or dismiss outright the hopelessly misogynistic, rigidly essentialist, or embarrassingly dated aspects of cultural nationalism, preferring instead the rendering of more hybrid, fluid identity categories that seem to articulate a "truly" liberatory politics.

Bearing this disavowal in mind, this essay tries to undertake a different kind of retrospective, one that is perhaps less quick to celebrate or criticize. It reviews some of the particular theatrical expressions of what might be called cultural nationalistic performance by looking at how such performances might function as *fetishes*, a term I have chosen both because it suggests the visceral impact and basic force that such racial performances invariably have and because such a term has also picked up – particularly in contemporary psychoanalytic and Marxist theory – a number of troubling associations. In the first two sections, I concentrate on how to assess cultural nationalism's unique racial performances, not only as such events present a "look" that might now be deemed somewhat outdated but also as this "look" indicates particular tensions of visibility and desire that are still very much alive. My aim is to try to understand better the connections between contemporary racial performance and some of the assertions and contradictions of racial representation that were brought into being several decades ago.

I. CULTURAL NATIONALISM AND RACIAL FETISH

Looking through contemporary plays written *about* the civil rights period, as well as plays written *during* that period, one can detect a recurring emphasis on how a change of consciousness must be linked with new modes of racial performance. In these particular moments of bodily transformation, onstage and offstage audiences are asked to re-evaluate how "race" is expressed and valued. One familiar example comes at the beginning of Act Two of Lorraine Hansberry's *A Raisin in the Sun*, in a moment when Beneatha proudly displays her newfound interest in Nigerian traditional dress and folk music. Her brother, Walter, springs up on the table and brandishes an imaginary spear, losing himself in a drunken fantasy of the African chief calling his men to war. This sequence begins as parody, a performance conditioned more by stereotype than by reality. Walter's chest-thumping declaration of "In my *heart of hearts* [...] I am much warrior!" rightly inspires the retort from his wife, Ruth, "In your heart of hearts you are much drunkard" (78). His comic rendition of the jungle warrior contrasts with the dignified urbanity of Asagai, the "real" African. In keeping with the play's gentle mockery of its African American characters' simultaneous idealization and ignorance of African culture and tradition, Beneatha parades her new clothing, *"fanning herself with an ornate oriental fan, mistakenly more like Butterfly than any Nigerian that ever was"* (76). At the same time, stage directions indicate a shift toward a different mode, where, in effect, we begin to see through "*the world of* Walter's *imagination*" (79). As he chants to his "Black Brothers," this turns from parody into a more compelling moment of transformation, one that is suddenly interrupted by the arrival of George Murchison, whose curt reply deflates Walter's hail of "Black Brother."

In this transformation, Walter's body is imagined as linking him to an idealized vision of his roots in Africa. In such a moment, he transcends his disenfranchised and debased state for a body that exudes masculine power and pride. Certainly this moment contrasts with his speech to his son, Travis, in the following scene, in which he promises Travis material wealth and prestige. If this later speech reinforces the ways in which Walter will continually disappoint his family, and himself, by relying on very limited notions of what the world has to offer him, the earlier moment of Walter's transformation into an African chief foreshadows the relief of the ending, when this repeated disappointment gives way and Walter finally comes into his manhood. This moment of transformation, then, is significant in how it performs a particular version of racial identity, one that gives power to the previously disempowered racialized body. A conception of race is central to the power of this moment, in which Walter's body is invested with blackness that brings to life his hidden but true identity. It is "*the inner* Walter *speaking: the Southside chauffeur has assumed an unexpected majesty*" (79).

What do moments such as these reveal about the larger workings of racial performance in this period, and how we should reassess these workings today? Certainly more is involved than surface changes in dress, hair, clothing, language, movement, elements that constituted the memorable "look" of more radical cultural nationalistic groups. Such stagings show that their particular modes of signifying race on the body were inspired not just by a taste for stylistic innovation and self-expression but by more deeply rooted desires and political principles. Theatre, like other forms of cultural expression, embodied the tension between liberal humanism's ideals of "integration" and cultural nationalism's insistence on the continued significance of racial difference.

Cultural nationalism differed most strongly from liberal humanist attitudes towards integration and civil rights in the very idea of performing race. Integrationists identified social progress with "the transcendence of a racial consciousness" (Peller 127). Integrationists saw race as the unfortunate product of long-standing racism: in order to eradicate institutional racism, one had not only to abolish racial categories but also to eliminate the performance of racial difference. Inherent in this idea was the figuration of race as simply a surface characteristic over an interior self that would be essentially the same for all people; in this view, once the legal barriers to racial equality were abolished, race would become obsolete. Thus integrationism rendered racial visibility in a way that both displayed it and made it ultimately meaningless, a surface characteristic over an essential self. Cultural nationalism saw this not only as a naive denial of the lasting effects of race but also, in fact, as a dangerous misjudgment. Racial stratification, deeply entrenched not only in legal segregation but also in the economic and social system, could not be so easily abolished; furthermore, to suggest that one does not see race is a pretense that allows racism to continue. In the words of Stokely Carmichael, "White America will not face the problem of color, the reality of it. The well-intended say: 'We're all human, everybody is really decent, we must forget color.' But color cannot be 'forgotten' until its weight is recognized and dealt with" (67). If integrationism advocated the discarding of racial markers as a false "mask" over the true self, the cultural nationalist relied on a particular performance – and a foregrounding of racial markers – as a political reminder of past and existing inequalities and a gesture of protest at the white domination of culture and power.

Thus these kinds of transformative stagings reflect certain cultural nationalistic principles in actively repudiating those potential erasures of racial difference. These moments insist on emphasizing – rather than devaluing – difference as manifested on definitively racialized bodies. The racial markers of skin, hair, facial feature, gesture, clothing, and language became signals of positive rather than negative difference: a difference that, moreover, must be intensified and heightened. Cultural nationalism's reinvention of race sought to stress what it felt to be an indelible and inescapable racial difference, both biological and cultural. In direct opposition to integrationism, cultural nationalism reiterated, even insisted upon, the racial body as a reminder – not just a declarative statement, but an imperative – of difference. Thus the characteristic way in which these performances made race not simply "reality" but, in fact, "larger than life" played up its spectacular qualities. If integrationism felt that race was a false "mask" over the deracinated real self, cultural nationalism insisted on the importance of the racial mask as a ritualized enactment that would bring forth the "true self."

Cultural nationalism unleashed not only a new vocabulary for the performance of racial identity but also a new paradigm for how one might relate to these bodies in the process of racial transformation as they become the objects of interest, attraction, and desire. These characteristic moments illuminate the new vision of the racial fetish that cultural nationalism produces and brings to the public eye. Again, although these kinds of newly racialized vocabularies of performance are sometimes criticized for being essentialist or self-segregating, they should be seen not just in their purely reactionary sense, as restating outmoded racial categories or promoting racial essentialism. Rather, they brought into being a less structured, less predictable *fetishism* – a projection of certain desires and fantasies on a particular form of the racialized body – in response to other, often programmatic erasures of race that were instituted in the spirit of integrationism and assimilationism. The heightening of racialized difference that is characteristic of these performances – the emphasis on see-ing certain elements or modes of bodily performance as distinctively "black" or "Chicano" or "Asian American" – presented yet another complex layer of sedimented meaning in the construction of race.

Relatively few plays wholeheartedly celebrated such moments; many choose to use them, as Hansberry's play does, to illustrate the tension inherent in these different conceptions of racial shape-shifting. Alice Childress's *Wine in the Wilderness* shows the misguided ideals of the artist, Bill, and his other college-educated friends through Bill's worship of his romanticized model of African beauty; it takes the "messed-up chick," Tommy, to show them the "true" face of black womanhood. The Chinese American Tam Lum in Frank Chin's *The Chickencoop Chinaman* experiments with a range of bodily and linguistic styles borrowed from African American cultural nationalism, ulti-mately never settling on a satisfactory language or body of his own. And in Ysidro R. Macias's satiric comedy *The Ultimate Pendejada*, the assimilated Robert and Mary Gomes convert into the more radical Roberto and María Gómez, only to find that their local Chicano Power friends are hypocritical and self-serving. It takes a trip to the *barrio* to show them that simply adopt-ing the "face" of activist politics is not enough: "Your ultimate pendejada was that you changed on the outside only, pero no en donde cuenta, not inside where it really counts" (164). Plays that work with these cultural nationalist racial fetishes, then, both celebrate potentially liberatory performances of race and, at the same time, express a wariness about them. By reinventing the expressive markers of appearance, gesture, language, hair, and clothing, cul-tural nationalism showed that it was possible to redefine both the form and the content of racial performances. At the same time, the desired fusion of such performances with coherent racial communities and liberatory politics was less successful.

Such works also stress the inherent problems in superficial equations of style and political action. Despite the calls for building political activism on a "cultural base" (Jones [Baraka] 124), there were obvious differences between changing legal and economic structures of power, on the one hand, and chang-ing culture, on the other. The uncertainty lay in determining the connection between these performances and an effective means of radical action. A change in dress, demeanor, and language did not guarantee political agency; in fact, emphasis on cultural expression alone potentially diverts attention away from activism. Moreover, the energy of racial reinvention could clearly be harnessed in less politically effective ways, turning such performances into what Tom Wolfe satirized as a form of "radical chic." Thus cultural national-ism had to insist again and again that its performances could not simply be reduced to empty posturing or mere "show," that they bore some deeper con-nection to liberatory philosophies and political action. But this intrinsic doubt was never resolved. Similar anxieties persist today, as certain multicultural initiatives are called into question for adopting the "face" of diversity without its political "heart." Contemporary corporate advertising, for instance, frequently employs not only a conspicuously multicultural-looking cast drawn from many racial groups but even elements of bodily style reminiscent of radical liberatory political movements. Hazel Warlaumont describes a 1972 *Cosmopolitan* advertisement for Smirnoff that featured an African American couple "dressed in stylish African apparel so characteristic of the 60s" and looking "casual, charismatic, and fun" (211); ads like these were the result of savvy marketing campaigns that targeted a "blossoming new youth market" (234). For Warlaumont, such "co-optation squeezed the novelty out of the threatening countercultural movement, reducing it to a worn-out cliché" (234). One might well argue that as time passes, such clichés lose even a minimal connection to the styles that spawned them. Appropriating the now familiar words of Gil Scott-Heron's 1970 poem, recent online advertisements for high-speed Internet connections and for Apple computers and others assure us that the "Internet Revolution will *not* be Televised" (emphasis added) or "the digital revolution will be televised."[3] Describing the 1998 Clio awards for television advertising, Jonathan Dee muses that "[e]very generation, every subculture, has its own icon of misappropriation by the advertising industry: Nike's use of the Beatles' 'Revolution,' for example, or Munch's 'The Scream' reanimated to sell Pontiacs, or Aaron Copland's 'Rodeo' used to encourage people to eat more beef, or Fred Astaire dancing with the vacuum cleaner, or Jack Kerouac posthumously hawking khakis" (67).

II. THEORIZING THE FETISH: THE "COLORED" BODY ONSTAGE

Magic opens doors to things we always knew because we carry the code in our bones, passing it along as blood memory and the murmured dreams of ancestors. (Cleage 161)

How best, then, to analyze and assess the mixed legacy of cultural nationalism? One way might be through an attempt to understand the different dimensions of fetishism. To call such signifiers fetishes is to confront headlong the complexity of desires for the racialized body and the different implications of staging these desires. It is precisely the fetishistic aspect of cultural nationalist performance that illuminates both its attractive powers and its attendant problems. How does one distinguish between the cultural nationalist fetish and other, less hallowed, versions of racialized styles – among them stereotypes, caricatures, and fantasies – that had previously been employed in the service of oppressive and exploitive systems? How do we evaluate such fetishism from the perspective of present-day corporate multiculturalism, in which the appearance of such "radical" bodies has less to do with revolution than with marketing?

The initial attraction to these bodies might first be explored through the most basic idea of the fetish, less Freudian or Marxist in conception (though these other conceptions of the fetish, as we shall see, will also come into play in important ways) than a so-called "primitive" fetish, an object that can lend its user extraordinary magical and transformative powers. To see this clearly, we might recall Frederick Douglass's account of his anticipated beating by the slave-breaker Mr. Covey in his *Narrative*. As he prepares to defend himself, Douglass is advised by another slave to carry on his person "a certain *root,* which, if I would take some of it with me, carrying it *always on my right side,* would render it impossible for Mr. Covey, or any other white man, to whip me." He does so and, despite his initial skepticism, becomes convinced of the "virtue of the *root*" (Douglass 102). Subsequently, he not only wins his fight with Mr. Covey but also gains a new sense of purpose:

This battle with Mr. Covey was the turning-point in my career as a slave. It rekindled the few expiring embers of freedom, and revived within me a sense of my own man-hood. [...] It was a glorious resurrection, from the tomb of slavery, to the heaven of freedom. My long-crushed spirit rose, cowardice departed, bold defiance took its place; and I now resolved that, however long I might remain a slave in form, the day had passed forever when I could be a slave in fact. (104–5)

A similar protective, empowering, and liberating potential is central to the fetishes imagined by these later cultural nationalisms' stagings of racially transformed and transformative bodies. These new racial identities were meant to be rebellious and subversive, their extreme demonstrations of dress, hair, language, and movement a direct affront to the erasure of racial differ-ence advocated by integrationism. They were also meant to be redemptive, to link their users to powerful sources of power, pride, and spirituality. The racialized body itself became a source of political and artistic "magic," a gen-erative creativity that fuels both artist and activist with a sense of domestic and diasporic collective identity. This fetishism of racial signification could well be put to effective use in the theatre, which, broadly speaking, endows bodies with its own kind of magic, power, eroticism, and potency.

The desire for a liberatory politics manifested *on* the body and through bodily performance – that one can "color" the once debased body in new ways – is one of the enduring legacies of cultural nationalism. That radical social change might be effected through witnessing these bodies, that they might awaken the consciousness and inspire transformation, remains at the heart of much of our conscious as well as unconscious sense of that theatre's power. A belief in such magic touches even the much more guarded hopes of contempo-rary theatre scholars, such as Dorinne Kondo, who seeks to "reclaim pleasure as a site of potential contestation that might engage, and at times be coexten-sive with, the critical impulse" (13), or José Muñoz, who suggests that queer artists of color work through a process of "disidentification" that involves "*recycling* or re-forming an object that has already been invested with power-ful energy" (39).

However, the desire for "colored" bodies – and the pleasurable and energizing magic that such bodies are thought to have – must also be viewed with some skepticism. This particular understanding of the fetish is inevitably shadowed by other, less optimistic ideas of what fetishism entails.

The racial fetish is certainly not unique to late-twentieth-century cultural nationalism. Much recent scholarship and criticism has called attention to how the "colored" body has been commodified, exploited, and exoticized as racial stereotype. These critiques often employ psychoanalytic readings to character-ize social desire, cultural fantasy, and theatrical pleasure. In this view, the fetish is the fantasized or literal image, object, or body part whose presence is psychologically necessary for self-gratification; the desire for the fetish is prompted by a deeply felt loss or anxiety over loss. This fetish is essentially a false front, something covering a "lack," signaling anxieties that can only be alleviated through repetitive and obsessive projections of signification. In his reading of Frantz Fanon, Homi Bhabha points out the parallels between the Freudian "primal scene" and the colonial encounter, those "dramas" that are "enacted *every day* in colonial societies" when "the child encounters racial and cultural stereotypes in children's fictions, where white heroes and black demons are proffered as points of ideological and psychical identification" (76). The racial stereotype, as Bhabha points out, is a type of fetish that is pro-duced out of the anxieties of the colonial encounter; it is out of his own "pho-bic myth of the undifferentiated whole white body" (92) that the colonizer produces the racial stereotype – fragmented, distorted, grotesque, repetitive – as a compensatory fetish.

Particular studies of theatre and performance have called attention to how larger social anxieties around race, nation, class, and gender manifest them-selves through these fetishisms of race. Eric Lott, for example, links the popu-larity of blackface minstrelsy to the anxieties felt by its primarily Northern, working-class white male audiences in antebellum America. Blackface min-strelsy, as performed by white male performers, signaled a racial dynamic that might be called the "pale gaze," a "ferocious investment in demystifying and domesticating black power in white fantasy by projecting vulgar black types as spectacular objects of white men's looking" (Lott 153). Such spectacular "black types" were clearly fetishistic in nature, and through the comic antics of blackface they turned into "uproarious spectacles for erotic consumption" (140). This kind of theorization of the racial fetish is also demonstrably useful in reassessing not only American popular theatre but also the works of well-known figures of modern drama (such as Artaud, O'Neill, Brecht, and Yeats, to name a few) whose appropriation of African and Asian traditional perfor-mance seems in keeping with the larger racial pathology of Western modern-ism. Shannon Steen, for instance, reads O'Neill's *The Emperor Jones* as "prompt[ing] and reflect[ing] a desire for control and mastery on the part of white spectators" and compensating for a particular "conception of self" held by O'Neill himself (347).

However effective in these instances, this understanding of the fetish as pathology cannot so easily be applied to cultural nationalism's renewed emphasis on race. However useful to illuminate the link between racist ideology and cultural representation, such models understand the fixation on racial difference only as the "improper" desire of the fetishist; the fetishist is cast primarily as a "white" racist, or, occasionally, as a person of color who has internalized racism and therefore may be guilty of "autoexoticizing" (Savigliano 2, 5, 144). Not only must the fetish then be "cured"; many cures entail a process of demystification, of destroying or divesting the fetish of any power that it has. The antidote most frequently prescribed is the healthy dose of the "real," some unexoticized, unfantastical version of representation (a cure often advocated in past calls for "minority" theatres to present "real" characterizations).[4] Cultural nationalism complicates this process by advocating new racial "types" to replace the old when it eschews the liberal humanist preference for a "deracinated" body.

Faced with overwhelming demonstrations of racial pathology (the obsessive preoccupation of "whiteness" with "Otherness"), it is hard to see the power of the racialized body as anything other than a symptom of some "white" illness. According to this view, we can see cultural nationalism's fetishism only as a misguided reaction to previous racial essentialisms, with the attendant worry that these new incarnations of racial difference will themselves become new forms of stereotyping. New versions of spectacular difference, then, become served up in order to placate social anxieties that – like racism – have never really gone away. This worry only intensifies if one understands fetishism as constructed through the ideology of capitalism as well as through the broader terms of racial pathology.

The psychoanalytic view of racial fetishism, as employed here, suggests that racism, while it may be deeply rooted, is ultimately correctable (through a reform of theatre practice and the strategic deployment of alternative, and presumably more "realistic," images). The terms of the commodity fetish pose a much more difficult problem. Commodity fetishism describes how capitalist society promotes a fetishistic consciousness, which invests objects and bodies with particular symbolic properties and value. Any desire to see the body of color, then, is tied to that body's value as spectacular commodity; the theatrical power of that body serves only to generate profit and becomes measured by its marketability. This problem is not prompted by bad intentions or even misjudgment on the part of theatre practitioners, but lies in the racialized body's transformation into commodity (as the body passes out of the hands of a specific local relationship and into circulation as a commodity). No longer are theatre productions calculated to rouse specific audiences, nor is their success necessarily dependent on their strong response, if, in fact, attendance is linked more to the need for entertainment or prestige (Baudrillard 49, 118) than to social reform. Theatre, like other forms of "recreation," may also be valued for its "distraction," the extent to which it actually prevents consumers from understanding the true nature of their alienation and dissatisfaction (Haug 120).

Again, such a view of fetishism complicates how we might understand the promise of cultural nationalist fetishes as magic: as challenging the social hierarchies and as instigating social reform. Michael Taussig has made the distinction between the precapitalist and the commodity fetish, the difference being that the precapitalist fetish is all about human relations ("person in product"), the commodity fetish about some independent value given to an object that in effect banishes its labor ("subjugate persons, who become dominated by a world of things – that they themselves created") (Taussig 28). Given this view, there seems little hope of rescuing some dimension of precapitalist fetish in this era of global capitalism. Such a situation makes us skeptical even of the recent successes of playwrights of color in producing for mainstream audiences. This wariness about the commodification of racial difference in the American theatre influences a number of contemporary readings. Using the Broadway and film productions of Luis Valdez's *Zoot Suit* as her examples, Yolanda Broyles-González suggests that the pressure to create a successful mainstream production may entail an "embellishment in production values" that may well overshadow "the play's actual substance" (190), thus "dilut[ing]" the play "for the sake of mass appeal" (213). Dorinne Kondo notes that Broadway plays such as *Rent* and *Bring in 'Da Noise, Bring in 'Da Funk* contain cogent political commentary on relevant social issues but also tend to "deflect attention from the political and from sharp social criticism through mobilizing the seductive pleasures of music, spectacle, and dance" (17).

The very terms of radical culture that seemed to promise "new voices" and the end of the white, masculine, heterosexual domination of the main stage seem instead to have been appropriated by an audience enthralled by their new ability to consume Others. The erotics of Otherness, so familiar to the American stage, is both reiterated and disguised by a new emphasis on liberal multiculturalism. Such a view denies the present stage frustration, complacency, and indecision inherent in contemporary American racial politics and suggests instead that there is real progress to be found in the selected inclusion of works by people of color. This imagining of theatre as both a cure for racism and the living proof of a newly pluralistic society would be targeted not so much at old racists but at more liberal audiences; here the consumption of these theatre works acts as a palliative, testifying to the myth that civil rights has actually worked to resolve racism. Thus racial fetishes in their new incarnation – as demonstrations of the power of colored bodies – work less to inspire audiences to social action and more to compensate for the loss of these radical energies. What is at stake is not so much whether these racialized bodies possess magic – for, judging by their entry into mainstream theatre, they undoubtedly do – but whether this spectacular power has any use other than the generation of profit. Thus a process is set up by which even the most rebellious words and images of cultural nationalism are ultimately co-opted into "radical chic," easily suiting corporate multicultural initiatives that embrace racial visibility only to disassociate it from political reform.

Such a co-opting seems part and parcel of the apparent demise of the spirit of radical activism in the decades after the early 1970s: political attitudes increasingly expressive of disillusionment, cynicism, complacency, and avoidance. The current state of progress toward racial equality has been characterized, since the 1980s, not only by excruciatingly slow or non-existent implementation of civil rights reforms but also by a powerful neo-conservative backlash and the persistence of racism in its many incarnations.

III. REINCARNATIONS

What other men have to woo and make exertions for can be had by the fetishist with no trouble at all. (Freud 154)

Ironically, then, the fetishist is the least likely of analysands to enter a psychoanalytic contract. He remains perfectly happy with his love object (an object unlikely to resist his wishes and fantasies). In all likelihood, if he enters analysis at all, it will be at someone else's request. (Grosz 145)

If we are to believe certain contemporary plays written well after the demise of this activism, the magic of cultural nationalist bodies refuses to die. Moreover, the continued resurrection of these outdated bodies cannot be explained away simply by nostalgia or postmodern pastiche. When they appear, they bring the full and complicated burden of their magical powers with them, challenging viewers to resurrect and harness the desire, pleasure, and energy of the racial fetish back into the service of radical politics.

Two examples may serve to illustrate the complex ways in which such bodies continue to be revived on the contemporary American stage. George C. Wolfe's 1986 revue *The Colored Museum* parodies a range of African American figures, including Aunt Ethel, a mammy figure; Normal Jean Reynolds, a teenage mother; Miss Roj, a finger-snapping drag queen; Junie Robinson, an African American soldier; and Lala Lamazing Grace, a flamboyant expatriate entertainer *à la* Josephine Baker. On the one hand, Wolfe's "museum" highlights the exaggerated and one-dimensional aspects of these characterizations; in his "The Last-Mama-On-The-Couch Play," a spoof of Hansberry's *Raisin in the Sun* and Ntozake Shange's *for colored girls*, characters such as "Walter-Lee-Beau-Willie" or the "Lady in Plaid" over-act their oppression until they are transformed into the cast of an "all-black musical" where "[n]obody ever dies" (29). On the other hand, these vignettes work not only to poke fun at stock characterizations but also to highlight more surprising secrets embedded within these flattened images. In the opening "exhibit," "Git on Board," Miss Pat, the perky stewardess aboard "Celebrity Slaveship" who tells her passengers "We will be crossing the Atlantic at an altitude that's pretty high, so you must wear your shackles at all times" (1), has her composure ruffled by the rhythmic drumming that persists throughout her attempts to control her passengers. The finger-snapping drag queen, Miss Roj, reveals a keen sense of political injustice and rage just barely contained by her drinking and dancing. Even the most wholly superficial of images, a glamorous couple who live "inside *Ebony* magazine. [...] where everyone is beautiful, and wears fabulous clothes" (9), describe feeling "[t]he kind of pain that comes from feeling no pain at all" (10). Many of these scenes suggest hidden emotions, anxieties, and secrets that inevitably arise to disrupt the seemingly imperturbable surface of these characterizations. This strategy holds true in "Symbiosis," in which a man "*in corporate dress*" (33) tries to throw away all the emblems of his youth. As he places various items in the garbage, mourning "[m]y first Afro-comb [...] My first dashiki [...] Eldridge Cleaver's *Soul on Ice* [...] The Temptations Greatest Hits" (33–34), he is confronted by a version of his younger self, the Kid. The Kid protests the Man's attempts to discard him, asserting that "regardless of how much of your past that you trash, I ain't goin' no damn where"; the Man finally winds up strangling the Kid, telling himself that he cannot afford even the ghost of his formerly radical black self ("I have no history. I have no past. I can't. It's too much. [...] Being black is too emotionally taxing; therefore I will be black only on weekends and holidays"). But just as the Man claims victory over his "rage," his younger self re-emerges from the trash can with a "*death grip on* THE MAN's *arm*," asking "What's happenin'?" (36–37).

This vignette satirizes the impulse to jettison the black activist past as if it were merely a fad; the Man treats his earlier body as simply a surface composed of choices in music, fashion, and books that he has outgrown. The Man's desire to kill his former self is, as he explains, a survival strategy in order to exist in a "changing" climate (34) that no longer values reminders of racial difference as *political* difference. However, the continued reappearance and power of the Kid illustrate the lingering power of the cultural nationalist fetish. The Man may seek to dispense with this past bodily incarnation as if it were simply one of these outdated, commodified styles that he can throw away, but the Kid cannot be put off so easily. "Symbiosis" states this tortured relationship between past and present most clearly, but the presence of cultural nationalism is felt throughout *The Colored Museum*, where "outdated" forms of racialized bodies maintain their hold over even the most seemingly apolitical "new" versions of the African American body.

A more extended example of this powerful intervention is Richard Wesley's 1988 play *The Talented Tenth*. Wesley depicts a group of African American men and women, former college activists now turned businessmen and professionals, whose affluence and conservative values contrast with the ideals of their youth. *The Talented Tenth* centers on the anxieties of one particular character, Bernard Evans, as he contemplates his personal and professional future. At the heart of Bernard's work ethic is W.E.B. Du Bois's charge that the "Talented Tenth," the relatively few African Americans who had access to education and power, should take responsibility for racial uplift. Bernard sees himself and his former classmates as

> the ones who were expected to build the ladder for our people to climb. [...] It didn't matter where you went to school, or how rich you became. You could even become President of the United States, or sit on the Supreme Court. The bottom line was always the same: helping the Race. Making our people's lives better. (408)

In the opening scene, Bernard reminisces about his interview with the successful African American businessman Griggs, who owns a small network of radio stations. Griggs charges Bernard to imagine racial progress as achieved through the arenas of money and power and to put aside his own self-indulgent notions of individual success:

> All you've got is duty, responsibility and the self-discipline that goes with it. It's the first seven generations after slavery that will suffer the most. They're the ones who have nothing to look forward to except struggle. They're the ones who have to bear the pain, make the sacrifices and fight the battles that have to be fought and won. Your trouble will always come when you begin to think that you deserve a good time; when you begin to think that the world is your oyster. You're generation number six, Mr. Evans. Your grandchildren can have the good time. Not you. For you, there's only struggle. (361)

Bernard takes Griggs's advice to heart, imagining his relationship to his work through a paradigm of racial progress, communal loyalty, and generational succession. In the first part of the play, this strategy seems to bear fruit. Bernard holds true to his mission, instituting a more confrontational and overtly political form of programming that will educate and inform black listeners; promoted to vice president, Bernard looks to "inherit" Griggs's radio stations.

However, the clear line of African American progress that is achieved through successive generations of "struggle" is soon threatened: first by the demonstrated penchant of Bernard's wife and friends for the emblems of material success and second by the proposed buyout of Griggs Broadcasting by Pegasus International, a white-controlled communications conglomerate. Bernard's college friends have lapsed into a state of narcissism and elitism;

their goals have become prestige and money rather than social change. Griggs, worn down by his own years of struggle to keep his company alive, finally justifies his decision to sell the company by telling Bernard that racial progress is best served by the material success of individual African Americans. He urges Bernard to accept the lucrative offer from Pegasus, telling him that it is better to be a "pragmatic businessman who looked the dragon in the eye ... and decided to wear an asbestos suit" than a "righteous revolutionary with no prospects" (387).

Bernard is the only one who defies this turn of events, criticizing and alienating his friends and seeking solace in an extramarital affair. What troubles him in particular is the widening gap between the poor and those successful African Americans like himself. Bernard is surprised by his own anger toward the "endless parade of poor downtrodden men holding squeegies [sic] in their hands, fighting each other over the privilege of wiping my windshield for fifty cents" (384–85). For him these men become living proof of his own failure to act as one of the "Talented Tenth":

> Instead of lamenting their sorry fate, I hated them because I knew there was nothing
> I could do to change their lives. They would always be there, day after horrible day.
> Their lives would never change. I had managed to grab the brass ring and I was
> being pulled up and away from them, floating higher and higher. I would survive the
> madness and they would not. (385)

Although civil rights presented more opportunities to middle-class African Americans, it did little to eradicate the poverty gap. In the present, the lack of true racial equality is often disguised by the new wave of middle-class affluence. Thus the affluent Bernard and his friends run the risk of thinking themselves "beyond" race, disassociating themselves from the continued poverty of other African Americans. The imagined link between rich and poor in the "Talented Tenth" model of race struggle will be disrupted if new generations of African Americans become enticed by their newfound luxury and privilege. Bernard thus experiences the conspicuous presence of poor African Americans as a kind of haunting; for him it presents an irreconcilable contradiction, the breaking of the promise of racial progress.

Such "haunting," as Avery Gordon suggests, infiltrates and interrupts the complacency of middle-class existence in America:

> But, and this is the very difficult part, haunting is *also* the mode by which the middle
> class, in particular, needs to encounter something you cannot just ignore, or under-
> stand at a distance, or "explain away" by stripping it of all its magical power; some-
> thing whose seemingly self-evident repugnance you cannot just rhetorically throw in
> someone's face. (131)

Interestingly, Bernard is haunted not only by these living reminders of the widening poverty gap but also by the memory of his former girlfriend, Habiba, who was killed fighting the revolution in 1960s Angola. Through actively conjuring up these various incarnations, Bernard keeps in mind the contrast between his current bourgeois lifestyle and the aspirations of his youth. In scene two, Bernard recalls how in college he and Habiba decided to join Martin Luther King's march to Montgomery and how Habiba's powerful "race memory" joined the protesters in the passion of collective revolution:

> Then, Habiba started shaking, gasping for breath, like she was convulsing. Suddenly, she opened her eyes and looked at me, saying she'd had a race memory. She was with a group of runaway slaves. Armed gunmen had chased them through a swamp. They were trapped with no way out. They began to sing, calling out to God, and the more they sang, the stronger they became. She saw the flash of the gunfire. She felt the bullets searing into her flesh. But she kept getting stronger. They ALL kept getting stronger. Then, Habiba screamed. Just like that. A scream like I'd never heard before. Everyone in the room just stopped. It was like we all felt what she felt. People began to moan and shout and chant. Bloods who'd stopped going to church and had sworn off the spirit possession of our parents and grandparents began to rock and shake and tremble – yea, they got the Spirit that night! (364)

Ironically, Bernard's powerful recollection is followed by his son's request for money to shop at the mall's "special holiday sale" celebrating Martin Luther King's birthday.

For Bernard, the bodies of both the living and the dead become fetishes that galvanize him into rejecting the pleasurable enticements of material success. Bernard's extramarital affair with Tanya is prompted both by his attraction to Tanya's resemblance to Habiba (both in her dark skin and "African" features and in her working-class background) and by his rejection of the values embodied by his wife, Pam (whose light skin and wealthy family connections originally made her attractive to the ambitious young Bernard). When Tanya angrily refuses to play the dead Habiba, rejecting his gift of a kente cloth and accusing him of living in the past, Bernard realizes that his dream of realizing Habiba in the flesh has to do with more than sexual novelty or simple nostalgia. His fetishism of Habiba becomes a means of reconnecting himself to his own desire to work in the service of a larger "racial uplift." By the end of the play, Bernard has refused Griggs's advice to work for Pegasus producing "infotainment" and lost his job; he has likewise ended his relationships with both Pam and Tanya. However, with the help of his African American consortium of backers, the "Diaspora Group," Bernard manages to outbid Pegasus and succeed Griggs as owner of the radio station. As he explains to Griggs, it is through making peace with the spirit of Habiba that Bernard can finally reconcile his past longing for revolution and his present, more pragmatic means of struggle. In keeping African American control over media and business, he succeeds in maintaining his own sense of the lineage of racial progress, even at the cost of his successful career and marriage. The final scene of the play mirrors its opening, with Bernard now lecturing his own son, who comes to him for a job, about his place in the "Talented Tenth" and the need for continued struggle.

In both *The Colored Museum* and *The Talented Tenth,* the emphasis is primarily on how former radicals have now been transformed into an upper-middle-class elite in danger of selling out along the lines described by Richard Wesley: "one day you cut your hair, shave your beard, put away your sandals, go from yippie to yuppie, nationalist to buppie. Everyone tells you you've done the right thing. And you wonder if you really have" ("One Struggle Over" 8). This transformation of the cultural nationalist body into yet another, far less radical mode of racial performance suggests the victory of conservativism, complacency, and capitalism, in which both psychoanalytic and Marxist versions of the fetish serve as key palliatives. As a sign of pathology or commodity fetishism, the fetish functions to compensate for loss and to ease anxiety or to reassure consumers of their social prestige and status and to distract them from other, less entertaining aspects of their lives. Still, these plays also stress how the ghosts of cultural nationalism – bringing to bear all their magical qualities – complicate these more comforting and comfortable varieties of fetishism that dominate contemporary American life. In both plays, the resurrection of the magic fetish of cultural nationalism is necessary in order to compel the fetishist towards a difficult reinvestigation of the past and a reassessment of the present.

Ultimately, it is the refusal of these bodies to go away, despite our continued disavowal, that signals the lasting importance of cultural nationalism's transformation of consciousness. Such racial performances have left their definitive mark on how we understand contemporary performances of racialized bodies, whether of the living or of the dead. At the very least, these fetishes maintain their hold in lingering desires continually seeking to realize themselves in the flesh, which disrupt our complacency, our security, and our ability to rest.

NOTES

1   *A Grain of Sand* premiered at the Los Angeles Theater Center in 1995. This excerpt is from an unpublished manuscript, courtesy of the author.
2   Omi and Winant have appropriated Karl Polanyi's terms for the introduction of market society in pre-capitalist England to illustrate the shift to a *socially* based politics in the contemporary U.S. (see Omi and Winant 194 note 2).
3   Advertisements for Medianet's FastPath DSL and for customers of Apple products

appeared in March 2001 at <http://www.fastpathdsl.com> and <http://www.apple.com/mediaarts/>.

4 See, for example, chapter 2 of my *Performing Asian America: Race and Ethnicity on the Contemporary Stage*.

Modernism and Genocide: Citing Minstrelsy in Postcolonial Agitprop

ALAN FILEWOD

The critical field marked by the term "modern drama" has from its earliest authorizations framed an intersection of rehearsable textuality and social subjectivity, or, as Raymond Williams famously put it in one of his earliest works, *Drama from Ibsen to Brecht,* of "convention" (3) and "structures of feeling" (8). The critical texts that have guided the development of the term "modern drama" organize the problem of theatrical modernism as one of giving form to the invisible and the unconscious and, through this, enacting a fantasy of the reclaimed "real" in which revelations embodied in performance supersede the reality of the external world. In this dominant mode, most famously summarized in English by critics such as Williams and Maurice Valency (and by several generations of contributors to *Modern Drama*), the fundamental subject of inquiry has been the explorations of playwrights and theatrical auteurs as changing material possibilities of theatre practice enable new dramaturgies and new narratives, typically coded as "perceptions" or "insights" into subjectivity.

Throughout the past century, these dialogues record a slippage between *modern, modernist,* and *modernity,* despite Williams's reminder that "[a]s catchwords of particular kinds of changes the terms need scrutiny" (*Keywords* 209). Under such scrutiny, the modern in "modern drama" marks an invented genealogy of critical and artistic practices that constructs a direct relationship between the prophecies of a select group of theatrical visionaries of the late nineteenth century and the increasingly localized and politicized practices of twentieth-century artists. (The definition of that select group, I might add, has been one of the favourite games of the genealogists of modern drama.) Against the recurring temptation to scrutinize "modern" to death, it might be useful to recall Walter Benjamin's caution that "[t]o determine the totality of traits by which the 'modern' is defined would be to represent hell" (544).

I want to approach a problem in the representations of race and empire in late-twentieth-century agitprop with the idea that "modern drama" has functioned as an instrument of canonization that enables structures of value in material practice – and has therefore functioned to disable, de-canonize, and devalue particular modes of production and representation. The texts to which I will refer are three panoramic historical agitprops from Australia, Canada, and Scotland. All three share markedly similar dramaturgical structures and performance strategies, which derive in some measure from a postcolonial populist nationalism produced by a common history of economic dispossession in the hinterlands of the British empire, and a shared resistance to the imperial coding of Englishness. But they also have in common tropes of racial impersonation that derive from the historical relationship between modernism and imperialism. My argument will be in two parts: first, that the decanonized location of agitprop destabilizes "modern drama" as a coherent category; and, second, that the recirculation of these tropes of racial impersonation reconfirms the imperial precepts of modernism in a narrative of cultural authenticity reclaimed through resistance. This resistance opposes the historical forces that have suppressed the imagined authentic and positions the consciousness of the modern against its invented prehistory. In this narrative, the act – and, through art, the declaration – of resistance proceeds from, recuperates, and witnesses authentic experience: of oppression, of community, of class, of nation. The rediscovery of this lost authenticity in the process of making and experiencing art is one of the defining conditions of theatrical modernism, a condition in which the situational aesthetics of agitprop have always been integral.

A longing for a fantasized authenticity, for a lost historical experience that can only be recovered through the nation-building projects of popular art and mass politics, underlies the fundamental precept of modernism in the theatre: that the enactment is in some way more real than the material world that enacts it. The terms of this recuperated reality have been historically variable, but they have in common an equation between recovery and resistance: they were racial for Wagner, national for Hauptmann, spiritual for Appia and theosophists like Roy Mitchell, political for Piscator and Brecht (and, on the other side of the ideological divide, for Coward; consider *Cavalcade*), psychical for Artaud. The quest to reconstitute an imagined authenticity recurs through all of these figures, suggesting that modernism is a metahistorical fantasy and, moreover, that as such it proceeds in large part from the European invention of race. In the social-Darwinist ethnographies that (re)scripted the racialized expansionist imperialisms of the late nineteenth century, the emerging teleology of the modern offered a fantasy of pan-European culture that rewrote the histories of nation-states as a discourse of organic bodies subject to biological processes of (invariably masculinist) growth, decay, and degeneration. As a metahistorical fantasy, modernism evoked the sphere of cultural production as a site of organic renewal, in which racialized national cultures were rescued from the degenerative oppressions of bourgeois sensibility.

In this reading, which is, of course, only one of many readings that decipher the complex of the modern, the field of contestation has been the cultural alignment of the avant-garde. In the theatre, the formative projects of modernity proposed by Wagner and later by Appia were predicated on the vision of a lost organic community made known and reconstituted through artistic practice both in the conventions and in the material organization of artistic work, which model the modernist vision of the national community. It is impossible to separate this vision – the vision of Bayreuth – from the imperial texts of racial and eugenic superiority. The fantasy of what Adorno, in reference to Wagner, called "repeatable acts of worship" (125) underlies the recurring inquiry into the relationship of form, ideology, and community codified in the idea of modern drama.

The compact between the avant-garde and fascism was the most extreme manifestation of the modernist recuperation of the lost community, especially in the early Nazi regime and in Italy, where Fascism itself was proposed as a modernist complex of technological futurism and racial community. But these examples are only the most sensationalistic of a tendency in which all of Western culture was deeply complicit. We tend today to be more at ease when speaking of modernism as politically and culturally resistant to the dominant ideologies that manufactured the militarized hell of the twentieth century. Williams contributed significantly to this tendency when he located Brecht as the climactic figure who reconfigured the tradition of modern drama. "Looking back from Brecht," he wrote, "we see the drama of the last hundred years differently: see its consciousness and its methods from the outside, in a fully critical light" (*Drama* 332).

Williams's attraction to Brecht was not just the result of an intellectual formation in the study of literature but also reflects the understandable ambivalence of a Marxist intellectual seeking uncontaminated models of left resistance at the point of the Cold War exposure of the crimes of Stalinism. His positioning of Brecht in the master narrative as the figure who rescued modern drama by clarifying its political possibilities is crucial because he elides the gap in which agitprop has been de-canonized. His location of Brecht was also a critique of what he called the "spectacular power" of the Piscatorian model of engaged popular theatre. Williams wrote of Ernst Toller that his "frantic typification" was a "narrow" dramatic method (*Drama* 297) that produced "a slogan summary of experience" (302). Brecht, in contrast, expressed "the power of a major writer: a way of seeing that permanently alters dramatic possibilities" (332).

The situational contingency of agitprop has been an unspoken problem in modern drama because it attacks the fundamental proposition of the dramatic as the repeatable, scripted text, and this problem has been compounded by the general, but by no means accurate, perception that agitprop was in its origins wholly identified with the propaganda campaigns of the Communist International. Virtually all studies of twentieth-century agitprop focus on the practices of groups and movements organized by or in sympathy with Soviet Communism. This is particularly true of studies of the workers' theatre movement of the 1920s and 1930s, but it is also the case with the second-generation agitprops of the 1970s. Few studies recognize the less organized, but no less real, relationship between agitprop and other political movements, including dissident anti-Stalinist Marxist tendencies and social democratic populist movements as well as right-wing populist organizations (especially in Germany and North America) in the 1930s. Despite the theoretical claims of mainstream Communist writers, the techniques of agitprop easily crossed ideological boundaries. The problem of agitprop has been not its complex relationship to discredited political movements but, rather, the fact that as a resistant theatrical form, it arises out of a partisan engagement with mass political practice, regardless of ideological location, and this engagement is an identifying condition of its textuality.

Notions of modern drama have always had an ambivalent history of engagement with practice. The recognition of performance practice as an unrepeatable textual element can be discerned as early as Stanislavsky and Meyerhold, who devised analytic structures that textualized the performing body of the actor and re-centred dramatic narrative to the *mise en scène*. But the notion of the rehearsable text has been inescapable to the extent that even Williams could not, in his very early work, see his way out of a canonicity framed by reproducible literariness. What he did not see in Toller, and in the vastly diverse field of agitprop that Toller drew on, was the literariness of *mise en scène*. For Williams, theatrical "techniques of production" had to be differentiated from dramatic convention, although they might be conventionalized into dramatic form by artistic genius (*Drama* 320).

Against this dismissal of agitprop as animated sloganeering, I want to propose that agitprop is not only an expression of theatrical modernism, and of its corollary, modern drama, but is similarly situated in a historical crisis of race. Although its theorists argued that agitprop was a counter-discourse that corrected the formalism of theatrical modernism, its machine aesthetics derived from the constructivism of early Soviet *mise en scène* and the theatrical expressionism of the Weimar republic – including the Bauhaus. No less than the psychosocial dreamscapes of Strindberg, agitprop proposed a reconstruction of the real. The transcendent reality was not the subjective consciousness of the spectator but the activation of political community through performance that creates, marks, and regulates moments of historical crisis. A crucial recurring element, and one that resurfaced in the 1970s, is that the contingent aesthetic conventions of agitprop reconstitute suppressed cultural properties of marginalized communities. This is the reverse side of Wagnerian modernism and its fantasy of organic community: race transmutes into class as the homogenizing community made known and recognized by its participation in theatrical conventions. In that sense, Appia and agitprop may emerge from the same set of cultural precepts. Like other modernists, the proponents of agit-prop in the 1920s and 1930s theorized its formal aesthetics as a modelling of consciousness.

The recovery of agitprop in the early 1970s similarly announced a set of discovered tactical processes generated by political necessity. But the forms of agitprop produced by groups such as the three I am concerned with here (7:84 in Scotland, the Mummers Troupe in Newfoundland, and the Popular Theatre Troupe [PTT] in Queensland) were also recovered through textual sources. This observation goes a long way towards explaining the transnational circu-lation of techniques and practices that – just as in the 1930s – generated per-formances that were remarkably similar but developed independently. For the generation of politicized theatre workers that sought to recuperate a practice of mobile people's theatre in the community, agitprop referred to a notion of working-class culture known by its resistance to the dominant dramaturgies and stagings of the professionalized theatre. This working-class culture was "discovered" to be anti-illusionist, gestic, presentational, bawdy, parodistic, and narrative – over and over again. The markers of iconoclasm – the announcements of refusal to participate in the dramaturgy of dominance – are commonly (re)presented as essential practices. This reworking of the trope of proletarian culture announces situational practices as class properties. It is per-haps most articulately argued by John McGrath (in *A Good Night Out*) and Chris Brookes (in his memoir of the Mummers Troupe, *A Public Nuisance*), both of whom write from an unproblematized structuring of class, nation, gen-der, and ethnicity.

The basic similarity of these agitprops was not simply a synchronic redis-covery of class-based structural principles but was in some measure produced by a material circulation of textual sources. The formative discovery of the counterculture of the 1960s' public protest had been the performative nature of the street demonstration. Locked out of access to conventional media chan-nels as a means of promulgating unpopular opinions, protesters discovered the "theatrical" power of taking to the streets to demonstrate dissent, just as they discovered the power of the underground press. "Performance" became a nat-ural mode of communication, which led to the discovery of cheap theatrical means to disseminate dissident views.

For theatre workers throughout the English-speaking world, much of this work was promulgated through the pages of radical theatre journals, such as *TDR*, *Theatre Quarterly*, and *Gambit*. They circulated what were in effect tex-tualized strategies that quickly become canonically dramatized. By the early 1970s, the explosion of guerrilla theatre in the student movement had gener-ated a dazzling variety of forms and texts, most of which were un-theorized and unrecorded. The canonical idea of agitprop was recovered both from textual searches for historical precedents that construct continuities with a history of engagement and from what Raphael Samuel has called the theatre of memory, that vast and unofficial archive of history as a "social form of knowledge," an "ensemble of activities and practices in which ideas of history are embedded or a dialectic of past–present relations is rehearsed" (8).

The recovery of agitprop sought historical sources to confer tradition and political coherence on this eclectic practice; in one sense it was an attempt to realign the counterculture with the working class that it had, in North America at least, repudiated.[1] The search for what Howard Brenton, in 1975, called "communist tools" (11) offered a way out of this impasse; to be effective, revolutionary theatre had to align with the working class (still undifferentiated as "the people," or sometimes "working people," in North America). And for that to happen, tools had to be found.

The textualization and recirculation of agitprop can be located in a set of publications in the early 1970s, as critics on the left began to interrogate the guerrilla theatre movement. In North America, three books published in the early 1970s were particularly important in this process. The first was Karen Malpede Taylor's *People's Theatre in Amerika* (1972), which identified the workers' theatre movement of the 1930s as a prehistory of contemporary radicalism, reiterated the transcendental libertarianism of the American counterculture movement, and valorized the most famous of the politicized avant-garde theatres, the Living Theatre. Her book was followed in the next year by Henry Lesnick's mass-market paperback anthology of several dozen guerrilla theatre texts, *Guerrilla Street Theater*, which attempted to document the range of the form and at the same time argue its limitations, chiefly identified as the anti-working-class bias of middle-class students. Arguing that the agitprop of the 1930s was "the major American progenitor of contemporary guerrilla theatre" (21–22), Lesnick appended a selection of documents from the American workers' theatre movement to his collection of street texts. In 1974, Jay Williams added another, less influential, link to this genealogical structure with his sentimental narrative history of the New York theatre scene of the 1930s, *Stage Left*.

At the same time, British researchers were undertaking more analytical research into sources in an attempt to clarify the fundamental problem of a radical theatre that seemed to have been successful and yet had obviously failed to bring about the revolution it so vehemently sought. From its inception in 1971, *Theatre Quarterly* systematically recuperated the "lost" history of the radical theatre, publishing articles on Unity Theatre, Theatre Workshop, the Workers' Theatre Movement in America, the Living Newspaper Unit of the Federal Theatre Project, and, of course, Brecht. Following the efforts of *TQ*, researchers sought to uncover not just historical data but the buried debates on aesthetics and class manifested in the work of these companies. Typical of many, but more diligent than most, were Richard Stourac and Kathleen McCreery, who took time out from their work with Red Ladder and Broadside Mobile Workers' Theatre in Britain to engage in the research that produced their 1986 book, *Theatre as a Weapon*. Similarly, in 1976 Robin Endres and Richard Wright excavated a suppressed history of Canadian workers' theatre texts in their collection *Eight Men Speak*, which reiterated the increasingly familiar argument of historical continuity of practice.

The obvious failure of the guerrilla street theatre movement clearly indicated a need to engage with a broader struggle, and the academic project of recuperating precedents offered theatrical models. As guerrilla theatre-makers carved out a niche on the fringes of the theatrical profession, they resituated their work; what had been guerrilla street protest was now historically legitimized agitprop. But the awareness of precedents, abetted by heavy doses of Brechtian theory, was not in itself sufficient to forge links with working-class struggle. The generational hostility to authority remained coupled with a naïve, occasionally arrogant self-righteousness. The central assumption of much of this early experimentation was that working-class people needed to be made aware of the nature of their exploitation. They needed Marxist analysis as a means of understanding the sources of their exploitation, and they needed an intellectual vanguard invariably composed of young, middle-class activists to explain it to them.

What audiences saw (and workers more often ignored) in these agitprops were clever pastiches that lampooned authority and communicated attitudes rather than analysis through gags and slogans. The dramaturgical forms of these shows derived from the implementation of the historical consciousness of agitprop with the practice of collective creation, which was both a political principle that enacted a critique of creative hierarchies and a material condition of theatrical organization. In 7:84, the Mummers, and the PTT we see the same operative vocabulary: documentary quotation, polemical direct address, and a heavy emphasis on citations of popular working class-culture (the ceilidh in 7:84; the evangelical meeting in PTT; and in the Mummers, vaudeville, Punch and Judy, and minstrelsy). These popular forms are drawn from a social archive of ideas of traditional culture; although they are always textualized, they are nonetheless presented as the authentic expression of a continuity of working-class cultural resistance. The fallacy of this presentation is particularly problematic in the recurrent citation of genocide that I have already suggested is one of the predicates of theatrical modernism and which these plays attempt to locate as a prehistory of contemporary political activism.

I focus on the Mummers Troupe as the typifying example because its work, largely unpublished and culturally remote, is the least known and, as such, lies outside the normative domain of "the drama."[2] I begin, then, not with a textual quotation but with a scrawled note and a memory. The note is an entry Chris Brookes wrote in his rehearsal diary while working on his first show, a panoramic comic-book history play variously known as *Newfoundland Night* or *Regular Weekly Entertainment: Cards 50¢, or, The Mummers History of Nfld* or *Cod on a Stick*.[3] Early in the collective process, as actors were plundering the social archive of traditional forms, Brookes envisioned "a bit w. merchant & fisherman as Legree and Sambo" (Rehearsal diaries n.pag.). That bit never made it into the show, although the underlying trope of racial impersonation certainly did. Three years later, it warped into the structural principle of a play called *What's That Got To Do With the Price of Fish?*, another panoramic agit-prop that examined the history of the fishery as a colonized Third World economy. This is my memory of the opening of the show as dancing fishery workers sing,

Newfoundlanders sing and dance
Do da, do da,
Inshore fishery got no chance
Oh da do da day. (Mummers Troupe, *What's That* 1)

This may not be a technically accurate citation of minstrelsy, but it is a citation of the Mummers' *idea* of minstrelsy as recovered from the theatre of memory. That Brookes was deliberately citing the minstrel show as a metaphor of Newfoundland's colonial history is clear from a rehearsal diary note in which he wrote (in words that I expect would cause him great embarrassment today but which clearly show their textual origins), "what makes a stage nigger a la minstrel show? what makes a caricature? how do we [...] make Nfld stage niggers?" (Rehearsal diaries n.pag.). The minstrel show, Brookes wrote, was "[o]bsequious yet subversive." He overlooked the minstrel show's origins in Jim Crow racism, preferring to see it as a subversive replay of stereotyped images. And so *Price of Fish* entertained audiences across Canada by legitimating its claim of oppression with a citation of white images of black America.

The claim to oppression was also a claim of aboriginality, just as it was in the Highland plays of 7:84. But that sense of historical displacement and erasure was problematic for the Mummers because Newfoundland's culture of working-class resistance was founded on the only act of total genocide in the British empire: "only" in the sense that Native aboriginal culture was not just enslaved and erased in Newfoundland, but every single indigenous Beothuk had been killed, through disease, famine, and murder, by 1830. Not that the Mummers overlooked the genocide of the Beothuks: in *Newfoundland Night*, the Beothuks are assigned a solemn episode in a play composed otherwise of insanely parodistic comic routines. But the sentimentality of the scene, a montage in which polyphonic voices recite the words of settlers who took part in genocidal hunting expeditions, is entirely directed to the fact of extinction. Beothuk culture is acknowledged only in the manner of its ending and represented only through the voice of a white actor who constructs a counter-

narrative to the documentary voices by reciting a sentimental inscription from
a settler gravestone that invites the audience to transfer familiar pathos to the
death of a people: "Your end was very sudden, you made us weep and cry. But
the saddest part of all dear Mary you never said good-bye" (Mummers
Troupe, *Regular Weekly Entertainment* 24). Newfoundlanders would recognize the point of transference in the name of "Mary," both a common local
name and an allusion to Mary March, the baptismal name of the last Beothuk.

In effect, the Beothuks provide a textual prehistory of oppression that
enables the Newfoundland settler culture to displace its complicity in genocide
into a shared history, in which the Newfoundland fisherman assumes the role
of imperial victim. This surrogation is iterated most succinctly in "The Five
Minute History Lesson" scene that begins the Mummers' most famous play,
They Club Seals Don't They?, a 1978 pro-sealing intervention in the international seal hunt controversy that had vilified Newfoundlanders as bloodthirsty
killers of baby seals. In this scene, a typifying fisheries couple replay 400 years
of displacement and exploitation by the English, the French, the English again,
and Upper Canadians. Sealing operates as a signifier of nation and, in effect, as
an aboriginal right. The scene concludes with a sentimental monologue by a
woman who remembers the last time she saw her father before he died on the
ice while sealing. In metonymic pathos, the monologue, like the eulogy transposed onto a memory of the Beothuks, enacts the death of Newfoundland, the
passing of tradition, the authenticity of local experience, and the reconstitution
of the postcolonial subject in the memory of a kind of pre-contact.

The claim of indigeneity that runs through the work of the Mummers, from
the foundation of popular traditions to the claim of ancestral right, requires a
conceptual renegotiation of aboriginality to resolve the deep and culturally
stressful contradiction between the sense of indigeneity and the awareness that
it is built upon a history of genocide and invasion. In the Mummers Troupe,
this contradiction found a resolution in the proposal of an ethnicity produced
by oppression.

At the same time that the Mummers were assembling their theatrical pan-
oramas from textualized citations and parody, John McGrath was producing a
very similar play with 7:84 in *The Cheviot, the Stag and the Black Black Oil*.
This is probably the most famous of the panoramic agitprops, in part because
of its cultural location and in part because of the international circulation provided by a major publisher, Methuen. Like *Newfoundland Night*, *The Cheviot,
the Stag and the Black Black Oil* encloses citations of racial impersonation in
a structure of documentary collage and traditional performance. In a notable
moment in the play, the cast follow the cleared Highlanders across the ocean,
to Canada, and replay the encounter with aboriginality. We hear the "[s]ound
of Indian drums, war-whoops, jungle birds, coyotes, hens, dogs barking. Book
turns to an Indian setting. Enter RED INDIANS. They dance and then freeze"
(23). The "Red Indians" creep up on the sturdy Highlanders with "toma-

hawks" raised, and their dialogue consists of the "ug" that confirms them as cited stereotypes reclaimed from popular culture. As was the case with the Mummers' plays, racial impersonation is a tactic of political alignment and shared history, a point underscored by the "French Northwest Trader" who says of the aboriginal figures,

> These are my little friends. They give me furs, beaver skins, Davy Crockett hats and all the little necessities of life. I give them beads, baubles. V.D., diphtheria, influenza, cholera, fire water and all the benefits of civilization. (*Cheviot* 27)

To ensure that the point is absolutely clear, an actor then steps out of character and announces,

> The highland exploitation chain-reacted around the world: in Australia the aborigines were hunted like animals; in Tasmania not one aborigine was left alive; all over Africa, black men were massacred and brought to heel. In America the plains were emptied of men and buffalo, and the seeds of the next century's imperialist power were firmly planted. (29)

That same structure of colonial genocide as an episode in European experience that traumatizes postcolonial modernity replays in the work of the Popular Theatre Troupe's 1975 *The White Man's Mission*, in which genocide is staged in the form of a Pentecostal tent meeting. The same pattern of popular culture citations appears: vaudeville turns, "I say, I say" cross-talk gags, and gestic cartoon metaphors. *The White Man's Mission* is an explicit attack on the policies of genocide that enabled the colonization of Australia, and, whereas the Mummers represented the victims of genocide through absence, and 7:84 through parody, the Australian actors signified aboriginality in the parodistic frame by means of a black cape: blackness reduced literally to material signification. Again, minstrelsy is explicitly cited as a tactic of political legitimation, as this episode indicates:

> NICK   ... To the American Indians, and the Australian Aborigines, who by so generously allowing themselves to be exterminated, and by giving so freely of their land, have made possible the fulfilling of the white man's manifest destiny.
> ALL   To the injuns and the boongs.
> NICK   To those Africans and Polynesians whose generosity in labour have laid the foundation of our common wealth.
> ALL   To the niggers and the Kanakas.
> NICK   Brother, would you give us a song to the departed blacks?
> DUNCAN   There was an old nigger
> And his name was Uncle Ned
> But he's dead long ago, long ago,

He had no wool on de top of his head
In de place where de wool ought to grow. (Fotheringham and Hunt 206)

It is not enough, I think, to observe that the re-inscription of minstrelsy that deploys white bodies to revive the cultural memory of racist imaging is problematic at best and callously racist at worst. Theatrical tropes are ways of knowing; they not only reconstitute imperial epistemes, and the gaze that fixes them, but actively constitute knowledge. In the struggle to enact postcolonial analysis in these plays, which are typical of many others, the engaged theatre workers could recognize the erased bodies only through the performative texts of imperial genocide. They articulate genealogies of aboriginality and victimization as the conditions of revolutionary refusal but finally reiterate the colonizing strategies that expropriated the text of aboriginal authenticity. I use "expropriate" here rather than the more common "appropriate" because this was not simply a process of *assuming* the properties of aboriginality; it was at the same time a *divestment* of those properties from their erased origin to articulate colonial nationalist difference and, ultimately, to enable narratives of immemorial nationhood. These three plays locate postcolonial nationhood in a history of popular resistance, but these histories are deeply complicit in the fantasy of rescued authenticity that is the vision of theatrical modernism. The failure of postcolonial agitprop lies in this notion of authentic resistance, in which the representation of resistance declares itself as resistance in praxis but in the end licenses the narrative strategies of oppression and replays the genocide that it expropriates.

NOTES

1 The discussion of the recovery of agitprop from textual sources in the 1970s borrows heavily from my work with David Watt on the history of labour-engaged theatre. See Filewod and Watt.

2 The work of the Mummers Troupe is largely unrecorded, and most of its playtexts remain unpublished. The papers of the Mummers Troupe are collected in two main collections. Correspondence and rehearsal diaries are the personal property of Chris Brookes and remain in his possession. They are indicated below as "Chris Brookes papers." The Centre for Newfoundland Studies at Memorial University of Newfoundland holds an archive of Mummers Troupe papers, including clippings, documents, videotapes, audiotapes, and typescripts. Both collections contain duplicate copies of promotional materials, typescripts, tapes, and administrative records.

3 The title of the Mummers' 1973 panoramic history changed several times, according to the time and place of the performance. Promotional flyers used both *Newfoundland Night* and *Cod on a Stick*. The typescript (itself a transcription of an undated performance) is entitled *Regular Weekly Entertainment: Cards 50¢, or, The Mummers History of Nfld.*

August Wilson, Doubling, Madness, and Modern African-American Drama[1]

HARRY J. ELAM, JR.

My first association with August Wilson came in the spring of 1987 when I was cast in the Studio Theater's production of *Ma Rainey's Black Bottom* in Washington, DC. This was the second professional production of the play, and so August Wilson came in from Minneapolis to see the production. It was a hit and ran for over twelve weeks, well into the swelteringly hot and humid DC summer. I played Ma's stuttering nephew, Sylvester. Sylvester's – and my – shining moment occurs well into the second act, when, after unsuccessfully stuttering through two previous attempts to record the intro to the title song, "Ma Rainey's Black Bottom," with Ma's coaxing he/I steps trembling up to the mike and produces a stammer-free rendition. "Alright, boys, you done seen the rest ... now, I'm gonna show you the best. Ma Rainey's gonna show you her black bottom" (Wilson, *Ma Rainey* 69–70). After performances, older black women would amble up to me and say, "Son, let me hear ya' talk!" And I would explain that I really did not, in fact, have a speech problem.

Sylvester marks Wilson's first venture into a form of character that becomes a repeated trope in his dramaturgy, one he develops through Gabriel in *Fences,* Hambone in *Two Trains Running,* Hedley in *Seven Guitars,* and Stool Pigeon in *King Hedley II:* figures who appear mentally or physically handicapped. Paradoxically, in Wilson's works those characters who appear mentally impaired, besieged by madness, unable to grasp the reality of the world around them, represent a connection to a powerful, transgressive spirituality, to a lost African consciousness, and to a legacy of black social activism. By "madness" here I mean a condition within these figures that operates on both symbolic and literal planes. Their madness has both individual and cultural significance; it both constrains and empowers these characters. Unlike the others, Sylvester does not suffer from madness; his sense of consciousness or activism is rather nascent. Nonetheless, his act of delivering the song intro without stuttering is a moment of personal and collective transcendence that benefits the gathered community. As such, it serves as precursor to the redemptive acts and transgressive rituals performed by these other figures in Wilson's subsequent dramas, rituals that will be the focus of this paper. In addition, as demonstrated by Ma Rainey's gestures of accommodation and support toward Sylvester and even by the comments of the older black women who hovered around me after performances, Sylvester's difference and deficiency do not isolate him from the community in Wilson's work. Repeatedly, others – women in particular – act to incorporate and nurture this difference within the bounds of the community. Wilson's mad figures operate in ways that reconnect their particular African-American community spiritually and psychologically to its history, to the African in African-American experiences. Madness enables these characters to mediate both figuratively and literally against discord, for harmony, and for communal and cultural change.

RACIAL MADNESS

Significantly, through his use of madness, Wilson repeats and revises a concept that I want to suggest has played a critical role in African-American modernism, its cultural practices as well as its social directives and philosophical treatises: the notion of "racial madness." This term refers to a trope that became operative in clinical practice, literary creation, and cultural theory in the modern period as artists, critics, and practitioners in all these arenas identified social and cultural roots for black psychological impairment. While I will ground racial madness within a particularly American context, I want to point out that in his theory and practice Frantz Fanon – the Algerian psychiatrist/ philosopher whose seminal works of the 1950s and 1960s became manifestos for black revolutionary change in the 1960s and 1970s and have re-emerged at the forefront of postcolonial studies in the 1990s – believed that the madness, the mental disorder and the melancholia of the colonial subject, was a direct product of the social and political circumstances of colonialism. As François Vergès argues, Fanon's "psychology was a sociology of mental disorders" that linked the symptoms of madness to the cause of freedom (52). Similarly, in modern America, racial madness was inextricably connected to the abuses of racism and oppression, as well as to the struggle for black liberation. My point here is not to pathologize blackness. Rather, by foregrounding this concept of racial madness, I want to recognize the relationship of and work between the clinical and the philosophical, between the literal and figurative symptoms and significance of this disease, always conscious of the cultural and social orientations of this condition. Racial madness was and is not simply a mental condition, nor simply a social one, but one that nevertheless demands a healing. Because of the complexities of the condition, this healing must conjoin the social and psychological and even the spiritual, and this, I believe, is where Wilson's madmen enter and what they attempt to accomplish.

As a critical trope, racial madness and its accompanying theories separate black modernism from the more recognized and established principles of white Western modernism. For if Western modernism, as noted by Jürgen Habermas and others, is characterized by a break with the past and a desire to experiment with new forms in the wake of progress, black modernism is marked, according to W.E.B. Du Bois and others, by a doubling and dichotomy: the desire to return to or renegotiate the past, the moments of initiating ruptures, the tragic separation from Africa, the horrors of the slave trade, the terrors of the Middle Passage, coupled with the push to move forward. Du Bois writes famously in *The Souls of Black Folk,*

[T]he Negro is a sort of seventh son, born with a veil, and gifted with second-sight in this American world, – a world which yields him no true self-consciousness, but only lets him see himself through the revelation of the other world. It is a peculiar sensation, this double-consciousness, this sense of always looking at one's self through the eyes of others, of measuring one's soul by the tape of world that looks on in amused contempt and pity. One ever feels his twoness, – an American, a Negro; two souls, two thoughts, two unreconciled strivings; two warring ideals in one dark body, whose dogged strength alone keeps it from being torn asunder. (45)

Du Bois suggests that this double consciousness provides African-Americans with a special and unique perspective on the American world, a "second-sight." Hortense Spillers argues that "DuBois was trying to discover – indeed, to posit – an *ontological* meaning in the dilemma of blackness, working out its human vocation in the midst of overwhelming social and political power. It was not enough to be seen; one was called upon to decide what it meant" (104). Thus, for Spillers, double consciousness requires a self-reflexivity on the part of black subjects as they consider who they are and how they are perceived within white America. Writing at the same time as Sigmund Freud, Du Bois argues that the struggle to be both African and American requires negotiating a duality that can be debilitating.

In a move that is purposefully provocative, then, let me suggest here that this double consciousness is a form of racial madness that has a direct impact on modern African-American cultural production. It is a madness because African-American subjectivity and identity must always be viewed in terms of a splitting, ruptures and loss, inclusion and exclusion: a maddening experience. Sandra Richards notes that through his twentieth-century dramatic cycle August Wilson intends to "help African-Americans more fully embrace the African side of their 'double-consciousness'" ("Yoruba Gods" 92). Accordingly, Wilson's accentuation of the African could be construed as a response to the dichotomy, to the madness, of double consciousness.

Within the modern period, American psychologists and social workers, in fields not unlike Fanon's, sought clinical solutions and social treatments for the madness produced in African-American experience. By 1948, the date in which Wilson sets *Seven Guitars,* ideas of racial madness and possible socio-logical and psychological treatments for it had become intricately intertwined with the so-called Negro Problem in America. While white supremacists believed that black inferiority made black people inherently insane, more left-ist-minded racial critics, both white and black, argued that conditions of oppression, racism, and restrictive prejudicial practices impressed on blacks a particular type of cultural neurosis. In her article "The Lunatic's Fancy and the Work of Art," Shelly Eversley notes that in April 1946, when the Lafargue Psychiatric Clinic opened in Harlem as the first clinic of its kind to offer treat-ment to an indigent, mostly black clientele, "one newspaper responded with the headline 'They're Crazy anyway.'" The Lafargue Clinic purposefully addressed the social roots of the psychological problems of its black patients. As Eversley explains, the Lafargue Clinic "rejected abstract notions of psychoanalytic neurosis to address what became understood as social and arti-ficially induced crises"; it "had the potential to demonstrate through psycho-logical discourses the social implications of the contradictory persistence of racism at mid century" (3). Through its clinical practice, the Lafargue linked the psychological and the social and identified racism as both a social and a psychological ill.

At this same historic juncture, African-American writers of the modern period, such as Ralph Ellison and Richard Wright, figuratively expressed the maddening effects of the American social environment on the African-Ameri-can psyche. As Eversley points out, Ellison and Wright were active supporters of the Lafargue Clinic who were interested not only in the practical implica-tions of social psychology but also in the metaphorical implications of mad-ness and schizophrenia. In their work, Eversley argues, schizophrenia becomes a metaphor that, not unlike Du Boisian double consciousness, "illus-trates ... what it means to live as a contradiction, as both Negro and Ameri-can." In a powerful and harrowing moment in Ellison's classic *Invisible Man* (1947), the madness of the social environment leads Brother Tod Clifton to sell Sambo Dolls on the corner. Social conditions of African-American life place Clifton, and the group of young Negroes on the subway train observed by the Invisible Man, outside of history: "For they were men outside of histor-ical time [...] They were outside the groove of history" (433, 436). Plunged outside of history, recognizing the madness of his existence, Brother Clifton dies in disillusionment, while the Invisible Man comes to appreciate an alter-native view to his earlier pseudo-Marxian perspective on historical progress.[2] Ellison's argument in *Invisible Man,* like that of Wright or Du Bois, is not that the race itself is insane but that the conditions of modern African-American life, the racism, alienation, and discrimination that black people face, induce this racial neurosis. Their argument is not one framed in Freudian psychoanal-ysis or one that fits neatly into white racist notions of black deviance but rather a social psychoanalytic approach professing that change within the social environment can and will affect the black psyche.

In a more radical reading, LeRoi Jones's foundational text in modern black drama, *Dutchman* (1964), identifies a racial insanity, fueled by years of racism and oppression, to which the only solution is not psychotherapy but violent social change. The middle-class black protagonist, Clay, attempts to divorce himself from the madness of race in his final apocalyptic speech to his white nemesis/seductress, Lula: "But who needs it? [...] My people's madness" (94). Still, despite his own desire to disassociate himself from the black majority, Clay understands and articulates that this collective psychosis can only be exorcised through the murder of whites, through violent black revolution:

> A whole people of neurotics, struggling to keep from being sane. And the only thing that would cure the neurosis would be your murder. Simple as that [...] Crazy niggers turning their backs on sanity. When all it needs is that simple act. Murder. Just Murder! (Jones, *Dutchman* 94)

Clay argues that madness is the relative state of modern black existence, but he rejects the more integrative social solutions to madness proposed by Du Bois, Ellison, or Wright by declaring that only murderous action will bring sanity.

Still, if we take the modernist perspectives of Du Bois through to Jones – the sense that modern black American existence is mad, suffering under a cultural neurosis – what happens when Wilson multiplies this madness through the creation of mentally impaired figures such as Gabe, Hambone, Hedley, and Stool Pigeon? Are they doubly mad or products of an even more fragmented consciousness? Does their madness within madness make them sane? My sense is that their particular madness places them in spaces removed from the normal trajectories of black difference, spaces that enable their individual predicaments to reflect back on the black whole, to double, double-consciousness in order to heal, to challenge, to renegotiate the collective black neurosis. Existing on the margins, outside behavioral norms and on the periphery of their plays' central conflicts, fiercely particularized, idiosyncratic, and iconoclastic, they exemplify subjectivity and interiority run amok.

WILSON'S MADMEN

As a consequence of their particular "madness," Wilson's madmen function in ways that evoke another sort of doubling: they are both culturally organizing and culturally organized. I classify their actions as "culturally organized" because they reflect specific cultural belief systems and practices. Each of these figures draws upon the past and reveals the African presence in African-American identities. Even as they escape the present madness, they embody the historical memory of primary ruptures, pains, and struggle within African-American existence, the legacies of forced separation from Africa, of the harsh Middle Passage, and of the terrors and pains of slavery. At once "outside of history," like Ellison's young Negroes on the train, they convey the significance of history and reinforce the impact of the past upon the present. Corresponding to the old adage "God looks out for fools and babes," Gabriel's, Hambone's, Hedley's, and Stool Pigeon's positions of marginality and "abnormality" grant them special access to God and provide them with unique spiritual powers.

I term these characters "culturally organizing," in other words, for their ability to explode and interrogate the meanings of madness. Their presence within the structure of otherwise realistic plays expands traditional cultural limitations of the form. Through these figures Wilson establishes a bridge between past and present, a way of connecting to tradition even in the face of progress. They operate, in Wilson's plays, both as symptoms of the American psychosis that limits black existence and as potential cures for this illness.

The madness of each of these figures results from symbolic or real confrontations with white power structures. These confrontations cause ruptures and schisms for the characters that parallel primal scenes of loss, rupture, and schism within the experiences of Africans in America. Thus they become representations of collective African-American social memories.

Gabriel Maxson is a mentally disabled World War II veteran and brother of the central figure, Troy Maxson, in *Fences,* Wilson's first Pulitzer Prize–winning drama (1987). During the war, Gabriel was wounded and a metal plate was placed in his head. Troy explains, "Man go over there and fight the war ... messing around with them Japs, get half his head blown off ... and they give him a lousy three thousand dollars. And I had to swoop down on that" (128). Gabe's fate reflects the legacy of all the black servicemen who fought in World War II in the jingoistic belief that they were keeping America safe for democracy, only to come home after the war to increased discrimination, second-class citizenship, and anything but democracy. Like these men, Gabe is alienated and dislocated from his social environment. Paradoxically, Gabe's mental condition locates him in a space of alternative consciousness where he has a special spiritual mission to fulfill. He is beyond the threat of earthly events; now he fiercely believes he is the archangel Gabriel, and he chases hellhounds throughout the play. Gabe claims, "I done died and went to heaven" (126). Significantly, the money the Government provided Gabe after his war injury provides the financing for Troy's home. "That's the only way I got a roof over my head ... cause of that metal plate. [...] If my brother didn't have that metal plate in his head ... I wouldn't have a pot to piss in or a window to throw it out of" (128). Gabe's disability is materially connected to the well-being of his family.

Cheated out of his just compensation, a ham, for painting the white butcher

Lutz's fence, Hambone in *Two Trains Running* (1992) has seen his mental condition deteriorate to the point where he only repeats variations of the phrase "I want my ham." Nine and a half years before the play begins, Lutz hired Hambone to paint his fence. According to Memphis, the proprietor of the restaurant that is the site of play's action, "Lutz told him if he painted his fence he'd give him a chicken. Told him if he do a good job he'd give him a ham. He think he did a good job and Lutz didn't. That's where he went wrong – letting Lutz decide what to pay him for his work" (23). Memphis points to the fault in black capitalist strategies that operate within or depend upon a system of white hegemony to assess their worth. Inevitably, such dependencies result in exploitation. Hambone's peculiar, particularized plight parallels repeated and unrequited African-American demands for reparations for the wrongs of slavery. His unfulfilled expectations reflect the historically promised, but never received, forty acres and a mule. Obsessed and possessed by his mistreatment, Hambone stands every day at the site of his indignity and demands from Lutz his just recompense: "I want my ham!"

While such obsessive behavior seems "mad," Wilson suggests that it implies a different level of consciousness, an unparalleled measure of commitment and focused "sanity." Holloway, the wizened older regular at the restaurant, explains to Memphis that Hambone "might have more sense than any of us" (29). Holloway explains that while Hambone refuses,

> We might take a chicken. Then we gonna go home and cook that chicken. But how it gonna taste? It can't taste good to us. [...] Every time we even look at a chicken we gonna have a bad taste in our mouth. That chicken's gonna call up that taste. It's gonna make you feel ashamed. [...] This fellow here [Hambone] ... he say he don't want to carry it around with him. [...] That's why I say he might have more sense than me and you. Cause he ain't willing to accept whatever the white man throw at him. It be easier. But he say he don't mind getting out of the bed in the morning to go at what's right. (29–30)

Holloway portrays Hambone's personal obsession as a singular effort against white hegemony and black complacency. The "bad taste in our mouth" brought on by accepting, cooking, and eating the chicken is in fact an internalized form of oppression, a racial neurosis that Hambone fights by returning each day to the originating site of rupture and terror: confronting Lutz. Lost on the other characters until after his death is the way in which Hambone's personal struggle against injustice reflects their own need for persistent, collective, revolutionary action.

In *Seven Guitars* (1996), the West Indian Hedley rants and raves about black social action. He rages against the white power structure, but his cries go unheeded by the other characters. Wilson, however, wants the audience to recognize the truth, power, and prophesy in Hedley's words. As a West Indian immigrant, Hedley stands as an embodiment of the black diaspora, a "Black Atlantic" traveler. Hedley constellates the history and memory of the West Indies as a transport zone for the slave trade, the images of West Indian plantation slavery, the legacy of colonialism and sugar cane economies, the heritage of the native uprisings and Toussaint L'Ouverture. These events constitute the site of his rupture, the sources of his madness and rage.

Hedley both contains and extends features of Gabriel and Hambone. His obsession, his singular focus, like that of Gabriel and Hambone before him, enables him to connect with the suppressed and oppressed African song of freedom in ways "a normal or sane mind" could not. Hedley shouts out a revolutionary sentiment that Hambone embodies but cannot speak: "the white man not going to tell me what to do" (24). Like Gabriel, Hedley, in his messianic prophecy and spiritual faith, syncretically blends the African and the Christian:

> The Bible say it all will come to straighten out in the end. Every abomination shall
> be brought low. Everything will fall to a new place. When I get my plantation
> I'm gonna walk around it. I am going to walk all the way round to see how big it is.
> I'm gonna be a big man on that day [...] I tell you this as God is my witness on
> that great day when all the people are singing as I go by ... and my plantation is full
> and ripe ... and my father is a strong memory ... on that day ... the white man not
> going to tell me what to do no more. (24)

Ironically, the historic site of black enslavement, the plantation, now becomes the environment for Hedley's mission of black liberation. Through Hedley's vision of the plantation, Wilson offers an intertextual linkage to and revision of William Faulkner's *Absalom, Absalom!* (1936), in which the white character Sutpen builds a plantation out of nothing on the backs of Haitian "wild Negroes" (27).

Hedley wants to be a "big man," free to determine his own fate. His name, "King Hedley," is significant in this regard. With the name Wilson riffs on both notions of royalty and the madness in Hedley's head. At times people suffering from various forms of psychosis imagine themselves to be kings, queens, or figures of royal standing, power, and privilege in order to combat their fragmented sense of self. Hedley reveals that he once killed another black man because, says Hedley, "He would not call me King. He laughed to think a black man could be King [...] After that I don't tell nobody my name is King" (*Seven Guitars* 67). The symbolic implications of naming take on life-and-death import for Hedley. Similarly, the value of names and naming has been critical to African-American identity; even the name for Africans in America has shifted through time from *colored* to *Negro* to *black* to *Afro-* and *African-American*, each one with real meaning and practical significance. Hedley is a black King, a mad King, mocking and signifying on concepts of sovereignty, royalty, power, and legitimacy. What *is* in a name, and who can be King? Wilson riffs further on these questions and continues the line of "Kings" with the title for his play of the 1980s and its central problematic figure, *King Hedley II*.

Hedley the first's father named him King after legendary musician King Buddy Bolden (1877–1931). Bolden, a builder and part-time barber, cornet player, and bandleader in New Orleans, has been called the first man of jazz and the first "King" of New Orleans cornet players. He was said to play the cornet so loudly and with such force that "he actually blew the tuning slide out of his cornet and it would land twenty feet away" (Zue Robertson, qtd. in Marquis 43–44). After repeated arrests, detentions, and struggles with mental illness, Bolden was committed to the Insane Asylum at Jackson, Louisiana, on 5 June 1907, where he remained for twenty-four years until his death on 4 November 1931. Bolden was a heavy drinker, and his outbreaks of dementia often followed his abuse of alcohol. Knowledge of mental illness in those days was rudimentary at best. Undoubtedly, contemporary psychiatry would find more sophisticated, neurologically based reasons for his illness. Nonetheless, the connection between Bolden's music, his race, his lifestyle, and his insanity suggests a continuum linking him to such tortured black geniuses as Thelonious Monk and Charlie "Bird" Parker. In each of these cases the music, the madness, the self-destructive behavior, the impacts of racism were all intertwined. Despite or perhaps as a consequence of their musical virtuosity, for these black artists the realities of being black and being an artist were at times overwhelming.

Hedley, at moments, finds the pressures and madness of race overwhelming. He refuses at first to be tested for tuberculosis, believing that such doctors and tests are a plot against the black man. Yet, as history has shown, his paranoia and racial conspiracy theories echo with the truth of cases such as the Tuskegee Institute experiment, where black men were left untreated for syphilis in a U.S. government plot to study the effects of the disease. Hedley recognizes that "[e]verybody say Hedley crazy cause he black. Because he know the place of the black man is not at the foot of the white man's boot. Maybe it is not all right in my head sometimes. Because I don't like the world. I don't like what I see from the people" (*Seven Guitars* 67). Thus, Hedley implicitly connects his madness to sociological sources and problems. He demonstrates a single-minded determination to restore the black man to his rightful position. This obsession eventually leads him to kill Floyd Barton, the central figure of the play. As Floyd attempts to recover his stolen bounty from its backyard hiding place, Hedley kills him. In this moment of madness and misplaced rage, Hedley mistakenly believes that Floyd is the legendary musician Buddy Bolden.

The murder of Floyd Barton in *Seven Guitars* has a direct connection to the madness of the character Stool Pigeon in *King Hedley II*. With *King Hedley II*, set in 1985, Wilson plunges characters and themes from *Seven Guitars* forty years into the future. In the second act, Stool Pigeon reveals to the title character that his real name is not Stool Pigeon but Canewell, a former friend of Floyd Barton's. In the concluding moment of *Seven Guitars,* Hedley shows Canewell a fistful of crumpled bills from Floyd's bounty. This action serves as Hedley's confession of the murder, a confession that the end of play leaves open as to possible consequences: Canewell may or may not keep the knowledge of Hedley's role in the murder secret. *King Hedley II,* however, closes off the possibility of conjecture. Stool Pigeon explains,

> Hedley showed me the money. Told me Buddy Bolden gave it to him. That's when I knew. I say I got to tell. What else cold I do? Ruby called me Stool Pigeon and somehow or another it stuck. I tell anybody I'm a Truth Sayer. She say I killed Floyd but she don't really believe that. (87)

Stool Pigeon's madness results not merely from his act of informing the white authorities of Hedley's crime but from the rupture it causes when he is ostracized from the community and branded Stool Pigeon.

Internal ruptures are the focus for the apocalyptic vision of the African-American community in the 1980s that Wilson imagines in *King Hedley II.* Wilson depicts a black wasteland devastated by black-on-black violence and crime. Significantly, Aunt Esther, an absent/present spiritual force that figures prominently in *Two Trains Running,* a woman as old as the black presence in America, dies of grief in *King Hedley II,* and her black cat dies, too. The set for the April 2000 production at the Seattle Repertory Theater imagined an inner city devastated by a holocaust of external neglect and internal disregard. The characters live in the shells of former buildings. The backdrop reveals the crumbling brick and worn-out remains of tenements. The lively backyard of some forty years earlier in *Seven Guitars* is now in a state of fragmented ruin. This "postmodern" apocalyptic set symbolizes the conditions Wilson perceives as endemic in black America both in the 1980s and today, a community destroyed by systematic abandonment, internalized oppression, and self-destructive violence and deeply in need of spiritual and social regeneration.

Stool Pigeon, not unlike his predecessors Gabriel and Hedley, prophecies a Day of Judgment in which God will right the wrongs of the earth. Stool Pigeon's faith is also a syncretic one. For him God is a "Bad Motherfucker." He repeats this mantra and warns the others of God's ability to bring devastating fires of retribution. Stool Pigeon is also a symbolic repository for lost history. Obsessively he saves newspapers, piling them up to a point where he can no longer fit into his own house. Mister asks him "Why you be carrying all them papers? Ain't they heavy?" Stool Pigeon replies, "See I know what went on. I ain't saying what goes on ... what went on. You got to know that. How you gonna get on the other side of the valley if you don't know that?" (24).

Stool Pigeon suggests that one cannot move into the future without knowing the past. His preservation of the newspapers holds on to history, protects the knowledge of what went on before. Wilson's vision of the 1980s plays out as a period of loss and rupture, not just in terms of black lives but in terms of history and collective memory. The lessons of black suffering, terror, and survival have been forgotten, and the way into the future is blocked as a result.

In a gesture that enrages his neighbor Ruby but subverts existing rules of power and privilege, Stool Pigeon repeatedly takes the covers off trash cans so that the neighborhood dogs can eat: "The dog got to eat too!" Symbolically, the gesture opens the spoils of the garbage cans to those without access. Using, again, the metaphor of food, Stool Pigeon's gesture reveals the inequities and hierarchies present in the rules of our social order as he provides the "under*dog*" with sustenance. Ruby and the others object on more practical and personal grounds: the dogs overturn people's property rights. In the Seattle Repertory Theatre production, director Marion McClinton blocked a continuing territorial war over garbage cans between Ruby and Stool Pigeon. As soon as he would remove the lids in one scene, she would recover them, with increasing frustration, in the next. Ruby's animosity toward Stool Pigeon reflects the fragmentation present within the picture of the 1980s black community in *King Hedley II*.

THE CONJUNCTION OF BLACK WOMEN AND MADMEN

While Ruby constantly chastises, rebuffs, and rebukes Stool Pigeon – "You old buzzard. Go on in the house!" (25) – Louise, Hedley's landlady and neighbor in *Seven Guitars,* pesters and provokes Hedley, but always with a concern for his health and well-being. Although Hedley refuses any attention, Louise attempts to compel him to receive treatment for his tuberculosis. Despite his obstinacy and difference, Louise and the others treat Hedley as an important member of their community. Correspondingly, Risa, the waitress and sole female figure in *Two Trains Running,* comforts Hambone and welcomes him into the community of Memphis's restaurant. After his daily confrontations with the butcher, Lutz, Hambone bursts into the restaurant to find Risa, who consoles and feeds him. At one point Risa even provides Hambone with a new coat so that he may be better prepared for the elements. In *Fences,* Rose cares for her brother-in-law, Gabriel, in similar fashion. She worries about his well-being and greets him warmly when he drops by her house, offering to feed him as well. In contrast to the tension between Ruby and Stool Pigeon, the nurturing of Risa and Rose brings Hambone and Gabriel into the community. These figures of madness are not abandoned but accepted. The picture is of a black community that embraces difference and that allows a space for those further marginalized by the larger society.

Still, the behavior of Risa and Rose as comforter and cook places them within very conventional gender roles and seems to leave them with little agency; they are always acting in service of and to the men around them. Moreover, all the figures of madness within Wilson's plays are male. Placed in relation to these traditionally gendered women, the masculinity of these madmen becomes more evident. Rather than being the product of universal default, their madness is grounded in a specific gender, race, time, and place. With these madmen, Wilson both comments on and repositions black masculinity. Black masculinity has historically been perceived, through racist paranoia, as a site of deviance. Within fields of representation and social organization, black masculinity has been associated with bestiality, with criminality, with uncontrolled sexuality. The stereotypes of the black male as criminal, as sexual predator, as savage, offer a threat to white hegemony, but one that is controllable, as historically and currently evidenced by practices such as lynchings, police brutality, overcrowded prisons filled with young black men, and racial profiling. Black masculinity has been codifiable and containable. Wilson, however, subverts expectations of black masculinity through Gabriel, Hambone, Hedley, and Stool Pigeon by literally taking them "outside of their minds" (Reese). As madmen, they exist outside the other images of black men that Wilson or society supply. While they affirm the madness of race, they defy norms, stereotypes, and accepted notions of black masculinity. Their neuroses make them no longer recognizable as an established type. Even as they reiterate their own idiosyncratic patterns of behavior, they disrupt conventional black male representations, as their irreducible peculiarities and sensibilities defy definition.

By placing these madmen outside the conventional constraints or definitions of masculinity, by constructing them as sensitive figures that disrupt normal processes of truth and reality through "hysterics," Wilson feminizes them. In fact, with their outbreaks of histrionics, their cries and sighs of madness, one could associate these characters with the "female" disease of hysteria, commonly identified with women in the modern period. This connection of Wilson's madness to hysteria has significant implications both for the form of Wilson's drama and for its content. In her important work on realism and hysteria, Elin Diamond argues that theatrical realism, at its inception in the modern period, is itself a form of hysteria. She notes that while realism "urged and satisfied the pursuit of knowledge, the production of truth," "Hysteria [...] has become the trope par excellence for the ruination of truth-making" (5). Diamond continues, "hysteria in feminist discourse has become meaningful precisely as a disruption of traditional epistemological methods of seeing/knowing" (5). Thus hysteria upsets the logic of gender roles and conventional expectations of gender. And yet, Diamond argues, realism functions as a form of hysteria, as it is subject to ideological distortions and to "a narcissism that deconstructs the mimetic referent upon which it is insisting" (7). Correspondingly, the actions of Wilson's madmen corrupt the logic of traditional realism even as they signify and represent their own truth. Gabriel, at the end of *Fences*, fulfills his self-imposed mission as the archangel Gabriel and actually opens the Gates of Heaven for his brother Troy to enter. His madness reforms realism even as it conforms to it.

Analyzing two race novels of the modern period, Frances Harper's *Iola Leroy* and W.D. Howells's *An Imperative Duty*, Michele Birnbaum points out that the racial dynamics of hysteria have been under-explored and identifies what she terms a "racial hysteria" (8) in which "*racism* [...] is the 'disease'" that contributes to female hysteria (18).The mulatto heroines of these texts experience hysteria as a result of internalized racial conflicts, their mixed blood, and their splitting of conscience. Birnbaum sees racial hysteria as a cultural sensibility and sensitivity. The racism of the social environment is the primal and primary source of this madness. In exploring the "consanguinity of the 'Race Problem' and the 'Woman Question'" in these novels' "'mixed blood' hysteric" (7), Birnbaum argues that the authors refigure feminine infirmity as a site of healing.

Thus, because African Americans represent the potent salvation of white America in both novels, *Iola Leroy* and *An Imperative Duty* strikingly reverse orthodox theories of African-American physical and civic degeneracy at the turn of the century. Structured by the medical discourse it seeks to exploit, Harper's racial uplift project and Howells's realist work risk the circulation of canards of social and feminine infirmity in order to reconceive them. [...] But by both novels' ends, the mulatta/o, in particular, is no longer the sign of racial entropy, but a medium for personal and national restoration. (17)

Wilson also reconceives madness as a medium for spiritual reaffirmation and for social and cultural change, and he locates the causes for the neuroses of his mad figures in the racial dynamics of their time. Yet both Birnbaum and Diamond associate hysteria with women. What of the women – Rose, Risa, Ruby – who care for, protect, and nurture these mad figures? How should we perceive them and their potential agency?

Certainly Wilson's women are not hysterics, nor do they respond principally to the disease of racism. Rather, they react to the patriarchal system that constrains them. Within the limitations of this system, they exercise a degree of freedom. Their relationships to Wilson's madmen provides them with space to display both resistance and desire. Prior to the first scene of *Two Trains*, Risa performs the "mad" action of scarring her legs with a razor. She acts to prevent men from objectifying her body, from seeing her only as a sexual object. This act and others' responses to it connect her to Hambone and his repeated act of madness in demanding his ham from Lutz the butcher. The restaurant owner, Memphis, says of Hambone, 'how ... in his right mind ... do he think Lutz is gonna give him his ham?" (29). Memphis similarly says of

Risa, "She ain't right with herself ... how she gonna be right with you?" (31). Determined to treat Hambone in a way that is "right," Risa invites him into the restaurant and feeds him, despite his lack of financial resources and the objections of her boss.

Disagreement over proper treatment for Gabriel is a site of tension for Rose and Troy from the outset of *Fences*. While Rose wants to commit Gabe for his own protection, Troy protests that he needs to be free. Later, when Troy is beset with the new financial expenses of an expectant girlfriend as well as those of his existing family, he has his brother committed so that he can receive money directly from Gabe's military pension. Rose uses her knowledge of his action to point out Troy's hypocrisy and to mark her growing awareness of their separation and distance:

> I said send him [Gabe] to the hospital ... you said let him be free ... now you done went down there and signed him to the hospital for half his money. You went back on yourself, Troy. You gonna have to answer for that. (169)

In this moment, Rose uses Troy's contradictory positions on his brother Gabe to strike back at him. Earlier in the play, just after Troy reveals to Rose that he has had an affair and impregnated another woman and before Rose has had the opportunity to digest this information and respond, Gabe, innocent of the circumstances, enters and literally comes between Troy and Rose. He interrupts their argument and offers Rose a rose: "Hey, Rose ... I got a flower for you. That's a rose. Same rose like you is" (161). Despite her rising emotions, her feelings of disbelief, pain, anger, betrayal over her husband's infidelity after eighteen years of marriage, Rose still attends to Gabriel and comforts him: "You go on and get you a piece of watermelon, Gabe. Them bad mens is gone now" (162). Her humanity, her inner resolve and compassion for others, shines through even in this crisis. This compassion must not be read as a return to domesticity that weakens this character and confines her to stereotypical gendered behavior; rather, it is an articulation of strength. At this time of intense conflict and emotional uncertainty, Rose finds the power and makes the choice to tend to the innocent and needy Gabe. This loving treatment of Gabe constitutes what bell hooks refers to as "love as the practice of freedom." hooks sees the giving of such love as an active choice that has transformative power to effect social as well as personal change:

such talk [of the transformative power of love] is often seen as merely sentimental. In progressive political circles, to speak of love is to guarantee that one will be dismissed or considered naïve. [...] However, if the leaders of such movements refuse to address the anguish and pain of their lives, they will never be motivated to consider personal and political recovery. (247)

Rose's act of love toward Gabe in this difficult time foreshadows the transformative power that love will have in both their lives and for the community around them. Rose goes on to recover from the anguish and deep pain of Troy's betrayal and to bloom.

Throughout the play, Gabe and Rose share a special bond. She offers him love and concern, and he responds in kind by bringing her gifts: "Rose ... hey, Rose. Got a flower for you. [...] Picked it myself. That's the same rose like you is!" (*Fences* 144). Like Gabe, Rose finds salvation in religion, and she is the only other character who speaks of "the judgment" as she warns Troy to mend his ways: "God's the one you gonna have to answer to. He's the one gonna be at the judgment" (118). Most significantly, when Gabriel returns, on the day of Troy's funeral, intent on opening the gates of Heaven for his brother to enter, he can perform his ritual only after he has communicated with and received the silent blessing and consent of Rose: "Hey Rose, I'm here! [...] Hey, Rose. It's time. It's time to tell St. Peter to open the gates. Troy, you ready?" (192). Within this relational context, Rose's role is critical. Employing René Girard's notion of triangulated desire, Rose functions as a mediating force, neither the object nor the subject of Gabriel's desire but an agent that enables that desire to reach fruition. As mediator, she is there, "radiating toward both the subject[Gabe] and the object," Troy's arrival in Heaven (Girard 2). In this poignantly spiritual scene, Rose and Gabe are both able to forgive Troy's transgressions and to recognize the transformative power of love as Gabe opens the gates of Heaven and brings personal and social change.

Perhaps the most profound example of the complex, complimentary, and contradictory conjunction of women and madmen occurs in *Seven Guitars,* when Ruby, forty years younger than she is in *King Hedley II,* sleeps with the mad West Indian Hedley. At this moment, Wilson describes Hedley as "*feverish with lust*" (89). Still, Hedley grounds his appeal to Ruby not simply in sexual need but in a confluence of race, spirituality, and masculinity:

> The black man is not a dog! He is the Lion of Judah! He is the mud God made his image from [...] I am a man, woman. I am the man to father your children. I offer you a kingdom [...] I offer you to be the Lily of the Valley. To be Queen of Sheba. Queen of the black man's kingdom. (88–89)

Hedley sees his power and his identity wrapped up in his image of manhood and his ability to pass on his legacy, to produce an heir. His sexual desire conjoins with his concern for racial uplift and his vision of a black messiah. His particular circumstances comment on black masculinity and the struggle of black men to find meaning within a social system that perceives only black inferiority.

Somehow the young, pregnant, seemingly self-interested Ruby decides to lie down with the now sex-crazed, formerly just crazed, Hedley. *"She lifts up her dress and gives herself to him out of recognition of his great need"* (90). Read simply, the gesture seems to reflect a male-centric dramaturgy that depicts women solely in relation to men. Where is the character development for Ruby to make this decision? It is in fact, then, an act of madness, an act that seems out of sorts with the character we have seen. Is it, perhaps, a hysterical response? After all, what normal woman would lie down with a figure so deranged with lust?

Ruby's act, however, is not simply the design of Wilson's male-centrism; it is an expression of practical agency within the constraints of her circumstances. The language of the stage directions is particularly significant here: *"She lifts up her dress and gives herself."* The "giving of herself" does not connote passive submission but needs to be read by critics, as well as actors undertaking the role, as an active choice. Ruby's giving of herself presumes self-possession, individualism, and subjectivity that can find representation in performance. Sandra Richards, writing about *Ma Rainey,* suggests that there are moments of absence in the written script that "in performance can be charged with potential" ("Writing" 83). This scene, how the director constructs it, and the way the actress as Ruby enacts it are "wonderfully charged in performance" (88). Richards continues,

Some feminists might wonder why I would choose to cover up or fix the chauvinist appropriation that Wilson has written. My response to both is to refer once again to an African-American folk aesthetic that understands as a generating motive, and values as an ideal in performance, the potency and heightened emotion arising from a dense interlock of competing energies. Thus, the unwritten, or an absence from the script, is a potential presence implicit in performance. (83)

The "dense interlock of competing energies" that Richards describes is equally present in any effective mounting of the Ruby/Hedley scene. Absent from Wilson's dialogue, or even from the revealing stage directions for this scene, is any notation of the time it should take Ruby to respond to Hedley or how she should use her body and gestures to embrace him and "give herself to him." How the actor conveys Ruby's thoughts and her rationale for action can be telling, for Ruby, too, has needs that this act of lying down with Hedley serve, and she, too, gets what she wants:

I'm gonna tell him it's [her baby] his. He's the only man who ever wanted to give me something. And I want to have that. He wants to be the father of my child and that's what this child needs. I don't know about this messiah stuff but if it's a boy – and I hope to God it is – I'm gonna name it after him. I'm gonna name him King. (*Seven Guitars* 95–96)

Impregnated by another, Ruby chooses Hedley as the father for her child. While Hedley speaks of transcendent visions, she responds to practical needs, to a child coming into the world without a father. Through this act she subverts conventions of legacy and paternity and usurps the power that traditionally lies solely in the domain of men, the seed of heredity, the power of masculinity. Ruby names both the father and the son. Here again Girard's notion of triangular desire is helpful, as Ruby mediates between Hedley and the unborn child. As mediator of desire, she enables Hedley to realize his vision, without subscribing to the patriarchal terms of it.

MADNESS, DEATH, AND RITUAL REDEMPTION

For Hedley, the possibility of fatherhood and the memory of his own father position him inside a history and condition his behavioral responses. Obsessed with the legacy of his father, he waits for the second coming of Buddy Bolden. Hedley expresses the sentiment that for his father, Bolden, the madman of blues legend was a sacred figure, a god. Hedley's vision of Bolden fuses the social, the cultural, the spiritual, and the financial. Bolden will provide financial resources for Hedley to transcend earthly limits, to overcome white oppression and to purchase his idealized "plantation." And yet his vision proves misguided. In a moment of ritualized violence, Hedley kills Floyd with his machete as Floyd stands before him resplendent in a white suit, a beacon of light whom Hedley, blinded by cheap booze, mistakenly believes is Bolden come to provide him with his birthright. This is a blues moment of tragic loss – the death of the talented, self-destructive blues musician Floyd – and a moment of misguided values as well. The pursuit of money and property result in black-on-black violence and betray Hedley's vision of black liberation.

Significantly, the final ritualized acts of all Wilson's madmen, including Hedley's killing of Floyd Barton, intimately involve music or are encoded in sound, and these soundings are intricately connected to the expression of madness. In *Dutchman,* LeRoi Jones proclaims black musical creation as a temporal curative for the neuroses of race. According to Jones's protagonist, Clay, "All the hip white boys scream for Bird. And Bird saying , 'Up your ass, feebleminded ofay!' [...] Bird would've played not a note of music if he just walked up to East Sixty-seventh Street and killed the first ten white people he saw" (*Dutchman* 94). As Clay articulates it, the music serves a channel for black rage. Creating music enables these figures to negotiate the pains and pressures, the "madness," of race. I would argue that Wilson's madmen build on this assertion. Through ritualized moments of sound and music that are possible only as extensions of their madness, they provide for communal healing, cohesion, and even resistance. The sounds and the madness intersect and interact.

As in *Seven Guitars,* in each case these rituals involve a death, a death that serves as a lesson and a benediction for the gathered community. Wilson suffuses the mourning for the death of Hambone at the end of *Two Trains Running* with a cacophony of sound. As the other characters listen to Memphis plan for his future, the sound of breaking glass and a burglar alarm are heard. Then the young rebel Sylvester enters, bleeding but carrying a ham stolen from Lutz's window, a blood sacrifice for Hambone's casket. Rather than asking Lutz for reparation, Sylvester claims for Hambone that which was long his due. His act and Hambone's death unite the community in celebratory revolution. In a manner reminiscent of black revolutionary dramas by Jones and others in the 1960s that concluded by inciting their spectators to participate in communal sounds of revolt, Wilson wants his audiences to leave chanting "I want my ham!" With Hambone's death we also learn that he "had so many scars on his body. [...] All on his back, his chest ... his legs" (91). Hambone bears the material legacy of the horrors of slavery. His madness is a modern response to that legacy.

At the conclusion of *Fences,* Gabriel, again through sound, also links the black past to the African-American present in a moment of ritual and spiritual possession. Gabriel summons his special faith to open Heaven's gates on the day of his brother Troy's funeral. His actions proclaim a new day for Troy and the Maxson family. In addition, Gabriel's ritualistic and spiritual enactment is an exhibit of a syncretic cosmology, the presence of African tradition within New World religious practice. Prior to opening Heaven's gates, Wilson writes, Gabriel endures "*a trauma that a sane and normal mind would be unable to withstand*" (192). At this moment, Gabriel's maddening experience, I believe, could be said to parallel the "tragic terror" that Nigerian playwright Wole Soyinka theorizes one must undergo when one enters the "fourth stage" of transition (149). In Yoruba cosmology, the fourth stage of transition represents the "metaphysical abyss both of god and man," the space between death and becoming (149). The world of the ancestors, the living, and the unborn are the prior three stages. According to Soyinka, the Yoruba god Ogun was the first to survive the fourth stage and disintegration within this tragic gulf by exercising control of his will (160). Soyinka argues that a "titanic resolution of the will" is necessary to rescue any person within this abyss. Soyinka also notes that the manifestation or ritual summons of this will "is the strange alien sound to which we give the name of music" (149).

Gabriel, placed and understood within a Yoruban context, must enter the transitional gulf, the fourth stage, to open Heaven's gates and transfer Troy from the world of the living to the world of the ancestors. He must transcend time and space. Most significantly, Gabriel survives his entrance into this transitional gulf because his mental capacity is not "normal." Gabriel wholeheartedly believes that he is the Archangel Gabriel, and his will is resolute. His dance and inaudible horn sounds, his attempt at song or what Wilson calls "*a song turning back into itself*" (192), are the embodiment of his "ritual summons" and the expression of his "titanic resolution of will." Gabriel's transcendent moment unites Yoruba ritual and Christian doctrine. The "Christian" Archangel opens the gates of Heaven by engaging in a Yoruban ceremony connecting himself and his family to African traditions. Gabriel invokes a racial memory, an African inheritance. His actions again reinforce the impact of the past on the present as the family's African heritage provides a benediction for their African-American present. This moment in *Fences* should be viewed not only as an expression of the redemptive power of madness but as part of Wilson's continuing project to critique the African American experience of Christianity and to define and structure a particularly African-American cosmology.

The concluding moment of *King Hedley II* continues this critique of Christianity as Stool Pigeon calls out to God, "Thy Will! Not man's will! Thy Will! You a bad motherfucker! Bring down the Fire!" (153). This exhortation follows the violent death of King Hedley II at his own mother's, Ruby's, hands, another senseless black death. Yet Ruby's accidental murder of King is also epic and ancient, as it recalls and inverts Orestes's act of matricide in Aeschylus's *Oresteia*. No furies seep out to haunt and follow Ruby, however; no Areopagus acts to resolve the line of killing and the demand for retribution. Still, there is a cosmic justice present, and Ruby's murder of King does serve to end a pattern of black-on-black violence. The shooting of the son by the mother who brought him into the word stops the violence because, unlike those murderous acts discussed previously within the play, it cannot provoke or compel retribution. There can be no subsequent act of revenge. The grief is too deep, too final.

In this bleak scene, a world seemingly devoid of hope, as Ruby collapses on the ground and King's wife, Tonya, runs screaming into the house, Stool Pigeon performs his ritual. Following the death of Aunt Esther and her black cat, Stool Pigeon had buried the cat in the back yard and enacted rituals over it. Repeating and revising blood sacrifices seen throughout the Wilson historical cycle, Stool Pigeon explains his plans for the cat: "I'm gonna take some bark off that tree and put that on there. You sprinkle some blood on there and she comin back in seven days if she ain't used up her nine lives" (83). Significantly, as Wilson's stage directions command, King dies over the grave of the cat, and his blood consecrates the ground. He is now literally the chosen one who is sacrificed in order to prepare the way for the regeneration and redemption of the greater community, for the good of those who live on. Standing over the body of the sacrificial King, Stool Pigeon might also be said to enter into the tragic abyss, the chthonic realm, as he sounds a chant that unites the Christian and African and extols God to act: "The Conquering Lion of Judea! Our Bright and Morning Star! I want your best! See him coming! We give you our Glory!" (153).

Stool Pigeon's call to God, reminiscent of Berniece's calling on her ancestors for assistance to help her brother Boy Willie in his battle with the ghost of the white plantation owner, Sutter, at the end of *The Piano Lesson,* is located in a particularly black vernacular culture and black religious tradition. Stool Pigeon, too, calls on ancestors as he calls for "The Conquering Lion of Judea," the name by which Hedley refers to himself in *Seven Guitars* and that King repeats in *King Hedley II.* The idea, then, is that Stool Pigeon is calling out to a God who looks like him, who understands the history of black struggle and survival, and who can and will respond to black needs. As the lights go down to end the play, Wilson directs that *"the sound of a cat's meow is heard."* The sound of the cat signals the success of Stool Pigeon's efforts, of King's sacrifice; it trumpets the potential rebirth of Aunt Esther and thus renews hope for the African American future. God has heard Stool Pigeon's plea, and the past renews the present.

The direction that Stool Pigeon and each of these mad figures takes is at once outside as well as inside history. They beacon toward what Paul Gilroy calls the "revolutionary or eschatological apocalypse" or "Jubilee" (56). During slavery times the notion of the Jubilee, a Judgment Day when they could truly overcome the terrors of slavery, offered the slaves hope in something after slavery, an afterlife, salvation. Faith in an eschatological transcendence in the future enabled the slave to survive and struggle in the present. Wilson's madmen and their ritualized actions similarly point to a secular spiritual revelation in which past and present conjoin, directing African-Americans to a future of social and cultural change. Within this ritual action, madness becomes a conduit for healing.

Wilson himself functions with a kind of creative madness that renegotiates the meanings of the African-American past and the madness of race. Paul Gilroy, describing Toni Morrison's work in *Beloved,* argues that her writing suggests a "minority modernism [that] can be precisely defined through its imaginative proximity to forms of terror that surpass understanding and lead back from contemporary racial violence, through lynching, towards the temporal and ontological rupture of the middle passage" (222). Wilson could be said to compose a similar black modernist project, as he is fundamentally concerned with the remaking and conservation of historical memory, the renegotiation of primal and initiating ruptures in African-American experience. Wilson, like Gilroy and Morrison, asks that we recognize the significance of race, slavery, and African-American thought and cultural production as not just conditioned by but constitutive of modernity.

NOTES

1 Special thanks to Michele Birnbaum for her reading of this article and her insights into the argument.
2 For a discussion of history in *Invisible Man,* see O'Meally.

Works Cited

Adorno, T.W. *Aesthetic Theory*. Trans. and ed. Robert Hullot-Kentor. Minneapolis: U of Minnesota P, 1997.

– *Ästhetische Theorie*. Ed. Rolf Tiedermann. Frankfurt-am-Main: Suhrkamp, 1970.

– *In Search of Wagner*. Trans. Rodney Livingstone. London: NLB, 1981.

Ahmad, Aijaz. *In Theory: Classes, Nations, Literatures*. London: Verso, 1992.

Albanese, Denise. *New Science, New World*. Durham, NC: Duke UP, 1996.

Aristotle. Poetics I *with the* Tractatus Coislinignus, *A Hypothetical Reconstruction of* Poetics II, *The Fragments of the* On Poets. Trans. and ed. Richard Janko. Indianapolis: Hackett Publishing, 1987.

Armstrong, Tim. *Modernism, Technology and the Body: A Cultural Study*. Cambridge: Cambridge UP, 1998.

Asmal, Kadar, Louise Asmal, and Ronald Suresh Roberts. *Reconciliation through Truth: A Reckoning of Apartheid's Criminal Governance*. New York: St Martin's, 1997.

Athey, Ron. *The Solar Anus*. Video and performance. Hot House Center for International Performance, Chicago. 7 Feb. 1999.

Auslander, Philip. *Liveness: Performance in a Mediatized Culture*. London: Routledge, 1999.

– *Presence and Resistance: Postmodernism and Cultural Politics in Contemporary American Performance*. Ann Arbor: U of Michigan P, 1992.

Barasch, Moshe. *Icon: Studies in the History of an Idea*. New York: NYU P, 1992.

Barbour, Floyd B., ed. *The Black Power Revolt: A Collection of Essays*. Boston: Porter, 1968.

Barlow, Judith E., ed. *Plays by American Women 1930–1960*. New York: Applause, 1994.

Barnard, L.W. *The Graeco-Roman and Oriental Background of the Iconoclastic Controversy*. Leiden: Brill, 1974.

Barrie, J.M. *Peter Pan. Peter Pan and Other Plays.* Ed. Peter Hollindale. Oxford: Oxford UP, 1995. 73–154.

Baudrillard, Jean. *For a Critique of the Political Economy of the Sign.* Trans. Charles Levin. St Louis, MO: Telos, 1975.

Baumgarten, Alexander Gottlieb. *Theoretische Asthetik: die grundlegenden Abschnitte der "Aesthetica."* 1750/1758. Ed. Hans Rudolf Schweizer. Hamburg: Meiner, 1983.

Behn, Aphra. *The Emperor of the Moon. The Works of Aphra Behn.* Vol. 3. Ed. Montague Summers. New York: Phaeton, 1967. 383–463.

Bender, John, and David E. Wellbery. *Chronotypes: The Construction of Time.* Stanford, CA: Stanford UP, 1991.

Bendure, Joan C. *The Newfoundland Dog: Companion Dog – Water Dog.* New York: Macmillan, 1994.

Benjamin, Walter. *The Arcades Project.* Trans. Howard Eiland and Kevin McLaughlin. Cambridge: Belknap/Harvard UP, 1999.

– *Gesammelte Schriften.* 15 vols. Ed. Theodor W. Adorno et al. Frankfurt am Main: Suhrkamp, 1972–1987.

– *Illuminations: Essays and Reflections.* 1968. Trans. Harry Zohn. Ed. Hannah Arendt. Trans Harry Zohn. New York: Schocken, 1969.

– *The Origin of German Tragic Drama.* 1977. Trans. John Osborne. London: New Left, 1985.

– *Selected Writings.* Ed. Marcus Bullock and Michael W. Jennings. Vol. 1. Cambridge: Belknap / Harvard UP, 1996.

– *Understanding Brecht.* Trans. Anna Bostock. London: Verso, 1998.

Bennett, Susan. *Theatre Audiences: A Theory of Production and Reception.* 2nd ed. London: Routledge, 1997.

Bentley, Eric. *The Life of the Drama.* 1964. New York: Atheneum, 1967.

– *The Playwright as Thinker: A Study of Drama in Modern Times.* New York: Harcourt, 1946.

Bernard, Claude. *An Introduction to the Study of Experimental Medicine.* Trans. Henry Copley Greene. New York: Collier, 1961.

Bhabha, Homi K. *The Location of Culture.* London: Routledge, 1994.

Birnbaum, Michele. "Racial Hysteria: Female Pathology and Race Politics in Frances Harper's *Iola Leroy* and W.D. Howells's *An Imperative Duty.*" *African American Review* 33.1 (1999): 7–23.

Bishop, Thomas. *Pirandello and the French Theater.* New York: New York UP, 1960.

Blažević, Marin. "The Story of Seeing." *Frakcija* 15 (1999): 61–69

Blau, Herbert. *Take Up the Bodies: Theater at the Vanishing Point.* Urbana: U of Illinois P, 1982.

Blitzstein, Marc. *Regina.* Adapt. of *The Little Foxes,* by Lillian Hellman. Original version restored by Tommy Krasker and John Mauceri. Scottish Opera Orch. and Chorus. Musical dir. John Mauceri. DECCA, 1992.

Bourdieu, Pierre. *The Field of Cultural Production: Essays on Art and Literature.* Ed. Randal Johnson. New York: Columbia UP, 1993.

Bové, Paul A. *Intellectuals in Power: A Genealogy of Critical Humanism*. New York: Columbia UP, 1986.

Bowlt, John E. *The Silver Age: Russian Art of the Early Twentieth Century and the "World of Art" Group*. Newtonville, MA: Oriental Research Partners, 1982.

Brecht, Bertolt. *Brecht on Theatre: The Development of an Aesthetic*. Ed and trans. John Willett. New York: Hill, 1964.

– *Der gute Mensch von Sezuan [The Good Person of Sezuan]*. *Gesammelte Werke*. Vol. 4. Frankfurt am Main: Suhrkamp, 1967. 1487–1607.

– "A Dialogue About Acting." 1929. *Brecht on Theatre* 26–29.

– "The Film, the Novel and Epic Theatre." 1931. *Brecht on Theatre* 47–51.

– *Life of Galileo*. 1938. *Collected Plays*. Vol. 5. Ed. Ralph Manheim and John Willett. New York: Vintage, 1972. 1–98.

– *The Measures Taken*. 1930. *The Jewish Wife and Other Short Plays*. Trans. Eric Bentley. New York: Grove, 1965. 75–108.

– *Mother Courage and Her Children*. 1938–1939. *Collected Plays*. Vol. 5. Ed. Ralph Manheim and John Willett. New York: Vintage, 1972. 133–210.

– "The Radio as an Apparatus of Communication." 1932. *Brecht on Theatre* 51–53.

– "A Radio Speech." 1927. *Brecht on Theatre* 18–20.

– *Werke: Grosse Kommentierte Berliner und Frankfurter Ausgabe*. 30 vols. Frankfurt am Main: Suhrkamp, 1988–1998.

Brenton, Howard. "Petrol Bombs through the Proscenium Arch." *Theatre Quarterly* 5.17 (1975): 4–20.

Brookes, Chris. *A Public Nuisance: A History of the Mummers Troupe*. St John's, NF: ISER, 1988.

Brookes, Chris. Rehearsal diaries, ms. 1973. Chris Brookes Papers. St John's, NF.

Brooks, Cleanth. *The Well-Wrought Urn*. New York: Harcourt, 1947.

Brooks, Cleanth, and Robert B. Heilman. *Understanding Drama: Twelve Plays*. 1945. New York: Holt, 1948.

Brooks, Cleanth, and Robert Penn Warren. *Understanding Poetry*. 1938. 3rd ed. New York: Holt, 1960.

– *Understanding Poetry*. 4th ed. New York: Holt, 1976.

Brooks, Cleanth, John Purser, and Robert Penn Warren. *An Approach to Literature*. New York: Appleton-Century, 1952.

Broyles-González, Yolanda. *El Teatro Campesino: Theater in the Chicano Movement*. Austin: U of Texas P, 1994.

Brustein, Robert. "Why American Plays Are Not Literature." 1959. *American Drama and Its Critics*. Ed. Alan Downer. Chicago: U of Chicago P, 1965. 245–55.

Buljan, Ivica. "Iconoclasm: A View on Theatre." *Frakcija* 15 (1999): 8–13.

Burke, Edmund. *A Philosophical Enquiry into the Origin of Our Ideas of the Sublime and Beautiful*. New York: Garland, 1971.

Butler, Judith. *Gender Trouble: Feminism and the Subversion of Identity*. New York: Routledge, 1990.

– "Performative Acts and Gender Constitution: An Essay in Phenomenology and

Feminist Theory." *Performing Feminisms: Feminist Critical Theory and Theatre.*
Ed. Sue-Ellen Case. Baltimore: Johns Hopkins UP, 1990. 270–82.

Bynum, W.F. *Science and the Practice of Medicine in the Nineteenth Century.*
Cambridge: Cambridge UP, 1994.

Caillois, Roger. *Die Spiele und die Menschen: Maske und Rausch.* Trans. Sigrid von
Massenbach. Frankfurt am Main: Wien, 1982.

Calinescu, Matei. *Five Faces of Modernity: Modernism, Avant-Garde, Decadence,
Kitsch, Postmodernism.* Durham, NC: Duke UP, 1987.

Carmichael, Stokely. "Power and Racism." Barbour 61–71.

Centre for the Study of Violence and Reconciliation Web Site. 1 April 2003.
.

Certeau, Michel de. *The Writing of History.* Trans. Tom Conley. New York: Columbia
UP, 1988.

Childress, Alice. *Wine in the Wilderness.* 1969. *Black Theater USA: Plays by African
Americans.* Rev. ed. Ed. James V. Hatch and Ted Shine. New York: Free P, 1996.
344–62.

Chin, Frank. The Chickencoop Chinaman *and* The Year of the Dragon: *Two Plays by
Frank Chin.* Seattle: U of Washington P, 1981.

Churchill, Caryl. *Light Shining in Buckinghamshire. Plays: One.* London: Methuen,
1985. 182–241.

– *Vinegar Tom. Plays: One.* London: Methuen, 1985. 128–79.

Clark, Anna. "Prostitution." *Victorian Britain: An Encyclopedia.* Ed. Sally Mitchell.
New York and London: Garland, 1988. 642–45.

Cleage, Pearl. Afterword. *Bearing Witness: Contemporary Works by African American
Women Artists.* Ed. Jontyle Theresa Robinson. New York: Spelman College /
Rizzoli Intl. P, 1996. 161.

Clément, Catherine. *Syncope: The Philosophy of Rapture.* Trans. Sally O'Driscoll and
Deirdre M. Mahoney. Minneapolis: U of Minnesota P, 1994.

Cocteau, Jean. *The Wedding on the Eiffel Tower.* Trans. Michael Benedikt. *Modern
French Theatre: An Anthology of Plays.* Ed. Michael Benedikt and George E. Well-
warth. New York: Dutton, 1966. 93–115.

Coetzee, Yvette. "Visibly Invisible: How Shifting the Conventions of the Traditionally
Invisible Puppeteer Allows for More Dimensions in Both the Puppeteer–Puppet
Relationship and the Creation of Theatrical Meaning in *Ubu and the Truth Commis-
sion.*" *South African Theatre Journal* 12.1–2 (1999): 35–51.

Cohen, Ed. *Talk on the Wilde Side: Toward a Genealogy of a Discourse on Male
Sexualities.* New York and London: Routledge, 1993.

Cornford, F.M. *The Origin of Attic Comedy.* London: Edward Arnold, 1914.

Cranston, Sylvia. *HPB: The Extraordinary Life and Influence of Helena Blavatsky,
Founder of the Modern Theosophical Movement.* New York: Putnam, 1993.

Crawford, T. Hugh. *Modernism, Medicine, and William Carlos Williams.* Norman:
U of Oklahoma P, 1993.

Csikszentmihalyi, Mihaly. *The Art of Seeing: An Interpretation of the Aesthetic*

Encounter. Malibu, CA: J. Paul Getty Museum / Getty Ctr. for Education in the Arts, 1990.

D.S. "N.B." *Times Literary Supplement* 22 Dec. 1995: 14.

David-Neel, Alexandra. *With Mystics and Magicians in Tibet*. London: John Lane, 1931.

David-Neel, Alexandra, and Lama Yongden. *The Secret Oral Teachings in Tibetan Buddhist Sects*. Trans. H.N.M. Hardy. San Francisco: City Lights, 1967.

Dee, Jonathan. "But Is It Advertising? Capitalist Realism at the Clio Awards." *Harpers* Jan. 1999: 61–72.

Derrida, Jacques. *Specters of Marx: The State of the Debt, the Work of Mourning, and the New International*. Trans. Peggy Kamuf. New York: Routledge, 1994.

– "The Theater of Cruelty and the Closure of Representation." *Writing and Difference*. Trans. Alan Bass. Chicago: U of Chicago P, 1978. 232–50.

Diamond, Elin. "The Shudder of Catharsis in Twentieth-Century Performance." *Performativity and Performance*. Ed. Andrew Parker and Eve Kosofsky Sedgwick. New York: Routledge, 1995. 152–72.

– *Unmaking Mimesis: Essays on Feminism and Theater*. New York and London: Routledge, 1997.

Diderot, Denis. *Le Paradoxe sur le comédien*. Ed. Robert Abirached. Paris: Gallimard, 1994.

– "The Paradox of the Actor." *Selected Writings on Art and Literature*. Trans. Geoffrey Bremner. Harmondsworth, UK: Penguin, 1994.

Dodd, Alex. "Face Up to Honest Reality." *Johannesburg Mail and Guardian* 11 June 1999. 31 Mar. 2000 <http://www.sn.apc.org/wmail/issues/990611/ARTS21.html>.

Dolan, Jill. "Geographies of Learning." *Theatre Journal* 45 (1993): 417–41.

Douglass, Frederick. *Narrative of the Life of Frederick Douglass, an American Slave*. Ed. Benjamin Quarles. Cambridge: Belknap-Harvard UP, 1960.

Dr. Faustus Lights the Lights. Dir. Robert Wilson. Libretto Gertrude Stein. Hebbel Theater, Berlin. 1992.

Du Bois, W.E.B. *The Souls of Black Folk*. 1903. New York: Knopf, 1993.

Eagleton, Terry. *Literary Theory: An Introduction*. 2nd ed. Minneapolis: U of Minnesota P, 1996.

Easthope, Anthony. *Literary into Cultural Studies*. London: Routledge, 1991.

Edwards, A.C. Foreword. *Modern Drama* 1.2 (1958).

Election Campaign Circus Chance 2000. Dir. Christoph Schlingensief. Berlin Volksbühne, Berlin. 13 Mar. 1998.

Eliot, T.S. Introduction. *Savonarola: A Dramatic Poem*. By Charlotte Eliot. London: Cobden-Sanderson, 1926. vii–xii.

– *The Superior Landlord*. Unpublished scenario. John Hayward Bequest. King's College, Cambridge.

– *The Use of Poetry and the Use of Criticism: Studies in the Relation of Criticism to Poetry in England*. 1933. London: Faber, 1955.

– *The Waste Land: A Facsimile and Transcript of the Original Drafts Including the Annotations of Ezra Pound*. Ed. Valerie Eliot. London: Faber, 1971.

Ellison, Ralph. *Invisible Man*. 1947. New York: Modern Library, 1994.

Endres, Robin, and Richard Wright, eds. Eight Men Speak *and Other Plays from the Canadian Workers' Theatre*. Toronto: New Hogtown P, 1976.

Eversley, Shelly. "The Lunatic's Fancy and the Work of Art." *American Literary History* 13.3 (2001): 445–68.

Eversmann, Peter. "Studying Theatrical Experience." International Colloquium of Theatre Studies. Tokyo. 2–8 May 2000.

Fabre, Geneviève, and Robert O'Meally, ed. *History and Memory in African American Culture*. New York: Oxford UP, 1994.

Fanon, Frantz. *The Wretched of the Earth*. Harmondsworth, UK: Penguin, 1967.

Faulkner, William. *Absalom, Absalom!* 1936. New York: Vintage, 1990.

Fergusson, Francis. *The Idea of a Theater: The Art of Drama in Changing Perspective*. Princeton, NJ: Princeton UP, 1949.

Filewod, Alan, and David Watt. *Workers' Playtime: Theatre and the Labour Movement since 1970*. Sydney: Currency P, 2001.

Fischer-Lichte, Erika. "From Text to Performance: The Rise of Theatre Studies as an Academic Discipline in Germany." *Theatre Research International* 24.2 (1999): 168–78.

– "Theatricality: A Key Concept in Theatre and Cultural Studies." *Theatre Research International* 20.2 (1995): 85–89.

– "Thoughts on the 'Interdisciplinary' Nature of Theatre Studies." *Assaph – Studies in the Theatre* 12 (1996): 111–24.

Foster, Barbara M., and Michael Foster. *Forbidden Journey: The Life of Alexandra David-Neel*. San Francisco: Harper, 1987.

Fotheringham, Richard, and Albert Hunt. *The White Man's Mission. Challenging the Centre: Two Decades of Political Theatre*. Ed. Steve Capelin. Brisbane: Playlab P, 1995.

Foucault, Michel. *The Birth of the Clinic: An Archaeology of Medical Perception*. Trans. A.M. Sheridan Smith. New York: Random, 1994.

Freud, Sigmund. "Fetishism." 1927. Trans. Joan Riviere. *Standard Edition of the Complete Psychological Works of Sigmund Freud*. Vol. 21. London: Hogarth, 1953–1974. 152–57.

– "Mourning and Melancholia." *Collected Papers*. Vol. 4. Ed. Joan Riviere. New York: Basic, 1959. 152–70.

– "Some Character-Types Met With in Psychoanalytic Work." 1916. *The Standard Edition of the Complete Psychological Works of Sigmund Freud*. Ed. James Strachey and Anna Freud. Vol. 14. London: Hogarth P/ Inst. of Psycho-Analysis, 1957. 309–33.

– "The 'Uncanny.'" *The Standard Edition of the Complete Psychological Works of Sigmund Freud*. Vol. 17. Trans. and Ed. James Strachey. London: Hogarth P and Inst. of Psycho-Analysis, 1955. 217–56.

Friedman, Hazel. "The Horror …" *Johannesburg Mail and Guardian* 8 Aug. 1997. 31 Mar. 2000 <http://www.sn.apc.org/wmail/issues/970808/ARTS60.html>.

Friedman, Milton. "Once Again: Why Socialism Won't Work." *New York Times* 13 Aug. 1994: 21.

Frye, Northrop. *Anatomy of Criticism.* 1957. Princeton, NJ: Princeton UP, 1967.

Fuchs, Elinor. *The Death of Character: Perspectives on Theater after Modernism.* Bloomington: Indiana UP, 1996.

Gallagher, Catherine. "The New Materialism in Marxist Aesthetics." *Theory and Society: Renewal and Critique in Social Theory* 9 (1980): 633–46.

Garfinkel, Harold. *Studies in Ethnomethodology.* 1967. Cambridge: Polity P, 1984.

Gassner, John. "An Answer to the New Critics." *Theatre Arts* Nov. 1952: 59–61.

– "There Is No American Drama." *Theatre Arts* Sept. 1952: 24–5, 84–5.

Gates, Henry Louis, Jr. "Editor's Introduction: Writing 'Race' and the Difference It Makes." *"Race," Writing, and Difference.* Ed. Henry Louis Gates, Jr. Chicago and London: U of Chicago P, 1985. 1–20.

Geertz, Clifford. "Blurred Genres: The Refiguration of Social Thought." *Local Knowledge: Further Essays in Interpretive Anthropology.* New York: Basic, 1983. 19–35.

Gilbert, Karen Wendy. "Urban Cyborg Sha(wo)man Manifesto, or, The City-Woman-Techne Machine." *Found Object* 8 (2000): 96–123.

Gilroy, Paul. *The Black Atlantic: Modernity and Double Consciousness.* Cambridge: Harvard UP, 1993.

Girard, René. *Deceit, Desire, and the Novel: Self and Other in Literary Structure.* Trans. Yvonne Freccero. Baltimore: Johns Hopkins UP, 1965.

– *Violence and the Sacred.* Trans. P. Gregory. Baltimore: Johns Hopkins UP, 1977.

Gonzalez, Jennifer. "The Appended Subject: Race and Identity as Digital Assemblage." *Race in Cyberspace.* Ed. Beth E. Kolko, Lisa Nakamura, and Gilbert B. Rodman. New York / London: Routledge, 2000. 27–50.

Gordon, Avery F. *Ghostly Matters: Haunting and the Sociological Imagination.* Minneapolis: U of Minnesota P, 1997.

Gordon, Eric A. *Mark the Music: The Life and Work of Marc Blitzstein.* New York: St Martin's, 1989.

Graff, Gerald. *Poetic Statement and Critical Dogma.* Evanston, IL: Northwestern UP, 1970.

– *Professing Literature: An Institutional History.* Chicago: U of Chicago P, 1987.

Graver, David. "The Actor's Bodies." *Text and Performance Quarterly* 17 (1997): 221–35.

– "Violent Theatricality: Displayed Enactments of Aggression and Pain." *Theatre Journal* 47 (1995): 43–64.

Gray, Eugene F. "The Clinical View of Life: Gustave Flaubert's *Madame Bovary.*" *Medicine and Literature.* Ed. Enid Rhodes Peschel. New York: Neale Watson, 1980. 81–87.

Greenblatt, Stephen. "Toward a Poetics of Culture." *The New Historicism.* Ed. H. Aram Veeser. New York: Routledge, 1989. 1–14.

Grossberg, Lawrence. *Bringing It All Back Home: Essays on Cultural Studies.* Durham, NC: Duke UP, 1997.

Grosz, Elizabeth. *Space, Time, and Perversion: Essays on the Politics of Bodies.* New York: Routledge, 1995.

Guillory, John. *Cultural Capital: The Problem of Literary Canon Formation.* Chicago: U of Chicago P, 1993.

Habermas, Jürgen. *The Philosophical Discourse of Modernity: Twelve Lectures.* Trans. Frederick Lawrence. Cambridge: MIT P, 1987.

Hale, Dorothy J. *Social Formalism: The Novel in Theory from Henry James to the Present.* Stanford: Stanford UP, 1998.

Handke, Peter. *Publikumsbeschimpfung: und andere Sprechstucke.* Frankfurt am Main: Suhrkamp, 1971. 6–48.

Hansberry, Lorraine. A Raisin in the Sun *and* The Sign in Sidney Brustein's Window. Ed. Robert Nemiroff. New York: Vintage, 1995.

Haraway, Donna J. *Modest_Witness@Second_Millennium. Female-Man©_Meets_OncoMouse*™: *Feminism and Technoscience.* New York / London: Routledge, 1997.

Haug, Wolfgang Fritz. *Critique of Commodity Aesthetics: Appearance, Sexuality, and Advertising in Capitalist Society.* Trans. Robert Bock. Minneapolis: U of Minnesota P, 1986.

Hegel, G.W.F. *Aesthetics.* 2 vols. Trans. T.M. Knox. Oxford: Clarendon, 1998.

– *Vorlesungen über die Ästhetik.* 3 vols. Frankfurt am Main: Suhrkamp, 1970.

Hellman, Lillian. *The Collected Plays.* Boston: Little, Brown, 1972.

Holiday, Anthony. "Forgiving and Forgetting: The Truth and Reconciliation Commission." *Negotiating the Past: The Making of Memory in South Africa.* Ed. Sarah Nuttall and Carli Coetzee. Cape Town: Oxford UP, 1998.

hooks, bell. *Outlaw Culture: Resisting Representations.* New York: Routledge, 1994.

Huizinga, Johan. *Homo Ludens: A Study of the Play Element in Culture.* 1944. London: Paladin, 1970.

Hurston, Zora Neale. "Characteristics of Negro Expression." 1935. *The Gender of Modernism: A Critical Anthology.* Ed. Bonnie Kime Scott. Bloomington: Indiana UP, 1990. 175–87.

Inglis, Fred. *Raymond Williams.* London/New York: Verso, 1995.

Ionesco, Eugène. *Rhinoceros.* Trans. Derek Prouse. *Nine Plays of the Modern Theater.* Ed. Harold Clurman. New York: Grove Weidenfeld, 1981. 471–572.

Irigaray, Luce. "The Forgotten Mystery of Female Ancestry." *Thinking the Difference: For a Peaceful Revolution.* Trans. Karin Montin. New York: Routledge, 1994. 89–112.

Jack, R.D.S. *The Road to the Never Land: A Reassessment of J.M. Barrie's Dramatic Art.* Aberdeen: Aberdeen UP, 1991.

Jakobson, Roman. "What Is Poetry?" *Language in Literature.* Ed. Krystyna Pomorska and Stephen Rudy. Cambridge: Belknap / Harvard UP, 1987. 368–78.

Jameson, Fredric. "Modernism and Imperialism." *Nationalism, Colonialism, and Literature.* By Terry Eagleton, Fredric Jameson, and Edward W. Said. Minneapolis: U of Minnesota P, 1990. 43–66.

Janko, Richard, ed. *Poetics*. Indianapolis: Hackett, 1987.

Jervis, John. *Exploring the Modern: Patterns of Western Culture and Civilization*. Oxford: Blackwell, 1998.

Jones, Basil, and Adrian Kohler. "Puppeteers' Note." Taylor xvi–xvii.

Jones, LeRoi [Amiri Baraka]. *Dutchman*. 1964. *Selected Plays and Prose of Amiri Baraka/LeRoi Jones*. New York: Morrow, 1979. 70–96.

– "The Need for a Cultural Base to Civil Rites & Bpower Mooments." Barbour 119–26.

Jordan, Ellen. *The Women's Movement and Women's Employment in Nineteenth Century Britain*. London and New York: Routledge, 1999.

Jordan, Tim. *Cyberpower: The Culture and Politics of Cyberspace and the Internet*. London: Routledge, 1999.

Kant, Immanuel. *Kritik der Urteilskraft*. 1790. Stuttgart: Reclam, 1976.

Kentridge, William. "Director's Note." Taylor viii–xv.

Kern, Stephen. *The Culture of Time and Space*. Cambridge: Harvard UP, 1983.

Kondo, Dorinne. *About Face: Performing Race in Fashion and Theater*. New York: Routledge, 1997.

Koselleck, Reinhart. *Futures Past: On The Semantics of Historical Time*. Trans. Keith Tribe. Cambridge: MIT P, 1985.

Krell, David Farrell. *Infectious Nietzsche*. Bloomington: Indiana UP, 1996.

Krog, Antjie. *Country of My Skull: Guilt, Sorrow, and the Limits of Forgiveness in the New South Africa*. New York: Random, 1998.

Kruger, Loren. *The Drama of South Africa: Plays, Pageants, and Publics since 1910*. London: Routledge, 1999.

– "Goat Island: *the sea & poison*." *Frakcija* 15 (1999): 70–75.

Kumar, Krishan. "The End of Socialism? The End of Utopia? The End of History?" *Utopias and the Millennium*. Ed. Krishnan Kumar and Stephen Bann. London: Reaktion, 1993. 63–80.

Kundera, Milan. *Immortality*. Trans. Peter Kussi. New York: Grove Weidenfeld, 1991.

Kushner, Tony. *Angels in America: A Gay Fantasia on National Themes*. New York: Theatre Communications Group, 1994.

La Berge, Ann, and Mordechai Feingold. Introduction. *French Medical Culture in the Nineteenth Century*. Ed. Ann La Berge and Mordechai Feingold. Amsterdam and Atlanta: Rodopi, 1994.

Lassus, Jean. *The Early Christian and Byzantine World*. London: Paul Hamlyn, 1967.

Lee, Josephine. *Performing Asian America: Race and Ethnicity on the Contemporary Stage*. Philadelphia: Temple UP, 1997.

Lefebvre, Henri. *Introduction to Modernity*. Trans. John Moore. London: Verso, 1995.

Lehmann, Hans-Thies. *Postdramatisches Theater*. Frankfurt am Main: Autoren, 1999.

Lentriccia, Frank. *After the New Criticism*. Chicago: U of Chicago P, 1980.

Lesnick, Henry, ed. *Guerrilla Street Theater*. New York: Avon, 1973.

Lessing, Gotthold Ephraim. *Laokoon*. 1766. Stuttgart: Reclam, 1964.

The Little Foxes. Screenplay by Lillian Hellman. Dir. William Wyler. Music by
  Meredith Willson. RKO, 1941.
Lott, Eric. *Love and Theft: Blackface Minstrelsy and the American Working Class*.
  New York: Oxford UP, 1995.
Macias, Ysidro R. *The Ultimate Pendejada: Contemporary Chicano Theatre*. Ed.
  Roberto J. Garza. Notre Dame, IN: U of Notre Dame P, 1976. 135–64.
Marquis, Donald M. *In Search of Buddy Bolden: First Man of Jazz*. Baton Rouge:
  Louisiana State UP, 1978.
Marx, Karl. *The Eighteenth Brumaire of Louis Bonaparte. The Marx-Engels Reader*.
  2nd ed. Ed. Robert C. Tucker. New York: Norton, 1978. 594–617.
– *The Eighteenth Brumaire of Louis Bonaparte*. Trans. Eden Paul and Cedar Paul.
  New York: International, 1963.
Massoutre, Gulaine. "Peau, chair et os." *Jeu: cahiers de théâtre* 69 (1992): 20–123.
McCarren, Felicia. *Dance Pathologies: Performance, Poetics, Medicine*. Stanford,
  CA: Stanford UP, 1998.
McConachie, Bruce. "Catharsis and the Materiality of Spectatorship." *Assaph –
  Studies in the Theatre* 12 (1996): 95–99.
McGrath, John. *The Cheviot, the Stag and the Black, Black Oil*. Rev. ed. London:
  Methuen, 1981.
– *A Good Night Out: Popular Theatre: Audience, Class, and Form*. London: Eyre
  Methuen, 1981.
McGrath, John Edward. "Trusting in Rubber: Performing Boundaries During the AIDS
  Epidemic." *The Drama Review: The Journal of Performance Studies* 39.2 (1995):
  21–38.
McHale, Brian. "Changes of Dominant from Modernist to Postmodernist Writing."
  Approaching Postmodernism. Ed. Hans Bertens and Douwe Fokkema. Philadelphia:
  Benjamins, 1986. 53–78.
McNally, Terrence, adapt. *Ragtime*. By E.L. Doctorow. 1976. Music by Stephen
  Flaherty. Lyrics by Lynn Ahrens. Ford Centre for Performing Arts, Toronto, 8 Dec.
  1996.
Mercer, Kobena. *Welcome to the Jungle: New Positions in Black Cultural Studies*.
  New York: Routledge, 1994.
Meredith, Martin. *Coming to Terms: South Africa's Search for Truth*. New York:
  Public Affairs, 1999.
Merleau-Ponty, Maurice. *Phenomenology of Perception*. Trans. Colin Smith. London:
  Routledge, 1989.
Micale, Mark S. *Approaching Hysteria: Disease and Its Interpretations*. Princeton, NJ:
  Princeton UP, 1995.
Miyamoto, Nobuko. *A Grain of Sand*. Unpublished playscript, 1999.
The Mummers Troupe. *Regular Weekly Entertainment: Cards 50¢, or, The Mummers
  History of Nfld*. Ts, 1973. Mummers Troupe Papers, Memorial U of Newfoundland.
– *They Club Seals, Don't They? Stars in the Sky Morning: Collective Plays of New-
  foundland and Labrador*. Ed. Helen Peters. St John's, NF: Killick P, 1996.

– *What's That Got to Do with the Price of Fish?* Ts, 1976. Mummers Troupe Papers, Memorial U of Newfoundland.

Muñoz, José Esteban. *Disidentifications: Queers of Color and the Performance of Politics*. Minneapolis: U of Minnesota P, 1999.

Niessen, Carl. "Aufgaben der Theaterwissenschaft." *Die Szene. Blätter für Bühnenkunst* 17 (1927): 44–49.

Nietzsche, Friedrich. *On the Genealogy of Morals*. Trans. Walter Kaufmann and R.J. Hollingdale. *On The Genealogy of Morals and Ecce Homo*. Ed. Walter Kaufmann. New York: Random, 1967. 3–198.

Nora, Pierre. "Between Memory and History: *Les Lieux de Mémoire*." Trans. Marc Roudebush. *Representations* 26 (1989): 7–25.

Nye, Robert A. *Crime, Madness, and Politics in Modern France: The Medical Concept of National Decline*. Princeton, NJ: Princeton UP, 1984.

– "The Medical Origins of Sexual Fetishism." *Fetishism as Cultural Discourse*. Ed. Emily Apter and William Pietz. Ithaca, NY: Cornell UP, 1993. 13–30.

O'Meally, Robert G. "On Burke and the Vernacular: Ralph Ellison's Boomerang of History." *History and Memory in African American Culture*. Ed. Geneviève Fabre and Robert O'Meally. New York: Oxford UP, 1994. 244–60.

Olmsted, J.M.D., and E. Harris Olmsted. *Claude Bernard and the Experimental Method in Medicine*. New York: Henry Schuman, 1952.

Omi, Michael, and Howard Winant. *Racial Formation in the United States: From the 1960s to the 1990s*. New York: Routledge, 1994.

Osborne, John. *The Naturalist Drama in Germany*. Manchester: Manchester UP, 1971.

Peau, chair et os. Dir. Gilles Maheu. Espace Libre, Montreal. 26 Nov.–21 Dec. 1991.

Peller, Gary. "Race-Consciousness." *Critical Race Theory: The Key Writings that Formed the Movement*. Ed. Kimberlé Crenshaw et al. New York: Free P, 1995. 127–58.

Phelan, Peggy. *Unmarked: The Politics of Performance*. New York and London: Routledge, 1993.

Pirandello, Luigi. *Naked Masks*. Ed. Eric Bentley. New York: Dutton, 1952.

Potter, Rosanne G. *The Little Foxes*. Iowa State University Play Concordances. Iowa State U. 15 Mar. 2000 <http://www.public.iastate.edu/~spires/Concord/foxes.html>.

Pryce, Jonathan, perf. *Hamlet*. By William Shakespeare. Dir. Richard Eyre. Royal Court Theatre, London. Apr. 1980.

Rebellato, Dan. *1956 and All That: The Making of Modern British Drama*. London: Routledge, 1999.

Reese, Venus Opal. Personal interview. 4 May 2000.

Reynolds, Oliver. "He Manipulates All Right." Rev. of *The Room* and *The Celebration*, by Harold Pinter. *Times Literary Supplement* 31 Mar. 2000: 20.

Richards, Sandra. "Writing the Absent Potential: Drama, Performance, and the Canon of African-American Literature." *Performativity and Performance*. Ed. Andrew Parker and Eve Kosofsky Sedgwick. New York: Routledge, 1995. 64–88.

– "Yoruba Gods on the American Stage: August Wilson's *Joe Turner's Come and Gone*." *Research in African Literatures* 30.4 (1999): 92–105.

Roach, Joseph. "Territorial Passages: Time, Place, and Action." *Of Borders and Thresholds: Theatre History, Practice, and Theory*. Ed. Michael Kobialka. Minneapolis: U of Minnesota P, 1999. 110–24.

– *Cities of the Dead: Circum-Atlantic Performance*. New York: Columbia UP, 1996.

Roberts, Elizabeth. *Women's Work, 1840–1940*. 1988. Cambridge: Cambridge UP, 1995.

Roden, David. "Iconoclasm and the Rhetoric of Energy in Societas Raffaelo Sanzio's *Hamlet*." *Frakcija* 15 (1999): 15–21.

Rokem, Freddie. "To Hold as 'twere a Mirror up to the Spectator: Catharsis – A Performance Perspective." *Assaph – Studies in the Theatre* 12 (1996): 101–9.

Rose, Jacqueline. *The Case of Peter Pan or The Impossibility of Children's Fiction*. London: Macmillan, 1984.

Roy, Parama. "As the Master Saw Her." *Cruising the Performative: Interventions Into the Representation of Ethnicity, Nationality and Sexuality*. Ed. Sue-Ellen Case, Philip Brett, and Susan Leigh Foster. Bloomington: Indiana UP, 1995. 112–29.

Rühle, Günther. *Theater für die Republik, 1917–1933: Im Spiegel der Kritik*. 2nd ed. 2 vols. Frankfurt am Main: Fischer, 1988.

Rutherford, Jonathan. *Forever England: Reflections on Race, Masculinity and Empire*. London: Lawrence, 1997.

Sadoff, Dianne F. *Sciences of the Flesh: Representing Body and Subject in Psychoanalysis*. Stanford, CA: Stanford UP, 1998.

Salome. By Oscar Wilde. Dir. Einar Schleef. Berlin Theatertreffen, Berlin. May 1998.

Samuel, Raphael. *Theatres of Memory*. Vol. 1. London: Verso, 1994.

Sarrazac, Jean-Pierre. *Théâtres du moi, théâtres du monde*. Rouen: Médianes, 1995.

Savigliano, Marta E. *Tango and the Political Economy of Passion*. Boulder, CO: Westview, 1995.

Savran, David. "Whistling in the Dark." *Performing Arts Journal* 15 (1993): 25–27.

Scarry, Elaine. *The Body in Pain: The Making and Unmaking of the World*. New York: Oxford UP, 1985.

Schell, Orville. *Virtual Tibet: Searching for Shangri-La from the Himalayas to Hollywood*. New York: Metropolitan-Holt, 2000.

Schiller, Friedrich. *Über die aesthetische Erziehung des Menschen*. 1795. Stuttgart: Reclam, 2000.

Schoenmakers, Henri. "Catharsis as Aesthetisation." *Assaph – Studies in the Theatre* 12 (1996): 85–93.

Sedgwick, Eve Kosofsky. *Between Men: English Literature and Male Homosocial Desire*. New York: Columbia UP, 1985.

Seel, Martin. *Eine Ästhetik der Natur*. 1991. Frankfurt am Main: Suhrkamp, 1996.

Segal, Lauren, and Henion Han. *Khulumani/Speak Out*. Johannesburg: Centre for the Study of Violence and Reconciliation, 1997.

– *Sisakhuluma: We Are Still Speaking*. Johannesburg: Centre for the Study of Violence and Reconciliation, 1997.

Segel, Harold B. *Body Ascendant: Modernism and the Physical Imperative*. Baltimore: Johns Hopkins UP, 1998.

Seltzer, Mark. *Bodies and Machines*. New York: Routledge, 1992.

Shimakawa, Karen. "Asians in America: Millennial Approaches to Asian Pacific American Performance." *Journal of Asian American Studies* 3 (2000): 283–97.

Sidnell, M.J. "Authorizations of the Performative: Whose Performances of What and for Whom?" *The Performance Text*. Ed. Domenico Pietropaolo. Ottawa: Legas, 1999. 97–112.

– *Dances of Death: The Group Theatre of London in the Thirties*. London: Faber, 1984.

Sinfield, Alan. "'Effeminacy' and 'Femininity': Sexual Politics in Wilde's Comedies." *Modern Drama* 37 (1994): 34–52.

– *The Wilde Century: Effeminacy, Oscar Wilde and the Queer Moment*. London: Cassell, 1994.

Smith, Susan Harris. *American Drama: The Bastard Art*. Cambridge: Cambridge UP, 1997.

Soyinka, Wole. *Myth, Literature and the African World*. Cambridge: Cambridge UP, 1976.

Spillers, Hortense J. "'All the Things You Could Be by Now, If Sigmund Freud's Wife Was Your Mother': Psychoanalysis and Race." *Boundary 2* 23.3 (1996): 75–141.

Sportstück. By Elfriede Jelinek. Dir. Einar Schleef. Burgtheater, Vienna. 23 Jan. 1998 (short version); 14 Mar. 1998 (long version).

States, Bert O. *Great Reckonings in Little Rooms: On the Phenomenology of Theater*. Berkeley: U of California P, 1985.

Steen, Shannon. "Melancholy Bodies: Racial Subjectivity and Whiteness in O'Neill's *The Emperor Jones*." *Theatre Journal* 52 (2000): 339–59.

Steinweg, Reiner. *Das Lehrstück: Brechts Theorie einer politisch-asthetischen Erziehung*. Stuttgart: Metzler, 1972.

Stevens, Wallace. "Le Monocle de mon Oncle." *The Collected Poems of Wallace Stevens*. 1954. New York: Knopf, 1961. 13–18.

Stone, Allucquère Rosanne. *The War of Desire and Technology at the Close of the Mechanical Age*. Cambridge: MIT P, 1995.

The Story I Am About to Tell. By Khulumani Support Group and the Market Theatre Laboratory. Dir. Bobby Rodwell. National Arts Festival, Grahamstown. July 1999.

Stourac, Richard, and Kathleen McCreery. *Theatre as a Weapon: Workers' Theatre in the Soviet Union, Germany, and Britain, 1917–1934*. London: Routledge/Kegan Paul, 1986.

Strindberg, August. Author's Foreword to *Miss Julie*. *Six Plays of Strindberg*. Trans. Elizabeth Sprigge. New York: Doubleday, 1955. 61–73.

Synge, John M. *The Complete Plays of John M. Synge*. New York: Random, 1935.

Szondi, Peter. "Theorie des modernen Dramas." *Schriften I*. Frankfurt am Main: Suhrkamp, 1978.

– *Theory of the Modern Drama: A Critical Edition*. Ed. and trans. Michael Hays. Minneapolis: U of Minnesota P, 1987.

Tate, Allen. *On the Limits of Poetry and Selected Essays*. New York: Swallow, 1948.

Taussig, Michael T. *The Devil and Commodity Fetishism in South America*. Chapel Hill: U of North Carolina P, 1980.

– *Mimesis and Alterity: A Particular History of the Senses*. New York and London: Routledge, 1993.

Taylor, Jane. *Ubu and the Truth Commission*. From the production by William Kentridge and the Handspring Puppet Company. Cape Town: U of Cape Town P, 1998.

Taylor, Karen Malpede. *People's Theatre in Amerika*. New York: Drama Book Specialists, 1972.

Trainspotting. Adapt. and dir. Frank Castorf. Berlin Volksbühne, Berlin. 26 Apr. 1997.

Truth and Reconciliation Commission. Amnesty Decisions 1999b: Case no. ac990292. <http://www.doj.gov.za/trc/decisions/1999/ac990292.htm>.

– Amnesty Decisions 2001: Case no. ac21002. <http://www.doj.gov.za/trc/decisions/2001/ac21002.htm>.

– *Amnesty Hearings and Decisions Index*. <http://www.doj.gov.za/trc/amntrans/index.htm>.

– Truth and Reconciliation Commission of South Africa: Final Report CD ROM. London: Macmillan Reference, 1999.

– Truth and Reconciliation Commission Web Site. 1 April 2001. <http://www.doj.gov.za/trc/>.

Turner, Jann. "Shocking Revelations from a Charming Man." *Johannesburg Mail and Guardian* 20 Sept. 1996. 31 March 2000 <http://www.sn.apc.org/wmail/issues/960920/NEWS46.html>.

Turner, Victor. *From Ritual to Theatre: The Human Seriousness of Play*. New York: Performing Arts Journal Pub., 1982.

Tutu, Desmond Mpilo. *No Future Without Forgiveness*. New York: Doubleday, 1999.

Valency, Maurice. *The Breaking String: The Plays of Anton Chekhov*. New York: Oxford UP, 1966.

van Gennep, Arnold. *The Rites of Passage*. Trans. Monika B. Vizedom and Gabrielle L. Caffee. London: Routledge, 1960.

Veltruský, Jiří. *Drama as Literature*. Lisse, Neth.: Peter de Ridder, 1977.

Vergès, François. "Chains of Madness, Chains of Colonialism: Fanon and Freedom." *The Fact of Blackness: Frantz Fanon and Visual Representation*. Ed. Alan Read. Seattle: Bay P, 1996. 46–75.

Veysey, Laurence R. *The Emergence of the American University*. Chicago: U of Chicago P, 1965.

Vogel, Paula. *How I Learned to Drive*. New York: Dramatists Play Service, 1997.

Warlaumont, Hazel G. *Advertising in the 60s: Turncoats, Traditionalists, and Waste Makers in America's Turbulent Decade*. Westport, CT: Praeger, 2001.

Washington, Peter. *Madame Blavatsky's Baboon: Theosophy and the Emergence of the Western Guru*. New York: Schocken Books, 1993.

The Waste Land. By T.S. Eliot. Dir. Marina Warner. Perf. Fiona Shaw. Gooderham & Worts Bldg., Toronto. Sept. 1998.

Weisgall, Hugo. *Six Characters in Search of an Author*. Adapt. of the play, by Luigi Pirandello. Libretto by Denis Johnston. Lyric Opera Center for American Artists. Cond. Lee Schaenen. New World 80454-2, 1994.

Welsch, Wolfgang. "Ästhetik und Anästhetik." *Ästhetisches Denken*. Stuttgart: Reclam, 1990. 9–40.

Wesley, Richard. *The Talented Tenth. Crosswinds: An Anthology of Black Dramatists in the Diaspora*. Ed. William B. Branch. Bloomington: Indiana UP, 1993. 359–411.

Williams, Jay. *Stage Left*. New York: Scribner, 1974.

Williams, Raymond. "Drama in a Dramatized Society." 1977. *Writing in Society*. London: Verso, 1983.

– *Drama from Ibsen to Brecht*. Rev. ed. London: Chatto & Windus, 1968.

– *Drama in Performance*. 1954. Rev. ed. Middlesex, UK: Pelican, 1968.

– *Keywords: A Vocabulary of Culture and Society*. 1976. New York: Oxford UP, 1984.

– *Keywords: A Vocabulary of Culture and Society*. London: Fontana, 1988.

– *The Long Revolution*. Harmondsworth, UK: Penguin, 1956.

– *Modern Tragedy*. London: Chatto, 1966.

– *Problems in Materialism and Culture: Selected Essays*. London/New York: Verso, 1980.

– *The Sociology of Culture*. New York: Schocken, 1982.

Wilson, August. *Fences. Three Plays* 95–192.

– *King Hedley II*. Unpublished manuscript, 16 January 2000.

– *Ma Rainey's Black Bottom. Three Plays* 1–93.

– *Seven Guitars*. New York: Plume, 1997.

– *Three Plays*. Pittsburgh: U of Pittsburgh P, 1991.

– *Two Trains Running*. New York: Plume, 1993.

Wolfe, George C. *The Colored Museum*. New York: Broadway Play P, 1987.

Wolfe, Tom. *Radical Chic and Mau-mauing the Flak Catchers*. New York: Farrar, 1970.

Yeats, W.B. *The Death of Cuchulain*. 1939. *The Variorum Edition of the Plays of W.B. Yeats*. Ed. Russell K. Alspach. London: Macmillan, 1966. 1051–63.

Zeami. *On the Art of the No Drama: The Major Treatises of Zeami*. Trans. J. Thomas Rimer and Masakazu Yamazaki. Princeton, NJ: Princeton UP, 1984.

Zola, Émile. "From *Naturalism in the Theater*." Trans. Albert Bermel. *The Theory of the Modern Stage: An Introduction to Modern Theatre and Drama*. Ed. Eric Bentley. Middlesex: Penguin, 1968. 351–72.

– *Le Naturalisme au théâtre.* Vol. 29 of *Œuvres complètes.*
– *Nos auteurs dramatiques.* Vol. 30 of *Œuvres complètes.*
– *Œuvres complètes.* 50 vols. Paris: François Bernouard, 1927–29.
– *Le Roman expérimental.* Vol. 36 of *Œuvres complètes.*

Contributors

Sue-Ellen Case is a member of the faculty at University of California at Los Angeles. She has published extensively in the fields of German theatre, feminist theatre, and lesbian critical theory and performance. More recently, her work focuses on the relationship between new technologies and performance. Her books *Feminism and Theatre* and *The Domain Matrix: Performing Lesbian at the End of Print Culture* are pioneer texts in their respective fields. Her numerous anthologies include *The Divided Home/land: Contemporary German Women's Plays* and *Performing Feminisms*. Her articles number over thirty and have been translated into several languages.

Elin Diamond is Professor of English at Rutgers University. She is the author of *Unmaking Mimesis: Essays on Feminism and Theater* (Routledge, 1997) and *Pinter's Comic Play* (Bucknell, 1985) and editor of *Performance and Cultural Politics* (Routledge, 1996). Her essays on performance and feminist theory have appeared in *Theatre Journal, ELH, Discourse, TDR, Modern Drama, Kenyon Review, Cahiers Renaud-Barrault, Art And Cinema, Maska*, and anthologies in the United States, Europe, and India.

Harry J. Elam, Jr., is Professor of Drama and Director of the Committee on Black Performing Arts at Stanford University. He is the author of *Taking It to the Streets: The Social Protest Theater of Luis Valdez and Amiri Baraka* (U of Michigan P) and co-editor of *African American Performance and Theater History: A Critical Reader* (Oxford UP) and *Colored Contradictions: An Anthology of Contemporary African American Drama* (Penguin). He has just finished a book entitled *(W)Righting History: The Past as Present in the Drama of August Wilson*. His articles have appeared in *American Drama, Theatre Journal*, and *Text and Performance Quarterly*, as well as in several critical anthologies.

Alan Filewod is Professor of Drama in the School of Literatures and Performance Studies in English at the University of Guelph, where he researches political and postcolonial theatre. His books include *Collective Encounters: Documentary Theatre in English Canada;* three anthologies of Canadian drama; and, with David Watt, *Workers' Playtime: Theatre and the Labour Movement since 1970* (Sydney: Currency Press, 2001). His most recent work, *Performing 'Canada': The Nation Enacted in the Imagined Theatre*, is forthcoming as a monograph published by *Textual Studies in Canada.* He is an editor of *Canadian Theatre Review* and former president of the Association for Canadian Theatre Research.

Erika Fischer-Lichte was a professor of modern German literature, comparative literature, and theatre research at the universities of Frankfurt-am-Main, Bayreuth, and Mainz from 1973 to 1996. Since April 1996 she has been Professor of Theatre Research at the Free University of Berlin; from 1995 to 1999 she was president of the International Federation of Theatre Research. Her numerous publications (twenty books and more than 100 essays in scientific periodicals, handbooks, journals, and essay collections) include *The Semiotics of Theatre* (1992), *The Show and the Gaze of Theatre* (1997), and, most recently, *Das eigene und das fremde Theater* (1999); *Theater im Prozeßder Zivilisation. Zur Geschichte von Körper-Inszenierungen* (2000); *Aesthetische Erfahrung. Das Semiotische und das Performative* (2001); and *History of European Drama and Theatre* (Routledge, 2002).

Stanton B. Garner, Jr., is Professor of English at the University of Tennessee, where he teaches courses in modern drama and dramatic theory. He is the author of *The Absent Voice: Narrative Comprehension in the Theater* (1989), *Bodied Spaces: Phenomenology and Performance in Contemporary Drama* (1994), and *Trevor Griffiths: Politics, Drama, History* (1999). His current research centres on the intersections of theatre and medicine.

Shannon Jackson is an associate professor in the departments of Rhetoric and of Theater, Dance, and Performance Studies at University of California, Berkeley. She published *Lines of Activity*, a study of performance and social change at Chicago's Hull-House settlement, in 2000 and has also published and performed in numerous journals, theatres, collections, universities, and art galleries in the United States. She is presently completing a second book, entitled *Disciplining Performance: Institutional Genealogies in the Arts and Humanities,* for Cambridge University Press.

Ric Knowles is Professor of Drama at the University of Guelph and at the Graduate Centre for the Study of Drama, University of Toronto. He is co-editor of *Modern Drama*, an editor of *Canadian Theatre Review*, and co-editor of *Staging Coyote's Dream: An Anthology of First Nations Drama in English* (Playwrights Canada, 2003). He is author of *The Theatre of Form and the Production of Meaning: Contemporary Canadian Dramaturgies* (ECW, 1999), *Shakespeare and Canada* (P.I.E. Peter Lang, 2003), and *Reading the Material Theatre* (Cambridge UP, 2003).

Loren Kruger is the author of *The National Stage* (U of Chicago P, 1992) and *The Drama of South Africa* (Routledge), as well as of recent articles on theatre and crime in Johannesburg (*Theatre Journal*) and, with Patricia Watson Shariff, on globalized culture and South African "life-skills" comics (*Poetics Today*). She teaches at the University of Chicago.

Josephine Lee is an associate professor of English at the University of Minnesota. Her *Performing Asian America: Race and Ethnicity on the Contemporary Stage* was published by Temple University Press in 1997. She is co-editor of *Re/collecting Early Asian America: Readings in Culture History*, an interdisciplinary collection of essays, to be published by Temple University Press. She has written numerous essays on modern and contemporary American and British theatre and is currently completing a book on racial politics and contemporary American theatre.

David Savran's most recent books are *The Playwright's Voice: American Dramatists on Memory, Writing, and the Politics of Culture* and *Taking It Like a Man: White Masculinity, Masochism, and Contemporary American Culture*. He is Professor of Theatre at the Graduate Center at the City University of New York.

Michael J. Sidnell is Emeritus Professor, University of Toronto; sometime Director of the Graduate Centre for Study of Drama, where he still teaches; and sometime Director of Graduate Studies in English at the University of Toronto. His books include *Dances of Death: The Group Theatre of London in the Thirties* (Faber, 1984) and *Yeats: Poetry and Poetics* (Macmillan, 1991). He has also edited two volumes of Yeats's dramatic manuscripts and is a contributing editor to the *Collected Works of W.B. Yeats*, now in progress, and to the *Complete Works of W.H. Auden: Plays* (Princeton, 1988), as well as the editor of the four-volume series *Sources of Dramatic Theory*, of which the two first volumes have been published. He is the author of many articles on theatre, drama, poetry, and kindred subjects.

Joanne Tompkins teaches theatre studies at the University of Queensland, Australia. She is the co-author of *Post-Colonial Drama* (with Helen Gilbert; Routledge, 1996) and *Women's Intercultural Performance* (with Julie Holledge; Routledge, 2000). She has published numerous articles on postcolonialism, multiculturalism, and interculturalism in Australian and Canadian theatres. She is also co-editor of *Modern Drama*.

Ann Wilson teaches in the School of Literatures and Performance Studies at the University of Guelph and is an editor of *Canadian Theatre Review* and *Essays in Theatre/Études théâtrales*. Her research interests focus on issues of gender and sexuality in relation to nation.

W.B. Worthen is Professor and Chair of the Department of Theater, Dance, and Performance Studies at the University of California, Berkeley. He is the author of *Shakespeare and the Force of Modern Performance* (Cambridge, 2003), *Shakespeare and the Authority of Performance* (1977), *Modern Drama and the Rhetoric of Theater* (California, 1992), and *The Idea of the Actor* (Princeton, 1984); he is also the editor of *The Heinle Anthology of Drama* (4th ed., 2003), past editor of *Theatre Journal*, and current co-editor of *Modern Drama*.